The Perspective of Love

The Perspective of Love

Natural Law in a New Mode

R. J. SNELL

PICKWICK *Publications* · Eugene, Oregon

THE PERSPECTIVE OF LOVE
Natural Law in a New Mode

Pickwick Publications
An Imprint of Wipf and Stock Publishers
199 W. 8th Ave., Suite 3
Eugene, OR 97401

www.wipfandstock.com

ISBN 13: 978-1-62032-713-5

Cataloging-in-Publication data:

Snell, R. J., 1975–

    The perspective of love : natural law in a new mode / R. J. Snell.

    xii + 208 pp. ; 23 cm—Includes bibliographical references.

    ISBN 13: 978-1-62032-713-5

    1. Religion and law. 2. Natural law. 3. Natural theology. I. Title.

BL65.L33 S62 2014

Manufactured in the USA

For all in the Templeton Honors College,
Fellows in the Apostolate of the Further Question

Man cannot live without love. He remains a being that is incomprehensible for himself, his life is senseless, if love is not revealed to him, if he does not encounter love, if he does not experience it and make it his own, if he does not participate intimately in it. This ... is why Christ the Redeemer "fully reveals man to himself."

—JOHN PAUL II, REDEMPTOR HOMINIS

Contents

Preface

ACCORDING TO THE RIGHTLY celebrated theorist J. Budziszewski, natural law is a fact, a "feature of the world having to do with the constitution of the human person, and behind that, with the constitution of created reality as a whole."[1] While it is, he suggests, possible to question that fact, if "we are serious about being Christian philosophers . . . we should already know the answer to that logically possible question," and it would "be frivolous—a squandering of what has been given to us—to waste breath on the question of whether the human person has a constitution."[2] In other words, we could, but ought not, ponder the existence and reality of the natural law—it is a fact.

Further, if we do exert the effort to theorize about the natural law, our questions should be humble before the factual reality; they should "come in second place, not in first," and accept as given knowledge of the world and the human person.[3] Consequently, theory "will not be the belly-button-searching kind . . . will not always be turning into metatheory of the natural law, a theory about theories."[4] Instead, theorists will get busy, engaging the pathologies and deceptions of the time—they will serve as signs of contradiction—a task frustrated by "turning . . . eyes skull-inward in a futile attempt to catch [themselves] at the act of contemplation."[5]

In this book, I do not heed his counsel, turning not only to metatheory but of the type attempting to catch itself in the act of contemplation (although I'll call that noetic exegesis). I do so cautiously, for his was good advice, and I'm well aware that such metatheory tends to sharpen knives

1. Budziszewski, *Line Through the Heart*, 2.
2. Ibid., 3.
3. Ibid.
4. Ibid.
5. Ibid.

without ever cutting anything, and our time may lack such luxury. Still, whatever the immediate crisis, there is a place for the long game, for understanding and creating conditions of inquiry and progress. I'm not so hubristic as to think my work will accomplish this, but I hope to pull in that direction. Further, Budziszewski allows that while metatheory may be frivolous for a Christian to ask "on his own behalf . . . it is not frivolous if we live among humans who deny the personal structure of their being."[6] Charity recognizes that the scandal of our time is so dire as to require inquiry into the obvious, and, moreover, Budziszewski suggests the Fall has rendered "our state . . . out of joint with our nature."[7] So while Christians needn't theorize about the fact of the natural law for themselves, the Fall and the revolt of modernity justifies explaining the obvious—or so his argument allows.

Oddly, however, it is the doctrine of the Fall which renders natural law a non-starter, a dead end theologically and culturally for so many Christians, mainly but not only Protestants. Culturally, the argument goes, the natural law fails to persuade anyone not already on board because it relies (generally under deep cover) on theological commitments about creation, design, purpose, and human identity. Theologically, natural law downplays the Fall, overlooks the noetic effects of sin, ignores salvation history, makes the Gospel non-essential to the moral life, confines grace to a heavenly or spiritual domain, and thinks that the human can know and act well without first knowing and acting like Christ and being formed by his Church and its sacraments. Not only does natural law smuggle in theology, it's bad theology (likely Pelagian).

But if the denial of natural law by non-believers justifies metatheory, so does friendly fire from Christians, which is now almost a barrage. This text engages metatheory in an attempt to show that the "Protestant Prejudice" should be incorporated into natural law theory, but also that the usual objections fail to distinguish the varieties of natural law theory; while the arsenals of the Protestant Prejudice may score direct hits on some modes—what I'll term the common sense and theoretical—they are far less troubling to what I'll term the modes of interiority and transcendence.

After a brief introduction explaining the project and its context, Part One differentiates natural law as common sense, as theory, and as interiority, explaining how the Protestant Prejudice tends to overlook interiority.

6. Ibid., 4.
7. Ibid., 5.

Part Two examines interiority in more detail, grouping together a range of contemporary thinkers beginning from the first person perspective of ethics. As opposed to earlier, or classical accounts, these thinkers do not begin with theoretical anthropology, metaphysics of the person, or metaphysical biology but share a methodology of noetic exegesis—adverting to the performance and intentionality of the concrete person's practical reason—and so can be grouped together, despite their differences: (1) John Paul II and Martin Rhonheimer, (2) contemporary natural law, or the so-called "new natural law" of Germain Grisez, John Finnis, Joseph Boyle, and others, and (3) the methodological phenomenology of the Canadian Jesuit, Bernard Lonergan. While these three "schools" do not agree on every detail, they provide a broadly similar starting point from which to address the usual Protestant concerns.

In Part Three, I outline natural law in the mode of transcendence, explaining how concrete subjects undergo both the reign of sin and the transformation of love. Without negating the natural, the Holy Spirit allows the proper function of natural reason again, and natural law operates as a normative account of human authenticity—an account of natural law rooted in value. Rather than denying the Protestant objections, I provide a non-abstract, non-conceptualist account of the natural law that (1) incorporates the Protestant objections, (2) avoids the usual philosophical problems, and (3) allows a normative and publically accessible account of human flourishing genuinely adequate to human nature.

This is natural law in a new mode, the mode and perspective of love.

My recollection is dim, but I seem to remember Wendell Berry writing that a person's life is best judged by the gratitude owed to others. If that's true, I've a good life developing, for I'm indebted to many, and I gratefully acknowledge the support of my colleagues at Eastern University, the Templeton Honors College, the Agora Institute, and many students, friends, and colleagues, especially Drew Alexander, Kate Bresee, Phil Cary, Austin Detwiler, Jeff Dill, Nate Farris, Kelly Hanlon, Sarah Moon, Amy Richards, and Jonathan Yonan. Also, Brad Wilson, Robert George, and the James Madison Program kindly included me in several working groups that clarified my thought; Pat Byrne, Kerry Cronin, Fred Lawrence, Susan Legere, and others involved with the Lonergan Center at Boston College generously provided time and space for several months of research; the Earhart Foundation supported early aspects of the work; Ryan Miller, Gilles Mongeau, and Jeremy Wilkins introduced me to the work of Martin Rhonheimer at a Lonergan Workshop. Finally, but most importantly, if we cannot live without love, then that little outpost of the Church that is my family has given me life—especially, and always, Amy.

Natural Law, Modes of Meaning, and Contemporary Disputes

A Brief Introduction

In March 2013, *First Things* published an essay by the noted theologian David Bentley Hart highly critical of natural law theory and its role in current moral and social disputes.[1] A remarkably gifted writer and polemicist widely known for *The Beauty of the Infinite: The Aesthetics of Christian Truth*, his essay garnered much attention, revealing significant fault lines between and within various theological schools.

According to Hart, whatever its pedigree, and however much his own theology affirms similar conceptions of the cosmos, he rejects a "style of thought whose proponents . . . believe that compelling moral truths can be deduced from a scrupulous contemplations of the principles of cosmic and human nature, quite apart from special revelation, and within the context of the modern conceptual world."[2] Such, declares Hart, "is a hopeless cause."[3] In attempting to converse with secular society in neutral terms, or at least terms acceptable to the secular mind, natural lawyers insist "that the moral meaning of nature should be perfectly evident to any properly reasoning mind, regardless of religious belief or cultural formation,"[4] an evidentness Hart believes not present or discernible, partly because of the knock-out delivered by David Hume's claim that value statements—an *ought*—can never be derived from factual statements—an *is*—and partly because

1. Hart, "Is, Ought, and Nature's Laws," 71–72.
2. Ibid., 72.
3. Ibid.
4. Ibid.

nature is interpreted from within a cultural tradition. Consequently, natural law is acceptable if and only if one "has prior supernatural convictions" grounding the law, so any attempt to use natural law as a purely secular and rational language "can never be much more than an exercise in suasive rhetoric (and perhaps something of a *pia fraus*)."[5]

Hart's proponents were quick to run with the notion of pious fraud. Writing in support, Michael Potemra suggested that boosters of the natural law argue "in a form along the following lines: *The moral desiderata of the American political Right are not an attempt to impose religious views in the public sphere, but a desire to make public morality conform to truths accessible to pure reason*."[6] But, he continued, if these truths are so easily accessible, even self-evident, "why do so many people deny them" unless we appeal to the false, not to mention unfair, accusation that either "the deniers have their minds darkened by sin" or "that the deniers are just plain stupid."[7]

Accounting for your position's failure by calling your opponents wicked or stupid lacks credibility, and others in the broader conservative milieu were quick to express similar reservations. Noah Millman doubted our grasp of human nature: "it's supposed to be an instance of deriving social 'oughts' from a natural 'is' . . . [but] there's another step to the argument: what is the epistemology that is necessarily prior to the determination of what this natural law is? In other words, how do we know what our essential natures are?"[8] Making a similar point, Rod Dreher suggested that natural law persuades only those already committed to the "metaphysical dream" undergirding the position, and that "you have to believe so that you may understand."[9] Alan Jacobs made a similar point: "Is it really the best we can do to say 'You fail to meet my standards of rationality; therefore I refuse to debate with you further'?"[10]

Not at all deterred by the criticisms, Edward Feser responded to Hart on both the form and substance of the argument, claiming that Hart

---

5. Ibid., 71.

6. Potemra, "A Bracing Challenge to Conservative Natural-Law Theorists." For my responses, see Snell, "Understanding Natural Law" and "Natural Law Is neither Useless nor Dangerous."

7. Ibid.

8. Millman, "What's Natural about Natural Law?"

9. Dreher, "Why Natural Law Arguments Fail."

10. Jacobs, "More on Natural Law Arguments."

"equivocates insofar as he fails to distinguish two very different theories that go under the 'natural law' label," and that the ambiguity is "essential to his case" for if clarified "it becomes clear that with respect to both versions of natural law theory, Hart is attacking straw men and simply begging the question against them."[11] Distinguishing between *classical* and *new natural law*, Feser, who sides with the classical account, articulates just how diverse contemporary natural law happens to be, and how undifferentiated and unnuanced the critics are with respect to the theory:

> Where the two approaches differ is in their view of *which* philosophical claims, specifically, the natural law theorist must defend in order to develop a system of natural law ethics. The "old" natural law theorist would hold that a broadly classical, and specifically Aristotelian, metaphysical picture of the world must be part of a complete defense of natural law. The "new" natural law theorist would hold that natural law theory can be developed with a much more modest set of metaphysical claims—about the reality of free will, say, and a certain theory of practical reason—without having to challenge modern post-Humean, post-Kantian philosophy in as radical and wholesale a way as the "old" natural law theorist would.[12]

More particularly, while Hart's objection rests on the force and persuasiveness of Hume's is/ought distinction as negating Aristotelian final causality, commitment to which, Hart assumed, was a *sine qua non* for natural law, Feser explains that one major difference between the classical and new accounts is precisely the status of final causes:

> if there were a version of natural law theory that both appealed to final causes in nature and at the same time could allow for Hume's fact/value dichotomy, then Hart's argument might at least get off the ground. But there is no such version of natural law theory, and it seems that Hart is conflating the "new" and the "old" versions, thereby directing his attack at a phantom position that no one actually holds. The "new natural lawyers" *agree* with Hume and Hart that one cannot derive an "ought" from an "is," but precisely for that reason do *not* ground their position in a metaphysics of final causes. The "old" or classical natural law theory, meanwhile, certainly does affirm final causes, but precisely for that reason rejects

---

11. Feser, "A Christian Hart, a Humean Head." For the extended debate, see Hart, "Nature Loves to Hide," 71–72, and Feser, "Sheer Hart Attack."

12. Ibid.

> Hume's fact/value dichotomy, and in pressing it against them Hart simply begs the question.[13]

According to Feser, then, natural law theory is not a monolithic enterprise without distinctions, schools, or traditions; yet, a reader as sophisticated and subtle as David Bentley Hart apparently overlooks these nuances. This oversight will be important for the thesis of this book.

Given such disputes, it's unsurprising to find Protestants involved in similar head-scratching. While natural law is sometimes considered "a Catholic thing," contemporary social issues like abortion, homosexual marriage, embryo-destructive research, and religious freedom have made for unexpected alliances, and have also strained the usual fences and demarcations. For instance, two years prior to Hart's essay, Matthew Lee Anderson's piece for *Christianity Today* on why "the brokenness of human reason" made evangelicals wary of natural law arguments about marriage prompted a torrent of (pixilated) ink, with tensions similar to the Hart debate.[14] In an interview with Robert P. George, a leading natural law thinker, Al Mohler summarized the thought of many evangelicals:

> I think one of the crucial points of distinction has to do with just how compelling we believe the natural law to be. . . . I have to come at this from a position that is more informed by Romans chapter one. When I believe that what we are told there is that humanity is dead set to suppress the truth in unrighteousness and that there is no law written within the heart nor within the role of nature that will keep them from doing what they are determined to do except by the regenerating power of God, the gospel of Jesus Christ . . . at the end of the day, I am not very hopeful that a society hell bent on moral revolution is going to be held in check by our arguments by the moral law, the natural law. . . . And as an evangelical, we have every reason to use natural law arguments, we just don't believe that in the end they're going to be enough.[15]

But which version of the natural law is being discussed, classical or new? In a later response, Anderson remarked that some of his respondents "were right to remind us that there are different strands of 'natural law.' If

13. Ibid.

14. Anderson, "Why Natural Law Arguments Make Evangelicals Uncomfortable," para. 5; Girgis et al., "What Is Marriage?" 245–87. See also, as examples, Carter, "Why Aren't Natural Law Arguments More Persuasive?"; Knippenberg, "Evangelicals and Natural Law Update."

15. Mohler, "Moral Argument in Modern Times," para. 46.

I conflated the versions, it's only because from what I can tell evangelical Protestants are no more amenable to Russell Hittinger/Jay Budziszewski style [natural law] than the new natural law. On this point, I would be delighted to be wrong."[16] He may be right in his judgment that evangelical Protestants are as wary of the old versions as they are of the new, but recognition of the distinction is not at all evident in the various discussions in either the popular or academic venues.

Whose Law? Which Nature? Historicity and Meaning

In both these episodes, fault-lines around politics, culture, ecclesiology, soteriology, tradition, nature, grace, and the status of reason emerged, and in both it was suggested that distinguishing natural law theories might aid the conversation. Apparently, *old* or *classical* natural law theory is distinct from *new* natural law theory, although how they differ or what this might mean for the various disputes was not evenly explored or precisely defined in the exchanges. The work of distinguishing the accounts—old and new—and making a case for why the distinction may matter is the task of this book. The question should be forced, "which natural law are you talking about?"

But even posing this question challenges natural law, a theory claiming that some things are self-evident, written on the heart, or cannot not be known by functioning persons.[17] If C. S. Lewis is correct, and the first principles of practical reason are "without question as being to the world of action what axioms are to the world of theory," then how can multiple theories of natural law provide a defense of natural law theory?[18] Wouldn't the plurality of accounts call into question any claim that natural law is basic, foundational, universal, normative, and known to all?

Tradition Dependencies, Tradition Independence

I agree with John Finnis, a prominent voice for what has been termed the "new natural law theory" (NNL), that the first principles of natural law are

16. Anderson, "Assorted Thoughts on Evangelicals and Natural Law," para. 4.

17. See Budziszewksi, *Written on the Heart*, 179–219; Budziszewski, *What We Can't Not Know*, 19–53.

18. Lewis, *Abolition of Man*, 40.

universal and non-revisable "however extensively they were overlooked, misapplied, or defied in practical thinking. . . ."[19] Certainly "there is a history of the opinions or set of opinions, theories, and doctrines which assert that there are principles of natural law" but there is a clear distinction "between discourse about natural law and discourse about a doctrine or doctrines of natural law."[20] If this is so, as I would also maintain, then the distinction between old and new theories reflects a division in discourse *about* natural law rather than a division *of* natural law itself—people talk about natural law in a variety of ways, which does not thereby render a variety in the law. The basic practical truths "are available to anyone," even though "truths find various modes of expression in differen[t] cultures and traditions."[21]

At the same time, I also agree with Joseph Boyle, a close collaborator with Finnis, that "all intellectual efforts, including their results in such things as theories, propositions, or arguments, appear to depend in a variety of ways upon cultural contingencies and particularities," and, moreover, that "the work of natural law theorists is obviously tradition-dependent" and "this is a kind of tradition dependence which natural law theory need not deny."[22] In one sense of tradition-dependence, there is no contradiction involved in accepting "that the same proposition or prescription can be expressed in different languages or arrived at by enquiries with very different starting-points," a claim supported, I should think, by most or all natural lawyers.[23] Additionally, Boyle suggests a stronger sense of dependence, "namely, the sense of tradition dependence which applies to those engaged in an enquiry and who recognize themselves to be developing a body of thought which prior thinkers have originated and developed but left incomplete."[24] This, too, is not particularly problematic, for it would be the most wooly-headed thinker who supposed that Thomas Aquinas had solved once and for all every possible elaboration and application of the natural law covering every conceivable domain of practical reason. Of course tradition develops in this way, although development here has a somewhat weak sense of extension and completion rather than the stronger

---

19. Finnis, *Natural Law and Natural Rights*, 24.

20. Ibid., 25.

21. George, *In Defense of the Natural Law*, 254, also 249–58.

22. Boyle, "Natural Law and the Ethics of Traditions," 5–6.

23. Ibid., 6. Lewis made the same claim; see *Abolition*, 44–48.

24. Ibid., 7.

sense of evolving. Suggesting also a third, strongest sense of tradition de-pendence, Boyle identifies the role of moral community or "common way of life," including those groups which "maintain a strong sense of group solidarity and identity" from which to live out their values and ethical stan-dards. While he does not mention any particular group, it's possible to read trends in contemporary ecclesial ethics, sometimes quite strongly opposed to natural law theory's claims of universalism, as fitting this third sense of tradition dependence.[25] Here natural law claims tradition independence, denying that practical reason is "based on and limited by the values lived within a community," claiming that "much of moral thought is not essen-tially dependent upon the lived values of a moral community," even though the third sense maintains that at least some principles or virtues are "not accessible to those who do not share the life of a community."[26]

We can begin to ascertain some of the tensions in contemporary thought, for as Hart claimed that natural law required cultural formation and supernatural commitments considered bizarre within the "the modern conceptual world," so might Hauerwas suggest the priority of the story-formed community, or Mohler that "the gospel of Jesus Christ" is "where we begin and . . . where we end."[27] Strange bed-fellows, perhaps, but all equally committed, albeit in their own distinct ways, to the inadequacy of natural law in the face of the distinctives of theology, the church, and the Gospel, distinctives which the natural law not only cannot include but which are potentially violated by natural lawyers, even if unintentionally.

Modes of Meaning and the Nature(s) of Intention

In addition to Boyle's three senses of tradition-dependent rationality, the last of which he judges foreign to natural law accounts, I suggest a fourth sense, one which on face seems rather at odds with the universalism of natural law, what I'll term the *modes and stages of meaning*. Meaning itself is tradition dependent, or historical, because meaning depends upon the operations of concrete human subjects who always operate as historical.

25. Ibid., 9–10. See, as examples, Hauerwas, *A Community of Character: Toward a Constructive Christian Social Ethic*; Kallenberg, *Ethics as Grammar: Changing the Post-modern Subject*; Wells, *God's Companions: Reimagining Christian Ethics*; Yoder, *Body Politics: Five Practices of the Christian Community Before the Watching World*.

26. Ibid., 16, 11.

27. Mohler, "Moral Arguments," para. 46.

This statement is rather more than the first sense identified by Boyle, for the claim here is not simply that the same moral principles are expressed in disparate cultural forms, something analogous to "dog," "Hund," and "le chien," all of which mean the same thing. In other words, the claim is not that the differences in legal systems depend upon a deeper underlying correspondence of first principles. (I think that's true, it's just not what the fourth sense intends to convey.) Instead, the very meaning and way that meaning is formed changes in time and culture, thus even concepts such as "nature," or "law," or "reason" do not mean the same thing in all places and times, nor is the way that humans make those meanings identical, although this is not, in any way, to suggest the absence of invariant, transcultural, or normative precepts for how meaning, in its various modes, is or ought to be made.

As an example: The meaning of nature differs quite dramatically in history, as does the way human intelligence functions to form the various meanings.[28] For Aristotle, "nature" is essentialistic, universal, necessary, and unchanging in its defining properties. Correspondingly, "nature" is comprehended through *episteme* or science, which is itself deductively necessary, derived from certain and self-evident first principles, unchanging in its conclusions or methods, governed by syllogistic logic, and strictly delineated in terms of object and governing principle. Such an account is most definitely *not* what is meant by "nature" in a philosophy of emergence, governed not by logic but by statistical probability, little concerned with essential properties but with patterns and functions of recurrence, and admitting less of universal necessity than of correlations, tendencies, and directions. To put it another way, Boyle's first sense suggested different terms for something universal, like nature, whereas I mean that a common term, say "nature," might be meaningful in radically disparate ways. Aristotle, Descartes, Newton, Leibniz, a caveman, a modern person with little scientific background, Einstein, and Bohr—they might all use the term nature, perhaps even recognizing a historical continuity of the term itself (Boyle's sense 2), but do they mean the same thing or utilize the same tools of thought in governing meaning?

For each, nature means some variable sought by the intellect, an x expected to be discovered at the end of the relevant inquiry, but the meaning of x and the way inquiry unfolds is not universal—"nature" seems to lack a nature other than as the heuristic, the "unknown towards which

28. Lonergan, *A Second Collection*, 43–53.

inquiry is heading."[29] And yet, or so I'll claim, there is something universal, fixed, abiding, and normative governing the inquiry, although history itself would be relevant to figuring out how.

Very briefly here, with more detail in subsequent chapters, Lonergan demonstrates the historicity of knowing, including the way knowing functions within stages of meaning. For Lonergan, knowing is the result of a series of operations—experiencing, understanding, and judging—rather than any single operation. While an empiricist may confuse experience with knowing and the idealist reduce knowing to understanding, fully human knowing includes the entire nexus of operations. The operations themselves, while invariant constants of human knowing, can be directed, synthesized, or coordinated in a variety of different patterns, and thus the same operations admit of quite distinct exigencies. If *nature* functions as a heuristic—the unknown x to be attained when one knows—our own experience provides ample evidence that we seek the unknown in a variety of ways. The car mechanic, the stock broker, the baseball pitcher, the psychiatrist, the theologian, or the theoretical physicist all have some unknown occupying their attention, and all seek the elusive x which, when known, provides them *what* they are seeking to know. The *what* or x differs—what is causing that odd noise in the fan belt, what is a good value for this equity, what mix of speed and location will strike the batter out, what therapy will bring wholeness to the client, what kind of particle could travel faster than light?—and yet each utilizes experience, understanding, and judgment to arrive at an answer, albeit in widely different exigencies or patterns of meaning. As Lonergan puts it, "[d]ifferent exigences give rise to different modes of conscious and intentional operation, and different modes of such operation give rise to different realms of meaning."[30]

The first distinction is that between *common sense* and *theory*. Both realms of meaning, for the most part, attend to the same objects from differing viewpoints.[31] Common sense considers objects as they relate to us, the world of persons and bodies *out there* for me to observe and interact with. Common sense brings with it a descriptive realm of meaning. The water coming from this tap is hot (or so it seems to me), my uncle is short (or in relation to me), and the car is speeding toward me (thus I jump back). These descriptions do not arise from some rarified method known only

29. Lonergan, *Understanding and Being*, 64.
30. Lonergan, *Method in Theology*, 81.
31. Ibid.

to experts, but still real knowing is involved. We name these in ordinary language taught to the members of the linguistic community, but the words serve not to grasp or explain the Form of the object, but rather to facilitate communication and use relative to us.

As an example, Lonergan highlights the confusion of Socrates's interlocutors. They really did know how to navigate the marketplace or gymnasium in Athens; no one thought them clueless or without knowledge, and they used the words in the proper and conventional ways, but Socrates pushed a different mode. Dissatisfied with conventional use, he asked for definitions—for the *nature* of justice or courage or piety—accepting only accounts which were universal and explanatory. Consequently, "the systematic exigence not merely raises questions that common sense cannot answer but also demands a context for its answers, a context that common sense cannot supply or comprehend. This context is theory."[32] For theory, the pattern of questions and judgments does not *describe* things as they relate to us, but *explains* things in relation to other things. Rather than suggesting the water is "hot," as in common sense, theory creates units of temperature, comparing the water to a scale of 0 to 100 degrees Celsius rather than to my sense perception. So, too, rather than suggesting the car is moving "fast," theory calculates velocity by the relation of data to other data ($v=d/t$). Remember learning the difference between weight and mass in your early schooling, and how puzzling that was to your ordinary experience? That's the difference between common sense and theory.

We find the distinction in many domains of human inquiry, not just science. Consider the difference between the Trinity of St. Patrick's shamrock and the *homoousious* of the Creed, or how we explain fairness to a child ("Would you feel good if they took your toy?") and principles of contract in the first year of law school. In each case, relatively similar objects are addressed, and perhaps even by the same people, but in quite distinct modes of inquiry. And as the mode of inquiry functions differently, so too does meaning, and so too does the heuristic of expectation change, the unknown but sought x which guides the query, the "nature."

Even noting the distinction between common sense and theory engages in a distinct mode, namely, to advert to the way(s) one's own intellect operates and functions to make and control meaning. Consequently, one "is confronted with the three basic questions: What am I doing when I am

---

32. Ibid., 82.

knowing? Why is doing that knowing? What do I know when I do it?"[33] In asking questions like this, one's intelligence turns from the objects of common sense and theory to oneself as an "object" of study, or at least to one's own intellectual performance and operations as "objectified," and thus the realm of *interiority*, the third stage of meaning.[34] Interiority is noetic exegesis, when consciousness becomes explicit to itself, when one's own consciousness is studied from within, so to speak, from the perspective of oneself as a knower, and when one's inquiry is about inquiry itself in a process of self-interpretation.[35]

The distinction between common sense and theory is significant in natural law, for that distinction separates naïve physicalism and naïve psychologism from a theoretical anthropology.[36] So, too, does the realm of interiority distinguish contemporary versions of natural law, rooted in a first person perspective, from the classical versions rooted in theoretical anthropology and its concomitant metaphysics of the person. Upon these distinctions all my arguments rest, and so much more explanation is to be expected in the following chapters.

As much as I borrow from contemporary natural law's use of interiority, the thrust of the book is to sketch an outline for natural law from a fourth realm of meaning, what Lonergan terms *transcendence*.[37] His articulation of this realm is somewhat brief, written after severe illness and more hinted at than actualized. He does tell us, though, that such meaning moves "beyond the realms of common sense, theory, and interiority and into the realm in which God is known and loved," or into a realm of what he terms "religious conversion," the "flooding" of our hearts by God's love and the fundamental remaking of our very selves and our consciousness.[38]

Consequently, we find not one natural law account but many, and those accounts can be differentiated not only by variations of content or articulation—this thinker says that, but that thinker says this—but more fundamentally by the realms of meaning in which differences operate and are formed. Such differentiation is, of course, fairly complex and demands

---

33. Ibid., 83. See also Lonergan, *Insight*, 343–71.

34. Ibid., 83.

35. Snell, *Through a Glass Darkly*, 78–97; Snell and Cone, *Authentic Cosmopolitanism*, 15–43.

36. Snell, "Protestant Prejudice," 21–30; Snell, "Performing Differently."

37. Lonergan, *Method*, 83.

38. Ibid., 83, 105.

"a rather highly developed consciousness" or phenomenological attunement.[39] One has to have appropriated one's own intellect.

The Argument

Following the hints made by Feser and Anderson, I suggest that many of the disputes in contemporary discourse about the natural law suffer from a lack of differentiation, thus confusing and conflating various accounts, merging together what should be distinct, and using arguments which may very well respond to one account as if they respond to another, even though they operate in widely different modes of meaning.

I claim, too, that the usual Protestant objections against the natural law are similarly undifferentiated, thus not particularly responsive to contemporary natural law, and can be accepted by natural law in the mode of interiority, and sublimated in transcendence.

To summarize the arguments I hope to demonstrate:

1. Natural law operates within stages of meaning, and thus there are natural law accounts articulated from the standpoint of common sense, theory, and interiority. Each mode of meaning brings different emphases and implications for the account.

2. The usual Protestant objections to natural law—the "Protestant Prejudice"—are objections directed towards natural law as it developed within the theoretical mode of meaning, and as such are reasonable and sensible objections, even if not entirely persuasive.

3. Contemporary natural law—here I'll include the work of John Paul II, Martin Rhonheimer, the so-called new natural law (NNL), and the cosmopolitanism of Bernard Lonergan—have moved beyond the theoretical mode into interiority, although the various thinkers express this in various ways: perspective of the acting person, first person accounts, subjectivity, internal point of view, phenomenological experience, intentionality, and so on. While these versions are not reducible to each other, and in fact disagree on several important issues, particularly in application, all operate from within the mode of interiority rather than theory.

4. Natural law understood from the mode of interiority is quite able to include the effects of sin on intellect and will, the role of grace, the

39. Ibid., 84.

importance of community, history (including salvation history), and the centrality of the Gospel. For Protestants to continue the usual objections without differentiation is to commit a straw man, attacking natural law as *theory* as if this defeats natural law as *interiority*.[40] To be sure, there are able and competent proponents of *classical* or theoretical natural law and by no means do they admit defeat to either the Protestant objections or those of contemporary natural law. In no way will I claim to have answered or refuted classical positions, but insofar as Protestants continue to argue the way they have, they will not be responding to natural law as it is currently understood by many schools.

5. An account of natural law incorporating history, sin, grace, and Gospel remains natural law, but it is natural law opening to a further mode of meaning beyond interiority. I am here attempting to articulate the broad outlines of natural law in a new mode, namely, from transcendence, *the perspective of love.*

A Final Word

In the following pages thinkers from quite distinct modes of thought and vocabularies are placed into conversation. In all of this, I can claim to represent no particular school, for while I am indebted to classical natural law accounts, I'm more sympathetic to the work of John Paul II, Martin Rhonheimer, and the NNL theorists, borrowing heavily from them all; but I don't claim any of these schools or thinkers would endorse my arguments or understand the modes of meaning as I do. My thought is enriched by them all, and I gratefully acknowledge my debts, just as I would be delighted if they found my arguments helpful, but in the end I take their arguments down different paths. Of course, the major influence in all my work is the late Bernard Lonergan (1904–1984), a Jesuit theologian-philosopher whose work on noetic exegesis governs the entirety of this project. As in my previous writings, I assume that Lonergan is not well known, and so I view this as a brief introduction to some aspects of his work, even as I take his thought into new conversations and directions.

In the end, I want to claim that natural law is more complicated in its varieties than is often thought, but that since the natural law is a work of

---

40. This is an argument I posited in "Protestant Prejudice," 21–30. See also my "Thomism and Noetic Sin, Transposed," 7–28.

human reason, and since human reason is also governed and ordered by love (*ordo amoris*), natural law is best grasped insofar as love is grasped. The human person can best be understood in terms of love, and since love is bent by sin and healed only by grace, an account of natural law can certainly include those very aspects which the usual Protestant objections find lacking. But before we get to that love which reveals the very meaning of the human, we start with common sense and with theory.

Part One

*Natural Law as
Nature and as Theory*

1

Natural Law as *Ordo Naturae*

In a very helpful essay, J. Budziszewski explains those elements common to all natural law theories. All "share a conviction that the most basic truths of right and wrong ... are not only right for everyone, but at some level known to everyone by the ordinary exercise of reason. They are an heirloom of the family of man."[1] Every natural lawyer would agree, he suggests, that basic truths are natural because somehow "embedded into the structure of creation, especially *human* nature, which includes the structure of the human mind," and all would agree that this structure obligates or binds.[2] True, known to be true, and right.

Particularly, he differentiates four aspects commonly affirmed by classical accounts, while new natural law demonstrates less commitment to the second and third: (1) a normative structure to practical reason; (2) an evident design to human nature; (3) the particular aspects of this design and the innate purposes and meanings of the designs; (4) natural consequences or discord to violating the good proper to our nature.[3] As Budziszewski indicates, much of the dispute in the natural law literature between classical and contemporary theories pivots around the status of teleology in nature: does nature reveal design, can design be known absent theological commitments, does design entail normativity and obligation, is the Aristotelian paradigm of final causality still meaningful, is metaphysical biology

1. Budziszewski, *The Line Through the Heart*, 199.
2. Ibid.
3. Ibid., 200.

sensible, and does natural law begin with and ground its conclusions upon nature? In short, what is the status of teleology?

As Leo Strauss articulated in his classic *Natural Right and History*, commitment to natural right seems reminiscent of a world existing no longer, part of a teleological universe "destroyed by modern natural science" and rejected by the social sciences in the name of "History and in the name of the distinction between Facts and Values."[4] Given the ateleological universe, historicism, and the fact/value distinction, it might appear quite unreasonable to maintain belief in natural law or natural right, for the intellectual substructure is, as Alasdair MacIntyre put it, echoed by David Bentley Hart, "unacceptable by the dominant standards of modernity."[5] Yet the cultural and scientific developments noted by Strauss have not resulted in the withering away of either natural right or natural law but instead contributed to a renewed vitality as some thinkers deepen the commonplaces of the tradition while others develop or stretch the tradition in new directions. This is to be expected, for challenges to a tradition cause crisis, irrational and wooden traditions either capitulating or refusing to engage while more supple and reasonable traditions ask new questions, pose new answers, transpose old answers, and articulate themselves in new and productive directions.[6]

This is not the first time that natural law has developed in response to a crisis presented by some theoretical or social challenge, so we should not be surprised to find it developing previously. And in each of these moments of challenge, I suggest, the crisis has been occasioned by the meaning of "nature." What is so natural about the natural law; what is nature?

INTENTIONAL DIFFERENCES

In the Introduction I claimed that "nature" functioned as a heuristic, which is to say that its meaning comes from what we seek to know, the unknown *x*, or from what we intend. Since what humans seek to know differs quite radically across cultures, times, places, and tasks, there are consequently many "natures." This is not an unknowable chaos, however, since paying attention to how our conscious operations work—noetic exegesis—allows

4. Strauss, *Natural Right and History*, 7–8.

5. MacIntyre, "Theories of Natural Law in the Culture of Advanced Modernity," 94.

6. For the rationality of Thomism as a tradition, see MacIntyre, *Three Rival Versions of Moral Enquiry*, 127–49.

us to explain the origin and development of the many "natures" by advert-ing to the disparate ways or exigences of how humans direct consciousness. Consequently, we can distinguish the multiple meanings of nature, includ-ing the historical development of those meanings and the various crises which have emerged in that history, by adverting to the different functions of consciousness.

According to Lonergan, Aristotle expressed something fundamental in the opening lines of the *Metaphysics*: "All men by nature desire to know." When the animal has its physiological needs met, it sleeps, but when the human has met its needs, we do math or theology or go exploring, for our intelligence is essentially dynamic love; so long as we want to know, so long as we care and direct our intelligence towards knowing, our consciousness continues to operate in a cumulative, self-correcting, and indefinite process of accumulating data and acquiring new insights.[7] This dynamism is for some unknown, and we seek this unknown spontaneously, by some innate tendency, although it "is a conscious tendency . . . we do so intelligently."[8] Children ask incessant questions, without prompting, according to some inner impetus, although the dull child, the one who does not care to know, can rarely be coaxed or coerced into knowing if he lacks the desire, for knowledge does not just happen because the external data is present but because of the interior condition of inquiry and the interior operations by which we arrive at knowing.[9] The interior condition manifests itself in questions, for we would not ask unless there was an unknown, and we could not ask unless we sought something. Something: what we seek exists as an ideal, but not clearly or explicitly or we would already have what we were seeking.[10]

The transcendental condition of our questions is the dynamic desire to know, and to know what is unknown, an x, and this unknown x func-tions as a heuristic, as an intended ideal that as yet is not appropriated or known. It is whatever is intended by the question. But what is intended by questions is not empty or abstract. The condition of questioning is tran-scendental—the "pure question"—but "no one just wonders. We wonder

---

7. Lonergan, *Understanding and Being*, 4–20; Snell and Cone, *Authentic Cosmopoli-tanism*, 1–12, 44–65.

8. Ibid., 4–5.

9. Lonergan, *Insight*, 29.

10. Lonergan, *Understanding and Being*, 5.

about something."[11] Of course, we can wonder about many things, in many different ways, and there are different heuristics at different times, in different communities, and so on. The pursuit is intelligent and conscious, but it is not conceptually explicit, and it differs and develops as questions differ and develop, so "how do you proceed methodically . . . to the attainment of something that you do not know, something which, if known, would not have to be pursued?"[12] According to Lonergan, the solution is precisely that metatheory by which we try to catch ourselves in the act of knowing which Budziszewski judged distracting:

> The solution . . . to this problem is self-appropriation. . . . The ideal we seek in seeking the unknown, in trying to know, is conceptually implicit. There does not exist naturally, spontaneously, through the whole of history, a set of propositions, conceptions, and definitions that define the ideal of knowledge. But to say that conceptually it is implicit . . . that these statements differ in different places and at different times—they are historically conditioned—is not to say that it is nonexistent. While the conception of the ideal is not by nature, still there is something by nature. The ideal of knowledge is myself as intelligent, as asking questions, as requiring intelligible answers . . . and if we can turn in upon these fundamental tendencies, then we are on the way to getting hold. . . .[13]

Denying any universal set of propositions and definitions may seem surprising for a proponent of natural law, but note as well his affirmation of a basic, universal, and innate tendency—the pure question—to which we pay attention as a clue.

The pure question is innate and universal, but the exigences of the pure question are disparate, with the plurality of "natures" tied to the plurality of patterns in which questions can develop. We should not be surprised to find within the natural law tradition serious differences of articulation and meaning, then; nor should this pose any threat to the coherence of the tradition and its claims of universal legitimacy, for any theory which claims to be inextricably caught up in human reason is thereby inextricably historical. Further, as tied to reason, which has its grounding in the pure question and the dynamic desire to know, we can investigate differences

---

11. Lonergan, *Insight*, 34.

12. Lonergan, *Understanding and Being*, 13.

13. Ibid., 14.

within the tradition as understandable because of the patterns and exigencies of questions.

COMMON SENSE AS MEANING

Intelligence has as its transcendental condition the desire to know; insofar as this desire is innate and operative, inquiry occurs spontaneously, for the conditions of inquiry are (a) desire itself and (b) something about which to inquire, which is provided through data. Not only is inquiry spontaneous, but so too are the insights arising from the questions of inquiry.[14] When we ask questions in response to some data, we experience the tension of inquiry (the not knowing) as well as a release of that tension when we have an insight into the data. Insights occur in response to asking "What is this?" and present a possible grasp of intelligibility immanent to the data. Of course, insights often turn out to be inadequate or incorrect, but the "Aha!" experience when we "see" or "understand" or "get" something, even if still vaguely and inchoately, is not at all unusual or recondite. This happens to us all quite frequently. Since intelligence is dynamic, an intelligence which follows out its innate desire or love of knowing hardly turns off whenever the first bright idea pops up; instead, one bright idea leads to another and another, allowing insights to accumulate in the process of learning.[15] Further, such insights can be communicated to others, even taught to others, and an intersubjective sharing of perceived intelligibility allows from "the communal development of intelligence in the family, the tribe, the nation, the race," since humans "are born into a community that possesses a common fund of tested answers."[16]

For Lonergan, the spontaneity of inquiry, the similarly spontaneous accumulation of insights, and the communication of insights are components of common sense. In its particular mode, common sense, unlike theory, exhibits little concern for universality. Rooted in the experiences of individuals and the promulgation of those experiences within particular communities, common sense is "not concerned with the universal definition of bravery or truth or justice" even though, of course, it wants "people

---

14. Lonergan, *Insight*, 197.
15. Ibid.
16. Ibid., 198.

to be truthful, brave, and just. . . ."[17] Common sense will develop under-standings of those virtues, will bequeath and educate members of the par-ticular community into them, and may even assume that its understanding is normatively and universally true, but it does not methodically develop symbolization attempting a universal account; it uses "our" language to convey "our" beliefs about how "we" live, and perhaps even "our" thoughts about how "they" live.

The reason for this unconcern is that common sense rests on how things of the world relate to us, and while persons of common sense very often think that how things relate and appear to them is self-evidently the way things are *in themselves*, common sense has no methodology by which to demonstrate this, nor would it be interested. In epistemological terms, as I discussed in the Introduction, common sense confines itself to descrip-tion in relation to us, not an explanation of data in relation to other data. So the water is hot, the man is tall, the car moves fast relative to us, as opposed to the relationship of data to data in degrees, mass, or velocity. The perspec-tive of data relative to us is not unintelligent, of course, but it is a *limiting of concern*, a particular stance towards the world under a certain description and use, and the world appears under the guise of concern and interest. The person of common sense approaches the world from a certain domain of interests, and whatever does not fit that domain of love and cares does not, in a certain sense, exist at all for them. It is meaningless and thus ignored or censored out: "It clings to the immediate and practical, the concrete and particular. It remains within the familiar world of things for us. Rockets and space platforms are superfluous if you intend to remain on this earth."[18]

Nor is this bigotry or provincialism. Most of us spend most of our time in the world of common sense, existing in a world of bodies "out there" as sources of pleasure, pain, use, comfort. When we drive our car or fix a meal, play a game or teach our children how to ride a bike, use a fork, or treat the neighbors justly, we are most often in the world of common sense. Common sense is not unintelligent, but a mode of intelligence by which we organize the concrete world in such a way that is predictable, manageable, and coherent: "the man of common sense wants a nucleus such that with the minimum of further insights he will be able to deal with any concrete situations that arise in his living."[19] As such, common sense tends to arise within multiple individuals and communities: "Far more

17. Lonergan, *Understanding and Being*, 87.

18. Lonergan, *Insight*, 202.

19. Ibid., 90.

than the sciences, common sense is divided into specialized departments. For every difference of geography, for every difference of occupation, for every difference of social arrangements, there is an appropriate variation of common sense."[20] The way "we" do it may work very well for the conditions of life we tend to find "here," which is why "they" seem like bumblers when "they" use the accumulated insights of their community "here" and also why we feel such vertigo when we are "there."

Common Sense as Law

Since common sense is intelligent, its accumulated insights are very often coherent and reasonable, but that which is coherent and reasonable has a claim to be true, even binding—"this is the way that we organize and do things here, and it is the way you ought to do it as well." Still, the way that common sense obliges or demands is peculiar to the mode of common sense; in the following sections I explain three variations of how common sense expresses natural law.

Natural Law as Inclination

Insofar as common sense confronts the world relative to our own perspectives, projects, interests, and concerns, it carries a latent possibility of reductionism whereby the being of the world *is* what it is insofar as it serves or frustrates my projects and concerns. The world, after all, is not given to us except through the mediation of our own awareness, an awareness which we govern through our own mode of concern:

> Both the sensations and the bodily movements are subject to an organizing control . . . there is, immanent in experience, a factor variously named conation, interest, attention, purpose. We speak of consciousness as a stream, but the stream involves not only the temporal succession of different contents, but also direction, striving, effort. Moreover, this direction of the stream is variable.[21]

---

20. Ibid., 203.

21. Ibid., 205. This is the underlying premise of Snell and Cone, *Authentic Cosmopolitanism* and its articulation of the education of love—the world is, for us, as we love it; if our loves are properly ordered, so too the world.

We do not inhabit the world as passive receptors, but rather as active organizers and censors, with our conation or attention the principle by which the world is organized. Of course, we can attend the world in a variety of ways.[22] Conation, or patterns of care, function as organizing principles which, in a sense, command consciousness and make the world. If "nature," in its plurality, is the *whatness* of the objects of our intention, and our intention can be governed by the interests of common sense—as biological, or aesthetic, or dramatic—then nature can be viewed as whatever our inclinations intend.

Plato gives us several characters who serve as symbols of this understanding of nature. Consider Thrasymachus from the *Republic*, for whom it is by nature right and just to seek the advantage of the stronger but unnatural to curtail and curb such advantage.[23] Similar views are expressed by Polus and Callicles in *Gorgias*, with Callicles particularly apt as an example. He enters by asking if Socrates is joking, then rebukes him for claiming to pursue truth but actually dragging "us into these tiresome popular fallacies, looking to what is fine and noble, not by nature, but by convention."[24]

> Nature herself makes it plain that it is right for the better to have the advantage over the worse, the more able over the less. . . . But if a man arises endowed with a nature sufficiently strong, he will, I believe, shake off all these controls, burst his fetters and break loose. And trampling upon our scraps of paper, our spells and incantations, and all our unnatural conventions, he rises up and reveals himself our master who was once our slave, and there shines forth nature's true justice.[25]

As Eric Voegelin interprets this scene, the dispute is over what form of love is to master and obligate our lives, either the Good (Socrates) or nature understood as "the stronger or weaker *physis*" (Callicles).[26] In the end, what occurs is an existential re-ordering by Socrates, for whom pleasure is not identical to the good, and for whom *eros* is the proper governing love, and thus for whom the "ordered universe," or nature, is a different world

---

22. For an exposition on these patterns of organization, see Lonergan, *Insight*, 204–12; Snell, *Through a Glass Darkly*, 86–91.

23. Plato, *Republic*, 338a–344d in *Collected Dialogues of Plato*.

24. Plato, *Gorgias*, 482e in *Collected Dialogues of Plato*.

25. Ibid., 483d–484b.

26. Voegelin, *Plato*, 32.

entirely.[27] Multiple natures, corresponding to the objectives of distinct loves, are at stake, but it is the existential ordering of loves—the therapy of desire—determining which nature prevails.

In a more contemporary context, the ambiguity of "nature" is observed in the moral and legal disputes about sexuality. On the one hand, homosexual acts are described by some as unnatural acts; on the other, the prevalence of same-sex sexual activity in animals is used to articulate the naturalness of homosexuality, as is the experience of same-sex attraction within humans. Some animals, and some persons, have sexual inclinations or desires for members of the same sex, and it is thus natural for them, while others find such desires alien and thus unnatural.

The unifying thread between Callicles and contemporary sexual politics is the role of inclination and desire in interpreting and defining nature. When we say of a person's behavior, "It's only natural," are we appealing to the statistically common inclination, or the inclination of this particular person whether statistically usual or unusual? In either event, nature is defined in reference to patterns of inclination, perhaps biological, but also aesthetic or dramatic. It's quite easy to find judgments on the naturalness or unnaturalness of a desire, a food, a behavior, even of religion, art, and architecture which seem to express the common sense understandings of how "we" or "they" organize and control our judgments.

Natural Law as Proverb

Common sense interprets data relative to us, and it was that aspect I stressed in natural law as inclination, but already by the conclusion of that section emerged the intersubjective or communal aspect of common sense. We don't have inclinations as individuals solely since inclinations are formed, educated, and interpreted within communities of meaning. Every parent, every tribe, every nation, and every tradition hands on certain tested and verified judgments about inclinations and desires in the hope of shaping both the behavior and inclinations of the other members. A parent wants not only to form their children's actions, but wants them to love certain things in certain ways.

Plato provides multiple examples of this as well. For instance, the opening exchange between Socrates and Cephalus in the *Republic* brilliantly reveals how accumulated insights pass into the habitual texture

27. Plato, *Gorgias*, 508a in *Collected Dialogues of Plato*.

of community life, and how philosophy (theory) disrupts such meaning. Socrates has accompanied a group of young men to Cephalus's home where they find him dressed in the regalia of ritual religious observance, as befitting a man of social position and wealth. Very rudely, and in some violation of the rules of hospitality, the polite conversation between the two elders is forced into *elenchus* by Socrates who asks of Cephalus how his money was obtained and whether Cephalus' own account of the justice with which he acted was sufficient. Entirely unperturbed, Cephalus draws upon the poetry of Pindar—"a fine saying and admirable"—in explaining justice as a kind of honesty and fairness in one's business with men and gods.[28]

In doing so, Cephalus relies upon the customs and education of his generation, for whom Pindar adequately states the laws and customs of the city and its form of life, its common sense. The appeal to Pindar is an appeal to authority, but not the authority of someone who explains, but the authority of someone who represents "our" way of doing things. Cephalus has no interest in explaining the reason behind the custom and has no sense of law's principles, for he is one of those kept lawful by the "force of tradition and habit . . . but they are not righteous by 'love of wisdom.'"[29] So long as no crisis threatens the community's ability to hand on its ways and mores, custom governs, and proverbs rather than explanations form the young; but such a community cannot explain or justify itself except by appeal to its venerable authorities, and they cannot justify themselves except by being accepted as venerable, and so in moments of crisis the old ways are exposed as *nothing other* than convention. Upon being challenged by Socrates, Cephalus departs, returning to the prayers and sacrifices mandated by his office in the *polis*, leaving the argument to his son, heir both of property and proverb, who begins with proverbs of his own before acknowledging his ignorance, the inadequacy of the poets, and the status of Socrates as superior and guide. Socrates, the symbol of theory, threatens the established order of custom, for theory and proverb attend to the same world in different ways.

In the *Oresteia* trilogy by Aeschylus, the hold and force of common sense is powerfully presented.[30] Duty-bound to avenge the murder of his father, Agamemnon, Orestes confronts the horrible reality that doing so entails the slaughter of Cassandra, his mother. Of course, one could read Cassandra as having justly restored the balance in her killing of

28. Plato, *Republic*, 331a–b in *Collected Dialogues of Plato*.

29. Voegelin, *Plato*, 57.

30. Aeschylus, *Aeschylus I*.

Agamemnon, for not only did Agamemnon sacrifice their daughter, Iphigenia, for favorable winds to Troy, but Agamemnon's family bore guilt for the murder of his cousins, the brothers of Aegisthus, and violation of hospitality to his uncle. On almost every level, some customary duty is denied and requires a righting of the scales.

In the matricide, Orestes demonstrates filial piety, earning for him the favor and protection of Apollo but also the hate of the loathsome Furies, chthonic and ancient spirits of revenge. Older than the Olympians, and protesting that their venerable rights have been ignored by the younger deities, the Furies demand Orestes' death, for he has killed his mother. He's also defended his father, and much of the play concerns the conflicts within common sense—for there are, recall, many common senses, and since they are little concerned for the universal they easily contradict each other: age versus youth, mothers and fathers, men and women, ground and sky, body and mind, blood and contract.

The dispute is resolved through the procedures of law in the court established by Athene on Mars Hill. The Aereopagus overcomes mere custom, for each side presents its case before the discretion of the jury, even though Athene arrives dressed for war in order to persuade the Furies to accept the court, and even though the deadlocked jury is resolved by Athene who admits her (arbitrary) preference for the male. Enraged, the Furies seek to reassert their rights, and Athene first threatens them with the force of Zeus before seducing them with the promise of enthronement in the soil below Mars Hill, from which their spirit will seep into the soil, water, plant life, and air of Athens. Revenge will be domesticated, but the law will be revenge shrouded with the robes of justice. Aeschylus reveal to us that the law of a city is nothing more than "common love" and "common hate" by which the city unites in its self-regard against all foreign and alien encroachments. What is one's own is obviously good, while the foreign is obviously bad. Such is the natural law of common sense made sacrosanct by time.

Natural Law as Nature

In distinguishing the first two varieties of common sense natural law, I've emphasized various aspects of common sense as a mode of meaning. For instance, common sense tends to (1) describe the world relative to us, and (2) tends to codify its insights in concrete and practical terms which while not concerned with universalizability are nonetheless handed on intersubjectively. Common sense also (3) tends to consider the real under the description of "bodies," and develops a version of objectivity in keeping with a world so described.

Unlike common sense, theory relates data to data and things to things, as, for instance, velocity is determined by the relation of distance to time or temperature is determined in terms of degrees Celsius in relation to water's freezing point. For theory, the world we sense is not so much described as it is explained, with explanations taking us into the realm of the intelligible more than the sensible; common sense, on the other hand, has no interest in leaving the sensible, and expresses its grasp of intelligibility with constant eye to sense and concrete action. Thus, not velocity but the fastness or slowness of the car relative to my safely crossing the street, or the hotness of the water relative to boiling an egg or scalding my hand. To distinguish the object of concern, or the way reality is grasped by the modes, Lonergan distinguishes *things* from *bodies*.[31] For the world of theory, the object of our conscious intention is understandable rather than necessarily imaginable, whereas common sense intends and thinks the real as imaginable. For the chemist *qua* chemist, water is a formula of intelligible relations, for the chemist *qua* person of common sense, water is something to drink. Water as *thing* is understood, but not imagined or touched, while water as *body* is always imagined as touchable. In the world of theory, God is three persons in one being united in a dynamic relationship of *periochoresis*; God for the child of common sense is an old man who sits on a throne up in heaven. In a way, both intend the same reality, but with different patterns of interest, with common sense intending bodies.

As such, "nature" for common sense 3 will be understood as *body*. This seems slightly counterintuitive, but as an example consider the way that the Platonic and Aristotelian version of "Form" is usually taught, with Plato's "Form" expressed visually as "up there," but Aristotle's as "down here and in things." Both express Form as invisible body, a common sense articulation, for body is understood by common sense as something which exists "already out there now real."[32] As "already," a real body exists prior to and independent of our perception; as "out there," not an idea but as possessing its own independent existence; as "now real," possessing temporal distinctness as part of its independence.

31. Lonergan, *Insight*, 275–82.
32. Ibid., 276.

Common Sense Objectivity and Innateness

Along with its "already out there now realness," a corresponding sense of objectivity in knowing attaches to bodies as opposed to things. While theory may demand a formula or a proof or an experiment to justify claims to know, common sense tends to think that knowing is like taking a good look at a body, seeing what is there, assuming anything not seen or imagined is not really real. (Imagine a child wondering if God exists because we cannot see Him.)[33]

This kind of objectivity is often mirrored in the language of "innateness." In ordinary discussion, natural law is often presented as if moral principles were somehow innate, as if we just had moral knowledge "in" our souls or minds. The "in" language corresponds to the body-language of "out there," since objectivity for common sense is usually thought of as getting what is "out there" somehow in the "in here" of mind.[34] The law, then, is objective because it exists independent of our perceptions and wishes, but fortunately we already know the law, it's just part of our mental structure and framework; we just have it "in here" even though its objectivity is modeled after the "already out there now real."

I'll save the question of the innateness of natural law for later, although clearly I doubt innateness as pictured by common sense. But this pattern of "in" and "out" pervades common sense 3, with natural law thought to reside *in* things, but by this they mean nature as the physical world. Natural law is modeled after the properties innate in physical reality, and natural law is the *ordo naturae*.

Law in Nature, Enchanted or Disenchanted

In one form, the *ordo naturae* is a kind of cosmic-mysticism where the divine ordering principle of the universe operates within nature to render it *cosmos* rather than *chaos*, with an isomorphism between the ordering principle of the macrocosm and the microcosm of soul or city. To live according

33. Snell and Cone, *Authentic Cosmopolitanism*, 23–31.

34. This need not be unintelligent. Descartes's whole project, one shaping the modern problematic for both empiricists and idealists was modeled on the image of the mind "in here," the world "out there," and ideas as a veil "in between." The best thinkers followed suit, all of them trying to solve the theoretical problems of epistemology and metaphysics with an image borrowed from an utterly distinct mode of meaning. See Snell, *Through a Glass Darkly*, 9–40.

to nature is to follow the principle of order (*arche, logos, physei dikaion, theios nomos*). In each formulation, the ordering principle is symbolized as governing the entire cosmos, with a unity or parallel between the laws of nature, the laws of the city, and the laws of the soul—metaphysics, physics, politics, and ethics are, in a real if confused sense, about the same thing.[35]

Following Eliade, Merold Westphal identifies in mimetic forms of religion such commitment to nature, "not simply or primarily because nature is the primary manifestation of the divine, but because through worship human existence is to be assimilated to the natural order," insofar as worship comports and imitates itself to the rhythms and forces operative in nature.[36] Through ritual imitation, religion "seeks to integrate human existence into the natural cosmos," in such a way that the distinction between ritual and mundane life is rather porous, but the order "in" nature becomes incorporated "into" one's own life through mimesis.

In philosophical rather than religious history, the natural philosophy of the pre-Socratics, "started by inquiring into the origin of the universe, its *physis*," was as much a metaphysical study as empirical, for the natural principles were thought to underlie and order "the comprehension of everything which proceeds from that order and now exists."[37] While each thinker and school presented their own account, the tendency was towards a greater connection between the laws governing the cosmos and all other aspects "in 'the nature of being' . . . in the spiritual world," so as to find order and method in human life."[38] The turn from natural philosophy to the human things, as Socrates recounted his own biography, was already underway: "The experience of being activates man to the reality of order in himself and in the cosmos . . . the experience of being is the primary experience of the cosmos in which man is consubstantial with the things of his environment, a partnership that in philosophy is heightened to the awake consciousness of the community of order uniting thought and being."[39]

In its pre-Socratic beginnings, philosophy, like earlier mythic or theological speculations, "attempts to find the origin of the cosmos in elementary forces," although "the gods of polytheism are excluded from it," leading

---

35. Voegelin, *Anamnesis*, 59.

36. Westphal, *God, Guilt, and Death*, 195.

37. Jaeger, *Paideia*, 155.

38. Ibid., 165. For the notion of philosophy as a way of life, see Hadot, *What is Ancient Philosophy?*

39. Voegelin, *Anamnesis*, 80.

to "the dissociation of a cosmos-full-of-gods into a dedivinized order of things."[40] Being, rather than the gods, is the unknown *arche*, the heuristic *x*, and thus metaphysics becomes the discourse concerning nature. Still, being is articulated as a material principle, whether as water, or air, or fire, or *logos*, but like mimetic religion the *arche* "stands at the beginning like a god from whose initiative a chain of events passes right down to the being that is experienced here and now," the study of which is not merely abstract but intimately connected to the right, or natural, way to live.[41] Asking, "what is right by nature?" still turns to forces outside of us, even if somehow coterminous (even innate) with our thought. Natural law *is nature* itself, or at least the principles of nature which comprise and govern all that is—us too.

Clearly I'm simplifying a complex development in the history of ideas and culture, but I'm trying to present a taxonomy rather than comprehensive history; my point is merely to demonstrate the possibility of a development in natural law which in its mode of inquiry is beholden to common sense in conceiving order as something which could be operative *out there*, or out there in nature, or *as* nature, even if mirrored in the "in here" of intellect.[42] Nor are attempts to read law in nature relics from a previous time. Martin Rhonheimer, for one, thinks that such "physicalist" accounts dominated both neoscholasticism and revisionism into the current century:

> This means that, within the perspective of certain academic trends (in which a large number of contemporary moral theologians have been educated), the natural law is frequently understood as an object of knowledge that lies, somehow, in the nature of things, over against the practical reason. . . . In close connection with this foreshortened conception of the natural law can be found a derivation of moral norms from a naturally ("physicalistically") understood reality. . . . This is a result of identifying the *lex naturalis*—in the sense of modern scientific law—with a natural order that lies in the being of things; it means understanding the concept of a "natural order" (*ordo naturalis*) that lies beneath the "ought" in such a way that the reason is reduced to an organ that merely "reads off" what "is" and prescribes what "ought" to be.[43]

---

40. Ibid., 75.
41. Ibid.
42. Snell, "Protestant Prejudice." See also Snell, "Saving Natural Law from Itself."
43. Rhonheimer, *Natural Law and Practical Reason*, 5–7.

For someone like Rhonheimer, however, *lex naturalis* does not mean what it is often taken to mean, as "some external standard 'out there'" or "in the heart," as we'll see.[44]

CONCLUDING THOUGHTS

I opened this chapter referring to J. Budziszewski's explanation that all versions of natural law, whatever their differences, hold that law is somehow "embedded into the structure of creation, especially *human* nature. . . ." No doubt this is true, but much depends on the little word "into." The history of natural law, including current proponents, includes common sense readings of "into," and, in fact, includes several different types of common sense readings: (1) natural law as found *in* inclinations, (2) natural law as found *in* the intuitive meanings of intersubjective community, and (3) natural law as *in* nature. Each expression operates within the common sense mode of meaning which (1) begins with and is largely limited to non-theoretical, albeit still intelligent, descriptions of very powerful experiences, (2) codified and shared within community and its educational forms, often through proverbs and authority articulating successful ways of living and acting, and (3) viewing the real in a common sense grasp of the bodies, or the "already out there now real," known through a kind of objectivity which grasps ordering principles of the real. For each type of common sense natural law, "nature" corresponds to a certain pattern of interest or care, emerging as the heuristic in keeping with that same pattern of care. Nature, for common sense, is the ordering pattern of that which is most real *to us*, as experienced by us, whether in our passions, or our community, or our religion, and even in our attempts to articulate the grounds of being. Law, for such meaning, is the order found in nature, an order which we do not create or constitute but rather find always already operative, not of our own devising; law is the order of nature, the *ordo naturae*.

Already, though, certain tensions and patterns emerge prompting the transition to a new differentiation of consciousness, a new mode of meaning. We see the transition in the history of ideas, of course, for Socrates asks hard questions about inclinations and custom, as does Sophocles, Aeschylus, Aristotle, the Stoics, and others; so, too, do the queries about the right way to live prompt further questions about the nature of "nature,"

---

44. Novak, "Bernard Lonergan," 248.

the genesis of order, political and moral systems best in keeping with that order, the distinction between appearance and reality, and so on. Despite the developments, common sense natural law 1—nature as inclination—is alive and well, for instance, in both sides of the debates about same-sex marriage. Common sense natural law 2—nature as proverb—appears whenever insights cluster and are shared within concrete communities of shared value and meaning, with the various common senses of different groups each appearing natural and normative to its membership. Common sense natural law 3—nature as nature—continues in both its mythic and philosophic forms whenever natural law is thought to reside *in* the world of nature, either as a function of the divine or as material order itself (*ordo naturae*), or as innately known.

Since the various common sense natural laws continue, so too the tensions and questions regarding their meaning and adequacy. It's not as though *Antigone* settled once and for all the difference between what it means to be a good citizen and what it means to be a good human, and Socrates certainly put no end to the sophists among us, or to the force of custom and habit. Consequently, while we can trace how the tensions and questions within the historical past prompted developments within natural law as it moved from common sense to the theoretical mode of meaning, those very tensions and questions can be discerned in contemporary scholarship and debate. Understanding the role of differentiation in how meaning is made requires a move from common sense to theory to explain how there are yet more "natures" to identify and grasp, yet more accounts of natural law to investigate. We turn, thus, to the second mode of meaning, the theoretical.

2

Beyond Common Sense

Natural Law as Theoretical Anthropology

The transition from common sense to theory occurs as a differentiation in consciousness when the same reality is attended to differently. As a result, the symbolization of that reality changes, as does the control of meaning and the corresponding account of objectivity. Rather than description, theory offers explanations; rather than the concrete, theory pivots between the concrete and the abstract; rather than bodies, theory deals with things. Such differentiation can be noted in intellectual history, but also in our own consciousness, as both persons and communities alternate between common sense and theory as their needs and interests demand.

Just as common sense underlies an account of nature and natural law, so too does theory. In this chapter I explore natural law in its theoretical mode, although theoretical articulations are so prevalent that they function as something like the default, as natural law *per se,* and can make a strong case to best represent and continue the classical natural law tradition, especially in its Aristotelian-Thomistic trajectory. A textbook on natural law, for instance, will very likely present the theoretical mode, perhaps why the usual Protestant objections generally respond to that account. Given its prevalence, I offer nothing like an exhaustive history but only a taxonomy, an account of types, claiming that classical natural law operates in the theoretical mode of meaning in its heuristic and control of meaning. Obviously this leaves out a good deal that is interesting in the various historical figures and proponents, but my claim is a metatheoretical one about how the classical tradition conceives of objectivity, knowledge, reality, and meaning.

FROM COMMON SENSE TO THEORY

If common sense can be summarized as (1) intelligence organized toward experience and practical life, (2) with intelligent achievements promulgated through community and convention, (3) and with an epistemology and metaphysics of body, then theory differentiates itself at each point, for as our intellects follow different exigencies of questioning, so too do differing modes of meaning emerge.

Theory as Meaning

For an infant, or a kitten, the world consists entirely of bodies, there being nothing other than bodies in their conscious grasp or intention; moreover, the bodies in their conation are generally directly in front of them, present at that moment. The infant cries when the bottle drops or a parent leaves the room because those comforting bodies no longer exist for the infant. In time, the baby grasps that the bottle has not gone out of existence but is just on the floor, so she looks down and points; her father still exists on the other side of the door or behind the hands covering his face, and peek-a-boo becomes a game of delight. Still, the world contains bodies and only bodies, even those no longer immediately present: "It is the world of what is felt, touched, grasped, sucked, seen, heard. It is a world of immediate experience, of the given as given. . . ."[45] Eventually, the infant will not need to point at a bottle just dropped but says "ba-ba" or "milk," thereby entering a new world, one mediated by meaning.

With language, we intend that which goes beyond the immediately present. Not only does language allow us to inhabit a world bequeathed from others in the tradition, but the world mediated by meaning goes beyond experience, for the meaningful is that which can be "intended in questioning," and questioning is not a function of experience but of intelligence.[46] While common sense and theory tend to encounter the same objects, "the objects are viewed from different standpoints" or exigencies

45. Lonergan, *Method*, 76.
46. Ibid., 77.

of our interest.[47] Common sense considers objects as they relate to us—the world of the hot water and the fast moving car—spontaneously exercising intelligence to accumulate insights in a cumulative and self-correcting process making sense of the world, particularly as we live and act in that world. Insights are spontaneously communicated to ourselves and others in the non-systematic, descriptive terms of ordinary language concerned more with accomplishing our purposes than of explaining the essence of things. For the meaning of common sense, the Socratic queries into the universal nature of moral properties, or the Aristotelian distinctions between formal and material cause, or the mathematical understandings of mass or thermodynamics are just simply "not objects."[48]

Theory as Invariance

When one moves beyond experience into the world of theoretical meaning, sense data is related not to us but to other data (the periodic table with its atomic numbers and weights, for instance) with "no immediate relation to us, to our sensible apprehensions."[49] Explanatory science often goes beyond what we sense, even beyond what we can imagine, which is disorienting to common sense—"What do you mean there might be 5, 8, 10, or 26 dimensions, or even more? How is that possible?" In moving into the relations of data, the theorist "builds up a world that is entirely different from the world of common sense, and he does so because of his pursuit of an ideal of which knowledge is universal, in which it is so exactly formulated that any strict logical deductions from his statements will also be found to be true."[50]

This tells us something quite important about theory in its classical structure, namely its anticipation of invariance, necessity, and universality. Recall that in pursuing an heuristic ideal, the unknown x anticipates answers of a certain kind.[51] Common sense thinks it understands when

47. Ibid., 81.

48. Ibid., 82.

49. Lonergan, *Understanding and Being*, 85–86.

50. Ibid., 86. Since I'm discussing classical natural law, I will here limit the discussion of theory to what Lonergan calls the classical heuristic structures, leaving out statistical or empirical structures for the moment. While doing so oversimplifies his thought, it allows for a pedagogical simplicity; other heuristic forms will come up in later chapters. For a good discussion, see Flanagan, *Quest for Self Knowledge*, 95–107.

51. Ibid., 64.

it can point, manipulate successfully, and use common language well. But physics doesn't think this, judging instead that "laws are reached by eliminating the relations of things to the senses of observers and by arriving at relations between the things . . . then there exists . . . the affirmation that principles and laws are the same for all observers because they lie simply and completely outside the range of observational activities."[52] In other words, theory, at least in its classical form, expects to find intelligibility as universal, invariant, and necessary, as that which cannot be otherwise than it is. It expects to find *laws*, as in classical laws of physics. The contingent is not fully intelligible, since we possess properly scientific knowledge, "as opposed to knowing it in the accidental way in which the sophist knows, when we think that we know the cause on which the fact depends, as the cause of that fact and of no other, and, further, that the fact could not be other than it is. . . . the proper object of unqualified scientific knowledge is something which cannot be other than it is."[53] Further, properly scientific demonstration "must rest on necessary basic truths; for the object of scientific knowledge cannot be other than it is," and consequently, the first premises must be basic, or self-evident, and the reasoning from them logically valid deductions, which would be necessarily true.[54]

Take an example from the *Theatetus* by Plato. In response to a query about the meaning of knowledge, Theatetus describes a recent conversation with his teacher, Theodorus, on the nature of mathematical squares. Beginning with instances, Theodorus proceeded sequentially to work through the numbers, "the power of 3 square feet and the power of 5 square feet . . . and he went on in this way, taking each case in turn till he came to the power of 17 square feet; there for some reason he stopped. So the idea occurred to us that, since the powers were turning out to be unlimited in number, we might try to collect the powers in question under one term, which would apply to them all."[55] Lonergan provides a similar example in the following series, "1+1=2; 2+1=3; 3+1=4; etc., etc., etc. . . ." suggesting that the most important aspect in the example is "etc., etc., etc. . . ." for ". . ." indicates that the process can go on indefinitely under a rule or formula.[56] Like Theatetus, one can stop, realize that the instances are potentially unlimited in number,

---

52. Ibid., 65.

53. Aristotle, *Posterior Analytics*, I.2 71b 10–15 in *Basic Works of Aristotle*.

54. Ibid., I.6 74b 5–10.

55. Plato, *Theatetus*, 147d.

56. Lonergan, *Insight*, 38.

and provide an explanatory formula rather than working through each and every instance. In so doing, one has grasped necessity in the relations, what must be present for the relations to be intelligible rather than accidental, and the "single term" or formula articulates what is necessarily present in the intelligibility of each instance covered by the formula, precisely the anticipation of the Socratic method's search for a definition including each relevant instance while excluding each instance of a different kind.

Theory and the Real

Although articulated differently, both Plato and Aristotle consider the formal necessity grasped in theory to be real and objectively knowable, and thus metaphysics became the master science. In common sense, the real was envisioned as *bodies*, as the "already out there now real," or presence, what could be seen or touched, because common sense begins with an anticipation of what exists in relation to me and my sensation. Since concern is for that which exists in relation to me, I expect that what exists is that which exists over and against me, and being is modeled after *bodies*. With theory, being is whatever is intended as meaningful, and only the invariant and necessary is fully meaningful:

> Metaphysics is said to be the most abstract and the most universal of sciences. All science must have some universality and therefore must be to some extent abstract. If we consider things with all their individual differences, there is no general truth that will apply to them all and no general law or principle that can be derived from them. It is only by leaving out of sight the individual differences and taking what is common to many individuals that we can formulate a universal law or principle. This is what we do when we abstract. We leave out what is peculiar to the individual and take only what is common. To abstract, therefore, is to universalize what is abstracted. Now Metaphysics, having for its object to study being as such, abstracted from all conditions under which reality exists, and considers only the reality itself. Therefore the notions we derive from such consideration of reality will apply to all reality, and consequently the science of Metaphysics is most universal.[57]

57. McCormick, *Scholastic Metaphysics*, 6.

Metaphysics is a science, and thus will follow the rules of the other sciences, just having greater extension and thus abstraction, but metaphysics follows entirely the rules implicit in theory's anticipation of meaning.

The shaping of metaphysics by our anticipations is true not only in the definition of metaphysics itself but also in its elements. For instance, in keeping with the notions of *episteme* found in classical theory, where demonstrative knowledge proceeds from necessary first principles, so metaphysics is "the science of first principles" providing those "things from which all reality derives," or ontology, as well as those "truths on which all knowledge depends," or epistemology.[58] For both studies, since metaphysics deals with the most abstract and necessary aspects, it is from metaphysics that our knowledge of the principles of both reality and knowledge are derived, "on which the validity of all our knowledge depends."[59]

Theory as Law

Within classical theory, a law is "an unchanging correlation among changing quantities that supplies . . . a standard for measuring. . . . A classical norm was assumed to be a universal necessary standard for judging all cases without exception."[60] And in looking for this, one "is concerned with an immanent intelligibility in the thing, event of process," meaning that one heuristically anticipates necessity to be discovered in the contingency and variability of the concrete, by abstracting from the contingency to discover intelligibility, which is necessary, unchanging, and explanatory.[61] Abstracting from contingency means abstracting from the individual, even abstracting from the world of bodies to the non-imaginable world of definitions, as when in geometry reference is made to points (which are not dots and cannot be imagined) or when the formula for calculating velocity in a free fall assumes the ideal of a vacuum (which is not to be found in this or that actual instance of a falling ball). The necessity is an abstraction, albeit an anticipated one, from which to attain the status of law.

Note the anticipation for data to "conform to some law." The heuristic shapes what we anticipate, and thus how we interpret what we find, in

58. Ibid.

59. Ibid., 6–7. McCormick continues: "Metaphysics is a first requirement for a true theory of knowledge."

60. Flanagan, *Quest for Self Knowledge*, 98.

61. Lonergan, *Understanding and Being*, 60–61.

an interesting pivoting of discovery and anticipation. We anticipate intelligibility under a certain heuristic, thereby discovering such intelligibility in the data given to us. For instance, Theatetus mentions that Theodorus began to teach about squares with the assistance of diagrams, namely, that which could be viewed and imagined, so to arrive at the formula after the intelligible principle was discovered through the use of the data supplied by the diagrams. But many people could look at the diagrams and find no intelligibility; only those anticipating finding something, only those looking for something, some unknown x of a certain type find x. Once found, the formula governs the anticipation of how additional instances will be understood, even before those instances are diagramed. So our anticipation allows for discovery which provides the basis for ongoing anticipation.

While common sense uses proverbs to articulate what wisdom has found to be true for the most part, helpful rules of thumb to get you through, more often than not, classical theories tend towards abstraction in "(1) their heuristic anticipation, (2) in the experimental techniques of their discovery, (3) in their formulations, and (4) in their verification."[62] In heuristic, classical theory looks to understand the intelligibility immanent to the data, expecting also that genuine understanding could be extended to all similar data, for the "nature to be known will be the same for all data that are not significantly different."[63] Further, concrete differences of time, place, or person, are to be ignored, and the techniques of experiment are to be applicable and repeatable for all. Consequently, the language with which intelligibility is formulated must not rely upon the vagaries of particular times or places, and thus a specialized and abstract language is required. Finally, a possible grasp of intelligibility is not verified with an isolated concrete instance but by a general and large number of instances; certainly the testimony of the wise person alone is not sufficient.

We see how the heuristic shapes conceptions of law, most obviously in the sense of a scientific law of nature: Law expresses a necessary principle based upon a grasp of the intelligibility within data, and which cannot be rationally denied. Of course, the question arises as to what allows such cognition to be *moral* law, as opposed to just a law of how intelligibility is anticipated. What makes law normative?[64] For theory, natural law looks

---

62. Lonergan, *Insight*, 113.

63. Ibid.

64. Hittinger, *The First Grace*, 39.

very much like a law of nature in its structure, for the forms of thought operate within the theoretical mode of meaning.

THEORETICAL NATURAL LAW—THE DEFAULT

Jacques Maritain summarizes much of the classical tradition of natural law when he writes:

> I am taking it for granted that there is a human nature, and that this human nature is the same in all men. . . . [P]ossessed of a nature, or an ontological structure which is a locus of intelligible necessities, man possesses ends which necessarily correspond to his essential constitution and which are the same for all. All pianos (whatever their particular type and in whatever spot they may be) have as their end the production of musical sounds. If they do not produce these sounds, they must be tuned, or discarded as worthless. But since man is endowed with intelligence and determines his own ends, it is up to him to put himself in tune with the ends necessarily demanded by his nature.[65]

There is a universal and essential nature, says Maritain, with teleology necessarily linked to the ontological constitution of the human, just as for "any kind of thing existing in nature, a plant, a dog, a horse, has its own natural law, that is, the normality of its functioning, the proper way in which, by reason of its specific structure and specific ends, it should achieve fullness of being either in its growth or in its behavior."[66] Consequently, the "first basic element to be recognized in natural law, is, then, the *ontological* element."[67]

For Maritain, and indeed for many others, all claiming the support of Aquinas, natural law obviously depends upon metaphysics of the classical type, where an essential constitution, universally and necessarily determinative of the nature and ends of every member of a species, provides the grounding by which to determine the proper function, and thus also the improper function, of an entity. Further, since natural law is written in nature in a necessary way, human knowledge of its basic principle is self-evident and the law is the "ensemble of things to do and not to do which follow therefrom in a *necessary* fashion."[68] Certainly it is the case that "every

---

65. Maritain, *Natural Law*, 27.
66. Ibid., 28.
67. Ibid., 29.
68. Ibid., 33.

sort of error and deviation is possible," that "our nature is coarse, and that innumerable accidents can corrupt our judgment," but this shows only that "our sight is weak," and "proves nothing against natural law, any more than a mistake in addition proves anything against arithmetic. . . ."[69]

Natural law requires necessity and invariance, but in a world of flux this is found only in the domain of *episteme*, and thus turning to the concrete human person is insufficient. Instead, natural law begins with a metaphysics of the person, with the universal, abstract, and unchanging. Heinrich Rommen puts it thus:

> The idea of natural law obtains general acceptance only in the periods when metaphysics, queen of the sciences, is dominant. It recedes or suffers an eclipse, on the other hand, when being . . . and oughtness, morality and law, are separated. . . . The natural law, consequently, depends on the science of being, on metaphysics. Hence every attempt to establish the natural law must start from the fundamental relation of being and oughtness, of the real and the good. Since the establishment of the natural law further depends upon the doctrine of man's nature, this human element has also to be studied. . . .[70]

Natural law depends upon a knowledge of being, of the being of the human person, and is derived from a theoretical anthropology whereby we first know what sort of beings we are, and only subsequently know what goods are proper to us, what goods we are obligated to pursue: "being and oughtness must in the final analysis coincide."[71]

Ontological and Epistemological Realism

By metaphysics, Rommen means the Aristotelian-Thomistic synthesis, committed to both ontological and epistemological realism, since natural law is "possible only on the basis of a true knowledge of the essences of things, for therein lies its ontological support."[72] Knowing essence begins with sense perception whereby the form of the thing is given to the intellect through the sensible and intelligible species. While the mode of the form's existence changes—existing in reality in the entity but intentionally

69. Ibid., 32.

70. Rommen, *The Natural Law*, 141.

71. Ibid., 143.

72. Ibid.

in the sensation and imagination—the actual intelligibility of the object is made present in sense and imagination or we could never understand the entity as it is. When we understand, our intellects are in-formed with the very same intelligibility possessed by the entity, the so-called *identity theory* of knowledge where the intellect *becomes* the object, possible since sensation and imagination possess the form and "present" it to the intellect.[73] The senses "are the gateway through which things or reality pass, according to the mode of the intellect, into the latter's immaterial possession."[74] This epistemological realism suggests that "things themselves are the cause and measure of our knowledge," for the intellect is moved by, informed by, and ultimately measured against the form of the thing itself: "At first, the intellect is passive. Reality exists prior to the intellect. The mental image is a copy whose original is the real."[75] A coherent understanding and a true judgment occur when the intellect corresponds to the form, when it matches up to the measure of the very nature of the concrete and sensible thing. Epistemological realism in which reality exists over and against the intellect, but which sensation bridges without remainder or interference, is a necessary condition of natural law, for unless we access essence as things are, we could never determine the goods proper to the essence.[76]

Sensation, while necessary, concerns individuals, whereas understanding, in keeping with the theoretical mode, is abstract, universal, and about that which cannot be otherwise. The concrete individuals of sensation, however, are never abstract, never universal, and always admit of contingency, so while our understanding is identical to the original, understanding, unlike sensation, concerns the universal essence which makes the thing the sort of thing it is. When I know this tree, or that human, I do not understand them as *this* tree or *that* human, but rather understand the essence whereby trees are trees and humans are humans. Understanding is of the universal, abstracted from the material accidents rendering tree-ness into this or that tree, this or that individual, and which makes Socrates distinct from Plato. Still, when I *know* Socrates, I also know Plato since their essence is the same: "The object of rational knowledge or cognition is therefore not the particular or the individual as such; this the senses lay hold of. The object of cognition . . . is what the thing is: the essence of the

73. Ibid., 148.
74. Ibid., 144.
75. Ibid.
76. Gilson, *Methodical Realism*, 127–44.

thing which lies hidden in the core of phenomena as an idea in every thing of the same kind; in a word, the form."[77]

Stressing the point, and demonstrating quite clearly the theoretical mode, Rommen continues:

> Sense perception grasps only the particularity of the existent being, of the individual thing, as e.g., this man or this concrete state. But cognition is founded on the perception of the universal, of that which is in all things of the same kind as their quiddity or essence. The thing is that which the abstract concept of the thing, the object of intellectual knowledge, represents, signifies, means; and this object of intellectual knowledge is really in the thing.[78]

Note his language: (1) the thing is understood in abstraction, without reference to the contingent particularities, (2) the thing understood is the *object* of intellectual knowledge, or that which is intended or sought (a heuristic anticipation), and (3) it is only as an abstract object intended by intellect that we have representation, significance, or meaning. Meaning obtains when we have abstraction to the necessary and universal present in the individual, when we have grasped, in the concrete, that which cannot be otherwise.

Nature as Principle of Motion

For natural law, the first task is metaphysical, grasping essence or form, since in Aristotelian metaphysics a grasp of the form is also a grasp of its final cause or telos. When explaining motion, Aristotle distinguishes the contingent and changeable matter from the "inner, enduring core, the form," with the form serving as the principle of act causing self-motion or self-change of the thing.[79] This is particularly evident in natural entities, those which possess their own nature from themselves and are not given it by an artist or craftsperson, for nature is an internal source of motion or change, an entelechy, whereby the form "unfolds itself in the matter."[80]

---

77. Rommen, *The Natural Law*, 145–46.

78. Ibid., 146. He continues, "the nature becomes universal and hence representative of the essence, the quiddity of the thing, when it is abstracted . . . when it is viewed apart from existence in things of the external world. . . ."

79. Ibid., 148.

80. Ibid.

Since a natural substance is self-moved and self-governed, the "unfolding" follows the intelligible structure immanent in form itself, and since everything which is seeks its own act and perfection—perfection meaning the completeness proper to the form—natural entities seek their own end. But the end or perfection, the finality of a substance, is its goodness, and thus form is intrinsically linked to final cause; the final cause is nothing other than the form having become fully itself, having accomplished its principle of unfolding until it has become its own essence. God, having no potency, demonstrates this principle most perfectly, for he is pure act—purely Himself without possibility of development or change—and thus is also his own perfection and goodness. All else is good insofar as, in an analogous matter, it becomes like God, or insofar as it becomes fully actualized in the form which it is. Goodness *is* the being of the thing; goodness is being, and being is goodness. Teleology is the unity of being and oughtness.[81]

According to Anthony Lisska, the metaphysics necessary for natural law entails accepting essential properties as "dispositional properties" with a corresponding teleology.[82] Dispositional properties are "potentially directed towards a specific development or 'end,'" they are the object's capacity to "do something."[83] The "something" is always a specific end, or act, "which is the fulfillment or completion of the potency."[84] Teleology is meaningful only in light of the relationship between the dispositional property, which is a real potency of the object, and the end, which is the actualization immanent to the dispositional property. As immanent, the "ends appropriate to human nature are built into the very nature or essence which determines a human person," and, further, are not non-moral goods understood as utility.[85]

Dispositional properties, which make up a thing's essence, are not static like a category, whatever our tendency to conceive of essence as rigid and closed, something like the properties which define a triangle. Rather, essential properties are more organic, something like a plant which has a form, and thereby develops and changes because of the immanent disposition of that form, although certainly the development is structured and directional.[86] Thus, in the famous article 94. 2 from the *Summa Theolo-*

---

81. Ibid., 150.

82. Lisska, *Aquinas's Theory of Natural Law*, 85.

83. Ibid., 87.

84. Ibid.

85. Ibid.

86. Ibid., 97.

giae where Thomas gives his most detailed account of the principles of the natural law, he is doing nothing more than identifying the structure of our dispositional properties: (1) Dispositions towards life, including continuation of existence, nutrition, and growth; (2) Dispositions towards animal sensation, including sense experience and offspring; and (3) Dispositions towards rationality, including sociality and understanding.[87] Whatever these dispositions have as their accomplishment or terminus, this is the human good.

Good and evil are defined by reference to the dispositional properties, for the good is the "harmonious completion of the dispositional properties," while the "hindering of any developing process" hinders the attainment of the act/good of the disposition, and thus also hinders or denies "the possibility of attaining human well-being."[88] Acts are wrong, then, not directly because a law-maker declares as such, even if that law-maker is God, but because "an immoral act prevents the self-actualization of human beings," or hinders the harmonious attainment of the disposed ends and the well-being constituted by that attainment.[89] In keeping with the earlier claims of the priority of ontology, it is clear that the ground of normativity is entirely shaped by metaphysics.

The notion of end is a prerequisite for understanding "good," for the good of an entity is nothing other than the finality, or full actualization, of the dispositional properties. Good, then, is coterminous with being, and a the good of the thing cannot be defined except in relation to the form of the thing. To say the same thing, but with a nod to metaethics, "moral theory is dependent upon the metaphysical theory."[90] If the metaphysics fails, so too does the moral account, and a moral account which operated antecedently to the metaphysics would be either arbitrary or impossible. Thus, not only does intellect rightly govern the will in action, but theoretical knowledge, operating as a metaphysics of the person or theoretical anthropology, is prior to ethics. *First* we provide an account of human nature, and *only then* can we do ethics: "ontology is a necessary presupposition for ... moral theory."[91] And not just any ontology will do, but only a metaphysics of essence, that is, of dispositional properties.

87. Ibid., 101.
88. Ibid., 103.
89. Ibid., 104.
90. Ibid., 88.
91. Ibid., 96.

CONCLUSION

Such oughtness may seem aridly metaphysical, hardly the demand of responsibility we sense governs our agency. We are free, after all, self-governed agents and a merely instinctual pursuit of our perfection seems inadequate to human dignity, precisely why Plato rejects Callicles's understanding of natural inclination. Rommen agrees, noting that the statement "we are free," is an ontological declaration of our nature. There is an ordering principle grasped by intellect, and while this governs animals in iron-like rigidity, for beings such as us, "endowed with reason and free will," those principles of necessary order obligate without thereby exerting efficient causality.[92] It is our nature, our essence, to be free, and so morality exists insofar as the "order of being confronting the intelligence becomes the order of oughtness for the will."[93] The order is objective, it exists independently of our reason, but yet we must choose to will and follow that objective order.

Still, though, the metaphysics is first. We discover form in knowledge, form presents the goodness of being, the drive to the good proper to the form, and it is this very good which the human as free is called to bring about. Practical reason, reason insofar as we bring about the truth of our being through our action, depends upon theoretical reason, for "moral philosophy, the science of moral action, is an extension of metaphysics, the science of being. . . . First the theoretical reason knows and . . . truth thereupon appears to practical reason as truth to be accomplished through the will."[94] Metaphysics, or a theoretical grasp of the real, is the basis upon which the natural law depends; the natural law derives from metaphysics, from theory. Law, insofar as it is practical or moral, arises from being, and is nothing more than the known truth which is to be brought about through action. Law tells us what we need to do, or not do, so as to live in keeping with the truth of our being, but we must know this being first, and only then can we act in keeping with the same law which being is for us. Having known being is to know oughtness, for the "supreme principle of oughtness is simply this: Become your essential being."[95]

From the perspective of interiority, the perspective of the acting person, however, the default model misses the point somewhat, for natural law

---

92. Rommen, *The Natural Law*, 153.

93. Ibid.

94. Ibid., 155.

95. Ibid., 156.

is not derived from metaphysics—*natural law is entirely underived.* That discussion will wait, for before turning to interiority, I examine the "Protestant Prejudice" against natural law, arguing that the usual objections refer to the default of theoretical mode. When we move away from theory to interiority, the objections dissolve as well.

3

Theory and the Protestant Prejudice

All claims to the contrary, natural law hardly seems self-evident in the contemporary context. While decades of Catholic undergraduates may have been taught natural law "as a kind of *lingua franca* for dialogue with non-believers," post-moderns, suggests Tracey Rowland, reject a stable view of nature, Liberals don't believe the conclusions, and "Protestants have never been all that keen on it, regarding it as something of Stoic, rather than biblical provenance. . . ."[1] In the end, this results "in a situation in which Catholics talk to other Catholics in an idiom which was devised for dialogue with unbelievers," while the unbelievers find the idiom largely irrelevant, or in the case of some Protestants, impious.[2]

Protestant views on natural law are quite diverse. On the one hand, and especially after Barth, "the great body of evangelical thinkers have generally avoided or explicitly rejected the natural law tradition, seemingly viewing it as a relic of scholastic Catholicism, tainted by its association with Rome, its errant appeals to common ground between the saved and the unsaved, and its unwarranted optimism regarding the power of human reason."[3] On the other hand, a sizeable literature reveals that the magisterial Reformers took natural law as an uncontroversial component of Christian tradition and made use of the theory without hesitation, just as a growing number

1. Rowland, "Natural Law," 374–75. See also Rowland, *Culture and the Thomist Tradition*, 136–58, and "Augustinian and Thomist Engagements with the World," 450–52.

2. Ibid.

3. Covington et al., *Natural Law and Evangelical Political Thought*, x.

of contemporary Protestants embrace it as Scripturally and theologically compatible and as necessary to fill the lacunae in Protestant political and ethical thought.

In this chapter, I explore several of the most common Protestant objections, arguing that these objections, however compelling they may be (or not), assume natural law within the theoretical mode of meaning. As arguments against the theoretical mode, they are coherent and powerful objections, and even if I find them ultimately insufficient, they are not irrelevant. In fact, rather than rebutting them, as is often the case, natural lawyers should embrace, incorporate, and sublimate them while moving into the third and fourth modes of meaning. "Protestant Prejudice" should be taken seriously, in part, because its worries demonstrate the suppleness and reasonability of natural law within interiority and transcendence. Properly understood, the objections are arguments *for* natural law in a new mode.

As in earlier chapters, I'm mostly interested in a taxonomy of types so as to explain the movement and function of meaning. As such, I'll not in this chapter provide anything like an exhaustive history of Protestant thought or grapple in detail with particular thinkers. That work is being done by others, on whom I rely, but their historical work remains to be situated within a narrative of meaning.[4]

The Protestant Prejudice

For those scholars attempting the historical retrieval of natural law within Protestantism, the very need to effect retrieval is somewhat odd, for they find in it no intrinsic disparity with the spirit of the Reformation:

> There is no real discontinuity be-tween the teaching of the Reformers and that of their predecessors with respect to natural law. Not one of the leaders of the Reformation assails the principle. Instead, with the possible exception of Zwingli, they all on occasion express a quite ungrudging respect for the moral law naturally implanted in the human heart and seek to inculcate this attitude in their readers. Natural law is not one of the issues on which they

4. Ballor, "Natural Law and Protestantism," 193–209; Charles, *Retrieving the Natural Law*; Charles, "Protestant Bias Against the Natural Law"; Charles, "Burying the Wrong Corpse"; Charles, "Protestants and the Natural Law"; Grabill, *Rediscovering the Natural Law in Reformed Theological Ethics*; VanDrunen, *Natural Law and the Two Kingdoms*; Cromartie, *A Preserving Grace*; McNeill, "Natural Law in the Teaching of the Reformers," 168–82; Johnson, *Natural Law Ethics*.

bring the Scholastics under criticism. With safeguards of their primary doctrines but without conscious resistance on their part, natural law filters into the framework of their thought and is an assumption of their political and social teaching.[5]

Despite the history, J. Darryl Charles notes that current opposition to natural law is fairly uniform among both revisionist and confessionally orthodox theologians—"there exists across Protestantism a broad consensus that rejects the natural law as a metaphysical notion rooted in divine revelation."[6]

Revisionists tend to worry that natural law is prescientific, with all the connotations of medieval superstition and metaphysical biology, and suspect that appeals to nature diminishes the plurality of voices within the tradition—there's not much space for "otherness" within universal and unchanging human nature.[7] The confessionally orthodox may share those same objections, but worry more that natural law "fails to take seriously the condition of human sin and places misguided trust in the powers of human reason, which has been debilitated by the fall."[8] Additionally, a constellation of further concerns emerges from questions about the fall, including the uniqueness of Christ, the necessity of grace, the autonomy of nature, and the status of works.[9]

As noted by Lutheran theologian Carl Braaten, there is a "longstanding commonplace in Christian thought that Protestantism distinguishes its moral theology from that of Roman Catholicism by its rejection of natural law," although Braaten suspects that "pressure to abandon the teaching of natural law stemmed not so much from the Reformation as from post-Enlightenment developments in philosophy, especially utilitarianism and positivism."[10] Protestant thought, in other words, followed the verdict of Hume or Mill on natural law more than that of Luther or Calvin. Nonetheless, the rejection has become very sharp. The objections are legion, but we'll examine them under three rubrics related to (1) natural law's autonomy, (2) Christocentrism and salvation history, and (3) the noetic effects of sin.[11]

5. McNeill, "Natural Law in the Teaching of the Reformers," 168.

6. Charles, *Retrieving the Natural Law*, 111.

7. Ibid., 112. See also Traina, "What Has Paris to do with Augsburg?" paras. 12–34.

8. Charles, *Retrieving the Natural Law*, 113.

9. Charles, "Protestants and Natural Law," para. 2.

10. Braaten, "Protestants and Natural Law," paras. 1, 14.

11. Rather than attempting to identify every objection, I provide three basic types

It is not my purpose to either defend or respond to these objections. Not only is that ground well-travelled, and by capable proponents of the various sides, but my interest is to *position* and sublimate the objections within an account of meaning rather than to respond to them point-by-point.

I should note, too, that while the chapter addresses the usual Protestant objections, I don't hesitate to draw upon Catholic thinkers expressing similar concerns. The objections are by no means exclusively Protestant, although they have been so closely aligned with Protestant thought as to become identified as such.

Nature or Creation? The Autonomy of Natural Law

The Roman Catholic tradition strongly affirms the integrity and autonomy of the created order. The Vatican II document, *Gaudium et Spes*, for instance, declares "... created things and societies themselves enjoy their own laws and values which must be gradually deciphered, put to use and regulated by men ... all things are endowed with their own stability, truth, goodness, proper laws and order. Man must respect these as he isolates them by the appropriate methods of the individual sciences or arts."[12] In this, the document continues with the mainstream of Thomism, holding in creative tension the belief that "at the very heart of things God is everywhere present and acting by His efficacy," while also rejecting any notion which "deprived natural things of their proper operations."[13] For Thomas, God does not deprive beings of their causality or integrity, so much as establish that very causality by his providence; neither does the freedom and efficacy of created reality deny God's glory, for it is precisely in granting efficacy that "the work manifests by its excellence the glory of the maker."[14] In fact, since effects are like their causes, every "natural form carries at bottom within itself the desire to imitate, by its own operation, the creative fecundity and pure actuality of God," showing that the world "can never be either too beautiful or too efficient, it can never realize itself too completely, can never tend too actively to its own perfection, in order to reproduce, as

---

of objections, a structure similar to that of Charles, "Burying the Wrong Corpse," 3–4.

12. Second Vatican Ecumenical Council, "Pastoral Constitution *Gaudium et Spes*," 36. See also *The Compendium of the Social Doctrine of the Church*, 45–48.

13. Ibid.

14. Ibid., 194.

it ought, the image of its divine model."[15] The glory of God is exalted when nature seeks its own perfections, as each thing seeks itself, or as Hopkins puts it, "*Whát I do is me: for that I came.*"

Not content to grant causality to creatures, or to interpret such causality as a likeness to God whereby God is glorified rather than diminished, Aquinas goes further, holding also that God wills persons for their own sake and the perfection of the universe requires free persons: "Hence, the complete perfection of the universe required the existence of some creatures which return to God not only as regards likeness of nature, but also by their action. And such a return to God cannot be made except by the act of the intellect and will."[16] Further, human intellect possesses its own light, its own active intellect, and God need not give natural knowledge to humans through divine illumination. As summarized by Ernest Fortin, Thomas valued autonomy, reason, and nature to an incredible extent, especially when compared to Augustine:

> Independent of Revelation and prior to the infusion of divine grace, man has access to the most general principles of moral action and, to the extent to which his will has not been corrupted by sin, finds within himself the power to act in accordance with them. There is thus constituted a specifically natural order apart from, though obviously not in opposition to, the higher order to which human nature is elevated through grace. . . . Speaking figuratively, Augustine had warned that one cannot safely appropriate the spoils of the Egyptians, that is to say, pagan leaning and philosophy, without first observing the Passover. Without much exaggeration, one could say that Thomas shows a greater willingness to postpone the celebration of the Passover until the Egyptians have been properly despoiled and, indeed, until such time as the whole land of Canaan has been annexed.[17]

Perhaps there's a bit of rhetorical flourish here, but Fortin's summary articulates the background of worries about natural law and autonomy.

---

15. Ibid., 199.

16. Aquinas, *Summa Contra Gentiles* II.46.3.

17. In Rowland, "Augustinian and Thomist Engagements with the World," 443.

Autonomous Nature?

According to Russell Hittinger, natural law can be considered in three distinct ways, as law in the human mind, in nature, or in the mind of God, and while the current literature reveals wide disagreement on how to unify these three strands, it is clear that the "theologian is (or ought to be) chiefly concerned with the third," for until "recently, the proposition that natural law is chiefly a theological issue was uncontroversial in Catholic moral theology."[18] Law in the human mind and law in nature were distinct but not foundational to natural law reasoning, which was a theological position about how God granted this "first grace" to humans. Considering natural law as if God did not exist would have been inconceivable, not to mention incoherent, to the Patristics or Aquinas, claims Hittinger.

Thomas, he suggests, always defined natural law in theological terms, as participation in the eternal law, and "never (and I must emphasize *never*) defined in terms of what is first in the (human) mind or first in nature."[19] Law may be discovered or discerned in the human mind, and it is "natural" with respect to our knowing, but it is defined by its cause, and thus natural law can never be understood as law without reference to God. Law as apprehended in our intellect is *not*, strictly speaking, the natural law so much as the effect of natural law for us, but the law in itself is defined without reference to our knowledge of it.[20] This is especially vital, says Hittinger, because while the law is immutable and unchangeable in the divine reason, its effects are quite alterable in the human, not only because only the bare foundations of the natural law are present to the ungraced mind, but also because concupiscence *destroys* the law of nature in sinful man.[21] Absent the continual work of God present in creation, and without the "remediation of divine positive law and a new law of grace," the human is so bent by sin as to not follow the law.[22]

Despite the textual evidence in Thomas, modern theology shifted its focus to the human mind and to nature, forgetting theology in articulating law and estranging it from the Church's domain. Oddly, in following "the

18. Hittinger, "Catholic Moral Theology," 2–3. See also Hittinger, *The First Grace*, 3–37.

19. Ibid., 6.

20. Ibid., 176 n. 17.

21. Ibid., 7.

22. Ibid., 8.

desperate modern need for consensus," Catholic moral thought has often followed modern rationalism, steadily departing from the theological basis of law and giving the perception that the most vexing issues "can be adequately directed by appeal to elementary principles of natural law" without need for theology, sacrament, or revelation.[23] As a result, the Church weakens itself, either by forgoing the storehouse of wisdom found in its treasuries in favor of a thin rationalism, or by presenting theological positions as if they were grounded in pure reason even though the arguments from reason alone are not particularly compelling or vigorous. On the one hand, nature seemed to teach whatever Church authority concluded, and on the other, every human was already supposed to know this—although the reaction of bored indifference or sharp skepticism should not be surprising.[24] Nor should it surprise if revisionist theologians find in autonomous reason a tool by which to discern the Church's "errors" about a whole host of social, political, and moral topics, for reason and nature have become unhooked and unhinged from theology and operate in a separate zone.

At this, Hittinger, a Catholic theorist, suggests Protestants may take note, concluding that Barth's insistence on theonomous ethics was not only correct but that Catholics have re-discovered the same. Some may press harder, suggesting that the tradition of autonomy within Catholic thought contains the seeds of its own undoing. The Dutch Reformed tradition, for instance, tends to present Thomas as committed to a two-storied view of reality, with a separate, or bottom, foundation of ungraced nature (*natura pura*). For an intellectual leader such as Herman Dooyerweerd, autonomous nature is Aquinas's major error:

> Within the natural sphere a relative autonomy was ascribed to human reason, which was supposed to be capable of discovering the natural truths by its own light. . . . In consequence, there was no longer a question of Christian philosophy. Philosophical thought was, in fact, abandoned to the influence of the Greek and Humanist basic motives . . . masked by the dogmatic acceptance of the autonomy of natural reason.[25]

Such autonomy is pagan rather than Christian and plants secular humanism, for philosophy is now untethered and hostile to faith since by

---

23. Ibid., 12.

24. Ibid., 16.

25. Dooyeweerd, *In the Twilight of Western Thought*, 44. See also Snell, "Thomism and Noetic Sin," 8–11.

"ascribing to the so-called natural reason an autonomy over against faith and the divine revelation, traditional scholastic theology merely gave expression to the false Greek view of reason as the center of human nature."[26]

Objections to Autonomy

As Carl Braaten notes, the Lutheran theology of "orders of creation" attempted to baptize natural law, preferring the *lex creationis* to the *lex naturae*, or the living God of the Bible to that of metaphysics.[27] There is something to this, of course, for the language of creation cannot be understood without reference to a Creator, while the more generic term "nature" has no similar connotation. Creation implies gift, or dependence; nature only facticity or there-ness. Still, while turning to creation might be sufficient to stem the worries about autonomy, it is by no means obvious that all worries would thus be resolved.

First, Barth's "Nein!" was directed as much at "orders of creation" theologians as it was at natural lawyers, including those who identified the law of Germany with the law of God.[28] Despite the language difference, both were tempted by supposedly "natural" or "reasonable" religion in keeping with human, or created, capacity; neither began with the Lordship of Christ and thus departed from the faith "revealed through Christ the living Word of God and Scripture as the mediator of the Word of God."[29]

> Barth's relentless attack on natural theology motivated his rejection of the orders of creation, because of its family resemblance to the idea of natural law. The family resemblance consists in the idea that people do not need to know Jesus Christ to have some knowledge of what is right and good through the law of creation and conscience, that is, by way of "the things that have been made" (Romans 1:20).[30]

In other words, the worry is not only whether moral theology makes reference in its system to God as origin, but whether "Jesus Christ, as he is

---

26. Ibid., 140. For similar claims from the broadly Kuyperian tradition, see also Schaeffer, *Escape from Reason*, 11–12; Pearcey, *Total Truth*, 74–95; Walsh and Middleton, *Transforming Vision*, 98–116; Goheen and Bartholomew, *Living at the Crossroads*.

27. Braaten, "Response," 35.

28. Ibid. See also Johnson, *Natural Law Ethics*, 7–8, 19–23.

29. Charles, *Retrieving the Natural Law*, 128.

30. Braaten, "God in Public Life," para. 8.

attested for us in Holy Scripture, is the one Word of God," and whether "apart from and besides this one Word of God" there are "other events and powers, figures and truths."[31]

The either-or aspect of this claim can be quite robust, leading to what Braaten describes as the theology of "one Word of God from which all structures, orders, commandments, and ethical norms for Christian living in the world must be derived," and which "succeeds in emptying the world of its own meaning as a realm of divine governance and human involvement prior to and apart from the biblical story of salvation culminating in Christ."[32] Given the divide, attempts to discover common, neutral, or universal ground can be interpreted as an attempt to abandon grace in favor of the "humanist project to bring about reconciliation apart from grace," the heresy of "non-Christians accepting the will of God."[33] As a consequence, and also the second objection, even a turn to creation, so long as the cross of Christ is not foundational, is "in competition" with the Gospel, pretending to provide a universal morality in rivalry with the uniqueness of Christ the Lord.[34]

Third, as a universalist project, natural law presents itself as "a set of timeless universal moral norms . . . as an objective 'thing' to use in theories. It becomes an immovable position rather than part of an ongoing intellectual investigation."[35] As a fixed "position," the theory assumes answers already worked out rather than supporting the friendship and imagination required by the narrative tradition of Christianity. As Hauerwas notes, "a people are formed by a story which laces their history in the texture of the world. Such stories make the world our home by providing us with the skills to negotiate the dangers. . . ."[36] While good communities use a narrative to live in the truth, natural law presents a set position, one which, in theory, is accessible to anyone without respect to their religious commitments, moral formation, or virtue, and thus becomes a dead thing, a tactic rather than a way to incorporate others, form the character of members, and

---

31. "Barmen Declaration," 8.11–8.12.

32. Braaten, "God in Public Life," para. 5.

33. Charles, *Retrieving the Natural Law*, 133. Here Charles is describing the work of Jacques Ellul.

34. Ibid., 134.

35. Bennett, "Stanley Hauerwas's Influence," 164.

36. Hauerwas, *Community of Character*, 15.

acknowledge the many moralities of many communities.[37] Rather than becoming story-formed people, Christians become systematic theoreticians.

Fourth, in attempting a common or universalistic project, even one articulated as creation rather than nature, the unique ethic of the Church is forgotten or minimized and given up to cultural assimilation and captivity.[38] Instead of the practices of the Christian community with their logic in the form of Christ, the prevailing, "neutral" norms of consensus govern action, but since the prevailing norms are unfaithful, fallen, and hostile powers and dominions, such consensus is a form of capitulation and even idolatrous collaboration. The unique narrative, practices, and virtues of ecclesial or *koinonia* ethics become replaced with the generic, and not only is Christian prophetic witness blurred, but so too the internal fidelity and formation of the Church and her members—the City of God begins to resemble the City of Man, and even to offer support for the violence intrinsic to the latter city.[39]

NATURE OR SALVATION HISTORY?

When commenting on John's Gospel, Aquinas distinguishes three meanings of the term "the world" in Scripture: (1) creation, (2) creation perfected by Christ, (3) creation as perverted by sin.[40] Presumably, "nature," specifically, "human nature," could be understood in an analogous way, as (1) originally created by God, (2) as perfected and graced by the work of Christ, and (3) as stricken with concupiscence. Which meaning does natural law use?

Unlike the differentiation of meaning, these distinctions refer to the changes wrought by actual events of salvation history which altered the meaning of the world/nature in their occurrence. As John Paul II began his first encyclical, *Redemptor Hominis*, Jesus Christ is "the center of the universe and of history," and attempting to understand either the world or human nature without drawing upon the revelation of Christ is to fail to understand either.[41]

---

37. Charles, *Retrieving the Natural Law*, 143.

38. Ibid., 142; Charles is summarizing the thought of John Howard Yoder and Stanley Hauerwas.

39. See Hauerwas, *Community of Character*, 111–28; Hauerwas, *The Peaceable Kingdom*, 51–64; Schindler, *Heart of the World*.

40. Rowland, "Augustinian and Thomist Engagements with the World," 444.

41. John Paul II, *Redemptor Hominis*, 1. See Rowland, "Augustinian and Thomist Engagements with the World," 445.

Universal and objective moral systems treating the world as generic facticity, even those beginning from "creation" without explicitly Christocentric and Trinitarian foundations, adhere to the *mythos* perpetrated on the Church by Enlightenment Liberalism.[42] Turning to nature as a static, a-historical given, denies the dynamics of Christian history, is mistaken about nature, and uses the Egyptian spoils to build the golden calf. In Rowland's terms, natural law without Christ exists neither in the City of God nor in the City of Man, but rather in the "neutral zone or 'third city.'"[43] Not only does that city not exist except as myth, but it splits nature and grace from each other, suggesting a two-end theory of human beatitude, with the natural end of humans still somehow intelligible when sundered from a supernatural vocation.[44]

Further, attempting to grasp the meaning of human nature outside the mediation of Christ's gift of love is Pelagian, claiming to understand the truth of the human through exclusively human understanding and agency. The Church as the sacrament of Christ becomes unnecessary to convey the meaning of human life and human dignity, or else reduces its scope to include only the supernatural ends of the human—heaven and the soul—while silent on the nature end. Autonomy, however strongly affirmed by *Guadium et Spes*, never meant anything like meaning, integrity, or dignity *without* Christ:

> If the expression "the autonomy of earthly affairs" is taken to mean that created things do not depend on God, and that man can use them without any reference to their Creator, anyone who acknowledges God will see how false such a meaning is. For without the Creator, the creature would disappear.[45]

---

42. Rowland, "Augustinian and Thomist Engagements with the World," 447. See also her book in the Radical Orthodoxy series, *Culture and the Thomist Tradition*, as well as RO's interpretation of the "secular," "neutrality," or "public reason." As discussed earlier, David Bentley Hart's position is similar on this point.

43. Ibid., 449.

44. The struggle between "extrinsicist" and "integral" accounts of nature and grace, between the *nouvelle theologie* of de Lubac, von Balthasar, and the *Communio* school, and the unlikely alliance between neo-Thomists and Rahnerians has been a major aspect of Catholic theology this past century. See Rowland, *Culture and the Thomist Tradition*, Schindler, *Heart of the World*, and Milbank, *Theology and Social Theory* for summaries.

45. Second Vatican Ecumenical Council, "Pastoral Constitution *Gaudium et Spes*," 36.

Consequently, any form of natural law beginning *as if there was no Christ* is heretical. Not only must natural law presuppose God, but the Trinitarian God revealed by Christ. All of which forcefully poses the question: Can there be a genuinely *natural* law which meets this test, or is natural law a branch of moral theology requiring Christian commitments, just as Hart and Hittinger, among others, suggest?

The centrality of salvation history in relation to nature is heightened even more by Barth, suggests Jesse Couenhoven, for whom temporality and salvation history point away from creation and towards the eschaton for a proper understanding of nature. In this reading, Barth "rejects not so much natural law theory *tout court* as certain ways of thinking about natural law that he finds problematic."[46] Barth's supposed distrust of postlapsarian reason overlooks his mature thought, says Couenhoven, particularly his insistence that natural law with an eye only to creation forgoes its eschatological fulfillment. Christ, the Second Adam, does not merely repristinate but provides "rather a new way of being human," such that the natural law of the garden is not the natural law of the kingdom, for the rule of Christ is something new.[47]

On this read, Barth need not be a fideist or voluntarist, for the divine command aspect of his ethics whereby God's commands are "right-making" and not merely "right-indicating," are not arbitrary but in "accord with and out of the love that constitutes the Father, Son, and Spirit as three in one."[48] The divine commandments relate to God's goodness and love, and express "the goodness that is suitable to creaturely lives of the particular sorts that God has elected to create," implying that commandments very much "relate to and indeed fulfill human nature" as God purposed in "creation and redemption."[49] Barth is presenting what might be termed "a natural law theory of divine command," where morality is ordered by "the nature of human existence, which itself is ordered to and by the divine nature."[50]

Consequently, no essential hostility exists between Barth and natural law, or at least a certain conception of natural law. And while Barth hesitates about postlapsarian human ability to properly know and judge

---

46. Couenhoven, "Karl Barth's Eschatological Natural Law," 1. See this work also in chapter 2 of *Natural Law and Evangelical Political Thought.*

47. Couenhoven, "Karl Barth's Eschatological Natural Law," 2–3.

48. Ibid., 4, 5.

49. Ibid., 5–6.

50. Ibid., 9.

our nature, so too does Aquinas, and the noetic reservations are not, says Couenhoven, the primary aspect of Barth's supposedly anti-natural law mood.[51] The most salient point is not epistemological but ontological, namely, the historical nature of humanity—"nature itself is open to grace in such a manner that our natures cannot be said to be a finished product but eschatologically forward-looking."[52] In its usual expression, natural law presents a static humanity with an unchanging essence, but because the logic(s) of creation and redemption are not merely repetitive or mechanistically developmental, God's moral commands change in "ways that cannot simply be predicted or inferred from the logic of the previous aeon," just as our natures change in light of salvation.[53]

Our natures are hardly erratic, of course, because the logic(s) all stem(s) from the divine life and its creation of human nature, and because Christ's own dual-nature implies "that human persons too are a being-in-act, and thus not a static state but a history."[54] Since nature is open to grace, nature is "not simply 'baked in' to the dust enlivened by creation."[55]

On this read, Barth does not deny natural law but only its traditional articulation; he accepts a relation between the created order, God's own order, and morality, but considers non-Christological versions to be "insufficiently teleological" in overlooking the eschatological dimension of the human.[56] One might add that static conceptions miss the theological point and are bad anthropology in looking for a substance rather than an act-in-development. For Couenhoven, then, Barth's most forceful criticism is not the noetic effects of sin but natural law's turn to creation rather than the future, a fundamental mistake.

What about Sin?

While Barth's main hesitation may not be the noetic effects of sin, for many "the trump card (or nuclear option) remains the fall, for even if prelapsarian Adam possessed and understood the natural law, human nature and human

---

51. Ibid., 12–14.
52. Ibid., 6.
53. Ibid., 17.
54. Ibid.
55. Ibid. See also O'Donovan, *Resurrection and Moral Order*, 31–75.
56. Couenhoven, "Karl Barth's Eschatological Natural Law," 18.

knowledge are so impaired as to render it non-existent or unknowable, or both."[57] Braaten describes the centrality of this objection to Protestants:

> The chief reason for this theological hesitancy to fully recognize natural law is the problem of sin. Natural law seems to suggest that the order of being in the original creation has not been totally disrupted by the fall and sin. Further, it suggests that human reason is not so blinded as to be incapable of reading the will of God in the natural structures of creation. On the contrary, Protestants have wanted to argue, the *imago dei* is so fully destroyed that there remains only a negative relationship to God.[58]

Or, as the noted Carl F. H. Henry once objected, natural law claims "(1) that independently of divine revelation, (2) there exists a universally shared body or system of moral beliefs, (3) that human reasoning articulates despite the noetic consequences of the Adamic fall," and such claims are unacceptable.[59]

This path is well-worn, and I'll only briefly summarize the objection, particularly as a later chapter deals with the topic in more detail. In some ways the objection is quite obvious, for if human nature is damaged or depraved, its inclinations are untrustworthy:

> How does sin affect the natural law? The sin question takes on at least two forms. (B.1) An epistemological question: how well can we know the natural law given that our reason is misguided by sin? (B.2) An ontological form: since sin has become a part of nature, how should we take account of sin in our account of the natural law? The answer to this question clearly has implications for proposition (1), concerning philosophical realism. Theologians often distinguish between prelapsarian and postlapsarian natural law, which suggests that the content of natural law has been altered by sin. Another way to get at the issue is to distinguish between an absolute and relative natural law. The absolute natural law addresses a circumstance without sin; the relative natural law contains modifications necessary to address the phenomenon of sin. (B.3) A subsidiary set of theological questions related to the

---

57. Snell, "Protestant Prejudice," 22.

58. Braaten, "Protestants and Natural Law," para. 17. In describing evangelicalism and natural law, Hittinger suggests that the theory "cannot be brushed away under the rubric of the 'epistemology of sin,' as some Protestants are wont to do" ("Catholic Moral Theology," 27).

59. Henry, "Natural Law and a Nihilistic Culture," para. 18. See also McGraw, "The Doctrine of Creation and the Possibilities of an Evangelical Natural Law."

ontological question concerns the relationship between nature and grace.[60]

Of course, the tradition is not naïve about this, recognizing that not every desire or impulse is to be followed:

> [Thomas] does not speak of all inclinations but only of natural inclinations; and not all inclinations are natural. One reason for this is that some are acquired. . . . The deeper reason is that the condition in which we human beings find ourselves today is not our natural condition even the feelings and desires with which we are born no longer function in the way that God intended. Had the Fall never taken place, every inclination would be a natural inclination. But the Fall did take place. . . . How, in our disordered state, can reason tell which inclinations are natural and which are not.[61]

Not only nature, but our reason and its ability to distinguish natural and unnatural impulses is disordered. Distinguishing natural and unnatural inclinations is fine, but reason seems little equipped or inclined to judge the distinction properly.

Reason's own perverted inclinations adds yet another dimension to the problem, for not only is human nature, apparently the source from which to read morality, a broken and corrupted source, as is the ability to read, but we don't want to read. Our will actively seeks ignorance, and in such a condition of incoherence it is almost impossible to imagine reason somehow overcoming the distortions of our willed desire, its own weakness, and the broken image to which we turn:

> Even in their prelapsarian state, their noetic powers intact, our first parents were tempted to "be like God, knowing good and evil" . . . How much more are we postlapsarians liable to this temptation, our noetic powers damaged by the Fall, our wills no longer innocent but depraved. . . . For natural law theory, the consequence of the fall is that we *don't want to hear* of natural law. We cannot fully ignore it, because its first letters are written on our hearts. But we resist the inscription, and the letters burn.[62]

---

60. Baer, "Some Reflections on the Problem of Natural Law," para. 9.

61. Budziszewski, *Written on the Heart*, 70.

62. Budziszewski, *The Line Through the Heart*, 18.

THEORY'S DOMAIN, THEORY'S PREJUDICE

While I do not take up a defense against these charges, plenty of natural lawyers have done so, and quite ably. Such arguments and counter-arguments operate either within the same mode of meaning or not: If within the same mode, the arguments clash on this or that premise, interpretation, inference, or bit of data, but if in distinct modes, arguments are often non-responsive, not actually clashing within the same argumentative space so much as missing the point. Rather than respond directly to the arguments, I accept them as genuine difficulties for natural law within common sense and theory, but claim they can be subsumed within interiority and transcendence, as I'll develop in the next two parts of the book. For now, however, I spell out how the default model of natural law—rooted in the meaning of classical theory—is structurally ill-equipped to deal with the three objections summarized above.

Consider some of the commitments of classical theory. First, "[p]roperly so called, science consists in the conclusions that follow necessarily from self-evident, necessary principles."[63] Second, as a consequence, there is "is no science of the accidental," but only of that which is abstracted from the particular and the concrete.[64] To know the human, third, is to abstract "from all respects in which one man can differ from another, there is left a residue named human nature and the truism that human nature is always the same."[65] Fourth, abstract and universal knowledge of the human privileges a metaphysics of the person, for metaphysics provides the necessary science of the soul:

> Thomism had much to say on the metaphysics of the soul. . . . Aristotle employed one and the same method for the study of plants, animals, and men. One was to know acts by their objects, habits by acts, potencies by habits, and the essences of souls by their potencies. The procedure was purely objective. . . . Human nature was studied extensively in a metaphysical psychology, in an enormous and subtle catalogue of virtues and vices, in its native capacities and proneness to evil, in the laws natural, divine, and human to which it was subject. . . . But such study was not part of some ongoing process: everything essential had been said long ago.[66]

63. Lonergan, *Second Collection*, 47
64. Ibid., 3.
65. Ibid.
66. Ibid., 48.

Fifth, given the universal and unchanging nature of the human, including the virtues and laws governing this essence, "[o]ne may fit out the eternal identity, human nature, with a natural law. . . . universals do not change; they are just what they are defined to be. . . . every good Aristotelian knows that. . . ."[67] Finally, and sixth, these controls are static; not only do they not allow for change, they presuppose that change is not meaningful:

> Truth is immutable. Human nature does not change. . . . It is true enough that times change and that circumstances alter cases. But all that change is accidental. The same eternal principles are equally valid and equally applicable despite the flux of accidental differences. . . . With meanings fixed by definitions, with presuppositions and implications fixed by the laws of logic, there resulted what used to be called eternal verities but today are known as static abstractions.[68]

Classical theory, classical Thomism, and classical natural law are all equally committed to these six aspects of meaning: (1) science begins from necessary first principles and proceeds to necessary conclusions; (2) no science of the accidental or particular is possible; (3) genuine knowledge of human nature abstracts from the accidental and particular in (4) a metaphysics of the person; (5) laws governing the person are fixed and immutable, and thus (6) there can be no system of change or development of the laws or metaphysics itself.

Classicism is structurally wooden, particularly in addressing the three objections articulated in this chapter. Consider autonomy in the relationship between nature and grace, and the worry about nature considered in isolation (*natura pura*), almost as if not created, sustained, and governed by God, or, even if created, following its own ordering principles without grace. Nature's relation to grace was a contentious issue throughout the last century, centered around the work of Henri de Lubac and the *Surnaturel* controversy.[69] As explained by Raymond Moloney, two issues stand out:

> The first . . . concerns the notion of a state of pure nature, which the received teaching of the schools considered to be necessary for the definition and vindication of the notion of the supernatural. This position saw the world in terms of what de Lubac called a

67. Ibid., 3.

68. Ibid., 47.

69. For a few examples, see Lubac, *Augustinianism and Modern Theology*; Lubac, *A Brief Catechesis on Nature and Grace*; Milbank, *The Suspended Middle*.

> dualism or a two-tiered universe. There is the reality of human na-
> ture defined by its orientation to a natural end in a state of natural
> beatitude . . . what Scholastics referred to as the state of pure nature
> . . . perfectly intelligible in itself without the need of recourse to the
> supernatural. In such a universe, grace and the supernatural are
> seen as additions from beyond human nature to a nature perfectly
> indifferent to them.[70]

Second, de Lubac understood nature "more historically than ontologically."[71] In his reading, the patristics, especially Augustine, nature referred to "that state in which we are born," and was more concerned with the historical existential order than with essence.

De Lubac did not hesitate to note the tendency toward essentialism in metaphysics, writing:

> . . . on the one hand we use a noun, "nature", and on the other
> an adjective, "supernatural". The nouns "supernature" . . . and
> "super-essence" were rarely used in ancient theology. . . . It was
> only recently, during the nineteenth century, that certain authors
> . . . began to speak regularly of "nature" and "supernature," thus
> completing in their language a deviation of thought whose history
> was already long. . . . this new terminology . . . has certainly made
> the traditional doctrine more obscure, and even falsified it. Let us
> say at the very least that it was the sign and the effect of the doc-
> trine's being obscured. . . . In reality, what we have here is not two
> juxtaposed realities (two "natures"), or, if one prefers, two realities
> the second of which would be superimposed on the other. . . . It is
> not a question of two substantial natures. . . .[72]

This may be, but the entire heuristic structure of classical theory seeks a nature with immanent intelligibility, with a closed-off substantial unity-identity. Consequently, in its very mode of meaningfulness, classical theory struggles to retain the existential and relational aspects of human nature, since it intends a nature which is substantial and where grace would be articulated as either accident of that nature or as substance external to it. Aquinas, his defenders will say, navigated this remarkably well, somehow articulating Augustinian insights in Aristotelian science, while his disciples were remarkably less adept at doing so.[73]

70. Moloney, "De Lubac and Lonergan on the Supernatural," 511.

71. Ibid., 512.

72. Lubac, *A Brief Catechesis*, 33–35.

73. Lonergan, *Verbum*, 3. David Steinmetz argues that Luther's apparent discomfort

If classical theory tends towards substantivist metaphysics, and if such metaphysics tends to think of grace in terms of an accident or a substance separate from nature, it would be no surprise for classical natural law to appear self-enclosed and immune to grace. So, too, would history be awkwardly related to nature in this mode; certainly a notion that the Christ event makes for multiple logics and natures within salvation history is not something classical theory could handle adroitly.

> One can apprehend man abstractly through a definition that applies *omni et soli* and through properties verifiable in every man. In this fashion one knows man as such; and man as such, precisely because he is an abstraction, also is unchanging. It follows in the first place, that on this view one is never going to arrive at any exigence for changing forms, structures, methods, for all change occurs in the concrete, and on this view the concrete is always omitted.... But this exclusion ... is not theological; it is grounded simply upon a certain conception of scientific or philosophic method ... and the omissions due to abstraction, have no foundation in the revealed word of God.[74]

With respect to sin, classical metaphysics does not see the problem. If sin were to destroy nature, as sometimes total depravity is (inaccurately) portrayed, then there would be no nature at all; it would be destroyed. For a nature to be sinful, nature must still exist, and, moreover, it must exist as specifically identical with the nature prior to the fall or sin would result in a substantial change, and a substantial change would mean either (a) a destruction or (b) an entirely new substance. If destruction, then Adam is no longer; if a substantial change, then pre- and post- lapsarian Adams are different species, and there is no fall or perversion of Adam, there is just an Adam-which-used-to-be-but-is-no-longer and this new, poor thing. Further, since sin is not natural, the whole language of "sin nature" is not particularly coherent, and sin begins to look like an accident, or even just like a loss of an extrinsic grace with nature maintaining its own integrity intact.[75] Further, since a nature possesses its own proper perfection(s) or act(s), any

---

with natural law was rooted in his desire for a vocabulary which was "relational rather than metaphysical," but that while Luther thought he targeted Aquinas in this, he didn't know Aquinas so much as Ockham and Biel. See Steinmetz, "What Luther got Wrong," and *Luther in Context*, 47–58.

74. Ibid., 5.

75. This is how Dooyeweerd and Schaffer read Aquinas, as if sin was a loss which left nature untouched in itself.

existing nature is ontologically good, and thus no matter how depraved, human nature remains good in precisely the same way (ontologically) as prelapsarian Adam was good.

That's all true, and from the standpoint of classical theory perfectly obvious and uncontroversial, and arguably was Calvin's view, too.[76] But that's not really the point. I suspect that those pressing hard the noetic effects of sin do not deny that human nature survived the fall, but consider that irrelevant, not what is at stake in the conversation. I agree, but then classical theory and its metaphysics may not be the language with which to have the conversation, but neither is this a reason to reject the very helpful and explanatory function of classical theory so far as it goes. We simply must go farther.

Conclusion

Lonergan spent years trying to raise his intellect to that of Aquinas's, and in so doing found Thomas to be a man of his own time, and that we, like Aquinas, must mount to the level of our time. Reading Aquinas requires historical consciousness, something his commentators, particularly in modernity, failed to recognize, thus sometimes presenting his ideas as eternal accomplishments. Some of his accomplishments were abiding, but even those occurred in response to particular problems at a particular time and with the science available.[77] Consequently, "St. Thomas ceases to be the arbiter to whom all can appeal for the solution of contemporary questions," even while recognizing his vital role in tradition, his abiding voice and accomplishments.[78] Rather than arbiter, Aquinas "stands before us a model, inviting us to do for our age what he did for his . . . a mature Catholic theology . . . will not ignore him . . . and it will be aware of its debt to him, even when it is effecting its boldest transpositions from the thirteenth century to the twentieth."[79]

The "boldest transpositions" of natural law reconsider how meaning works. As we shift to interiority in the next chapters, we shift the controls of meaning, from (1) logic to method, (2) classical science to probability,

---

76. Torrance, *Calvin's Doctrine of Man*, 117–20.

77. Lonergan, *Insight*, 11–24; Lonergan, *Verbum*, 3–11; Lonergan, *Grace and Freedom*.

78. Lonergan, *Second Collection*, 49.

79. Ibid.

(3) soul to subject (or metaphysics to phenomenology, of sorts), (4) nature to history, and (5) first principles to transcendental method, all of which, remain to be explained.[80] All this, I claim, cheerfully allows a natural law incorporating reasonable autonomy, salvation history, and the noetic effects of sin, or the Protestant Prejudice.

80. Lonergan, *Second Collection*, 50–53.

Part Two

Natural Law in a New Mode

Ordo Rationalis

4

The Perspective of the Acting Person

John Paul II and Martin Rhonheimer

In Part Two, I explore natural law from within the *mode of interiority*, summarizing natural law in the work of John Paul II and Martin Rhonheimer, new natural law, and Bernard Lonergan. By no means do these various thinkers present anything like a unified account with exact agreement; in fact, Finnis is sharply critical of Lonergan, Rhonheimer expresses disagreements with new natural law, and Rhonheimer's read of John Paul II is contested by some. Nonetheless, all these thinkers accept a natural law distinct from the theoretical model of classical Thomism. Among those to be discussed, John Paul II retains the closest link to the metaphysics of the person while incorporating subjectivity, while Rhonheimer and the new natural lawyers deny natural law's dependence on theory, and Lonergan creatively retrieves the Thomistic spirit.

Not only is the relationship to classical theory and its metaphysical presuppositions altered, but each thinker turns to the concrete human subject as foundational to the project. While Rommen thought that natural law flourished under metaphysics, these thinkers see no reason natural law cannot develop coherently when subjectivity, phenomenology, practical reason, first person perspectives, and intentionality analysis are utilized— what I would call the turn to the subject, or what John Paul II termed "the perspective of the acting person."[1]

1. John Paul II, *Veritatis Splendor*, 78.

No Longer Strangers to Ourselves: A Working Definition of Interiority

While common sense intends bodies in relation to us, and theory intends things in relation to other things, both heuristically anticipate the real, or nature, under a certain description, an *x*. Neither, however, made anticipation the object of study; they attended to the real rather than to *how* they attended. To put it differently, both presumed and enacted an account of meaning without ever asking about the meaning of meaning. Interiority does.

Just as common sense "gives way" before the systematic questions of theory, so too do critical questions place both common sense and theory in relief. Having differentiated the two modes, certain questions arise:

> So man is confronted with the three basic questions: What am I doing when I am knowing? Why is doing that knowing? What do I know when I do it? With these questions one turns from the outer realms of common sense and theory to the appropriation of one's own interiority, one's subjectivity, one's operations, their structure, their norms, their potentialities. Such appropriation, in its technical expression, resembles theory. But in itself it is a heightening of intentional consciousness, an attending not merely to objects but also to the intending subject and his acts.[2]

For Lonergan, asking these three questions and appropriating the answers to them by attending to the operations of one's own intellect is the key to interiority. While epistemology busies itself with the standards of objectivity, and metaphysics wonders about the nature of reality, cognitional theory asks about the concrete human subject doing epistemology and metaphysics, asking not only "What is knowing?" and "What is known?" but also "What am I doing when I am knowing?" What am *I* doing, and what am I *doing*—this is a turn of attention to myself, and a turn to myself as operating and performing.[3]

Classical theory attended to a metaphysics of the person—human *qua* human—using the very same method to know humans as to know animals and inanimate objects. However precise and true that knowledge was, it alienated us from the definition of ourselves, for the concrete and existing *I-self* was abstracted away. Lonergan, as I noted in the conclusion of the

2. Lonergan, *Method*, 83.

3. Ibid., 25.

preceding chapter, suggests that Thomism should pay less mind to the soul as an abstract nature and more to the subject in their concrete existence, and in so doing allow philosophy to meet real persons for the first time.

Natural law from the mode of interiority begins with subjects who are not strangers to themselves, having asked "What am I doing when I am knowing?" and using the self-knowledge gained by this reflexivity for "the basic anthropological component" of natural law.[4] All natural law holds that law is in some way accessed or known through anthropology—the dispute is about the meaning, access to, and role of anthropology. Interiority provides the basic anthropological component, a version of human nature, by attending to what we *do*, not what we *are*, and claims to *understand* rather than *derive* the law.

THE ACTING PERSON: JOHN PAUL II

Karol Wojtyla, later John Paul II, exercises noetic exegesis in a highly creative way; while rejecting any idealistic phenomenology of pure consciousness whereby the object is constituted by intentionality, he nonetheless retrieves Thomistic metaphysics within a study of the person in a way Thomism alone could not accomplish. For Wojtyla, Aristotelianism inadequately grasped the person, reduced persons to an entity in the world, a cosmological meaning and a reduction needing expansion: "only by probing the subjectivity of human beings can we understand them in all their personhood."[5]

Deeply informed by the phenomenological tradition, particular with Max Scheler's work on value, Wojtyla sought "neither to reform nor to replace traditional Catholic philosophy" and its realistic commitments in metaphysics and epistemology, but his "particular attention is drawn, however, toward our contemporary situation and to prevailing currents of thought."[6] Consequently, he grapples with "the dramatic shift that has taken place in Western thought since the late Middle Ages. For there has been a deep fascination with and cultivation of the inner character of human consciousness in modern times. . . . Wojtyla is confident that modern techniques and approaches, and above all phenomenology properly modified,

4. Ibid.

5. Crosby, *The Selfhood of the Human Person*, 82, see also 82–123.

6. Schmitz, *At the Center of the Human Drama*, 36; Cf. Buttiglione, *Karol Wojtyla*, 120.

can help us to explore the inner region of human experience."[7] As Wojtyla put it, the "problem of the subjectivity of the human being seems today to be the focal point of a variety of concerns.... *Today more than ever before we feel the need—and also see a greater possibility—of objectifying the problem of the subjectivity of the human being.*"[8] Turning away from pure consciousness toward the "full concrete existence of the human being, to the reality of the conscious subject," or the acting person, he embraces contemporary developments: "we can no longer go on treating the human being exclusively as an objective being, but we must also somehow treat the human being as a subject. . . ."[9] Turning to the concrete person—the "I" who acts—and objectifying subjectivity is noetic exegesis.[10]

Indebted to Aristotelian anthropology, Catholic tradition defined the human in terms of genus-species, as rational animal. As true and fecund as the definition is, its cosmological assumptions consider humans as "basically reducible to the world."[11] Of course humans have specific differentiation—rationality—but the method considers the human as an object among objects, whereas the irreducible personhood of the human requires a method adequate to subjectivity. While rationality opens to phenomenological attention, the tradition viewed rationality from within a "metaphysical terrain," a landscape "foreign" to lived experience.[12] The irreducible was overlooked, and it could not but be overlooked by the metaphysical method used alone, or, as I might term it, by the mode of classical theory alone.

The oversight of subjectivity truncates the distinction between human actions (*actus humani*) and those actions which humans do in a cosmological mode (*actus hominis*): "And so when we say, for example, that 'an animal acts,' this means something different from when we say that 'a human being acts.' This is understandable since a different nature lies at the basis of the one activity and the other."[13] Aristotelian categories provide the distinction, of course, precisely because of the rational and voluntary nature proper to the human, but still metaphysical categories miss the irreducible. For persons, the issue is "the revelation of the person as the subject *experiencing* its

7. Ibid., 37–38.

8. Wojtyla, *Person and Community*, 209.

9. Ibid., 210.

10. Wojtyla, *The Acting Person*, 4.

11. Ibid., 211.

12. Ibid., 212.

13. Ibid., 96.

acts and inner happenings, and with them its own subjectivity,"—and thus lived experience must become the center of our self-interpretation.[14] Such self-experiencing subjectivity "cannot be derived by way of cosmological reduction" but instead turns to the concrete person as "an 'eyewitness' of his or her own self."[15]

Wojtyla is particularly sensitive to the role of "nature" in this, for as a realist for whom philosophies of consciousness risk losing the body, his commitment to metaphysics requires greater sophistication than the abstract reduction.[16] In "The Human Person and Natural Law," for instance, Wojtyla attempts to resolve the apparent conflict between natural law and the person, expressing a reserved sympathy for those rejecting natural law by "spontaneously rising up in defense of the special character of human action, in defense of the reality of both the action of the person and the person as such."[17] Nature, he responds, is not univocal and at least two meanings jostle in the dispute. For the Thomist, nature is not that of phenomenalism, where "nature is equivalent to the subject of instinctive actualization."[18] Instinctive actualization is involuntary, so to say that something "happens by nature, we are immediately emphasizing that it *happens*, that it *is actualized*, and not that someone performs an action or that someone acts."[19] Nature is "it," the instinctual or physical which "in this sense excludes the person as an acting subject, as the author of action, because nature in this sense points to a thing's being actualized," very much like nature as instinct discussed in the first chapter. On such a reading, natural law reduces to "biological regularity" outside of personal control.[20]

Understood as such, natural law would be, if not opposed, at least indifferent to the person as responsible moral agent. For the Thomist, nature is not so limited, referring to "the essence of a thing taken as the basis of all actualizations," including the person.[21] Since law is an ordinance of reason, and reason is intrinsically integrated to personhood, natural law is

---

14. Ibid., 213.
15. Ibid., 214.
16. Ibid., 169–70.
17. Wojtyla, *Person and Community*, 181.
18. Ibid., 182.
19. Ibid.
20. Ibid., 183.
21. Ibid., 182.

"something proper to the human being as a rational individual," as a person, although not in any way forgetful of God.[22]

While the two meanings of nature and natural law are quite disparate, based in conflicting theories of knowledge and cognition, and while any conflict between nature and person occurs only for non-Thomistic meaning, the concepts are conflated or "somehow transposed" into each other, a "kind of shifting or transposing of concepts and meanings [which] goes on all the time."[23] In other words, to get nature right, differentiation is necessary, and not merely that of a genealogical tracing of historical variance but rather of the modes of cognition. Getting nature right, getting the *humanum* or the *personale* rather than the entity or genus-species, requires the differentiation of meaning, and that, in turn, requires a metaethics rooted in an account of lived experience.[24]

Even within the modern turn to the subject, overlooking lived experience is not unusual, and a woodenly reductionistic reading of natural law interpreted as instinct, regularity, or laws of nature should not surprise us: "The traditions of philosophical anthropology would have us believe that we can, so to speak, pass right over this dimension, that we can cognitively omit it by means of an abstraction that provides us with a species definition of the human being as a being, or, in other words, with a cosmological type of reduction (*homo=animal rationale*). One might ask, however, whether . . . we do not in a sense leave out what is most human. . . ."[25]

Given the Continental philosophy of the time, it might be tempting to read the concern for lived experience as a turn to intentionality, and the opening lines of Wojtyła's magnum opus, *The Acting Person*, might suggest this:

> The inspiration to embark upon this study came from the need to objectivize that great cognitive process which at its origin may be defined as the experience of man; this experience which man has of himself, is the richest and apparently the most complex of all experiences accessible to him. Man's experience of anything outside of himself is always associated with the experience of himself and he never experiences anything external without having at the same time the experience of himself.[26]

22. Ibid., 184.
23. Ibid., 182–83.
24. Wojtyła, *Man in the Field of Responsibility*, 4.
25. Wojtyła, *Person and Community*, 215.
26. Wojtyła, *The Acting Person*, 3.

Yet, while the person faces themselves by coming "into a cognitive relation with himself," Wojtyla thinks that humans are revealed not in thought but in action.[27]

Experience is not merely sensation, even though an experience is related to the data given to us, including "the dynamic totality of 'man-acts.' It is this fact that we take as the starting point, and on it we shall primarily concentrate our argument."[28] And insofar as "man-acts," then "*action serves as a particular moment of apprehending—that is, of experiencing, the person.*"[29] Of act, we distinguish the *actus humanum* from mere happenings within us by the presence of deliberation and freedom; only the *actus voluntarias* is the *humanum*, only the conscious and willed act reveals the person.

The Scholastics knew this, but while not "entirely disregarded, its presentation was vague, and, as it were, only implied in it."[30] Properly concerned with reason and will's reality as an aspect of reason, consciousness tended to be "as it were, hidden in 'rationality,'" as if rationality was sufficient to explain the person.[31] As true as it is to say that *homo est animal rationale* or *persona est rationalist naturae individual substantia*, these definitions only inchoately hint that "man not only acts consciously, but he is also aware of both the fact that he is acting and the fact that it is he who is acting. . . ."[32] Nature, as construed in the definition of person as "individual substance of a rational nature," may never exist apart from a subject, but still if we "prescind from the nature of every human being, in whom it actually exists, then we may conceive it as an abstract being, which stands in relation to all men," especially if "solely the consequence of birth . . . inborn in the given subject of acting, as if it was determined in advance by its properties."[33]

At the core of lived experience is the experience of duty: "the lived experience strictly connected to every concrete subject when that subject is the cause of an act and experiences its own efficacy. The lived experience of duty ('I ought to . . .') is always strictly personal and connected to the

27. Schmitz, *At the Center of the Human Drama*, 70; cf. Buttiglione, *Karol Wojtyla*, 123–41; Wojtyla, *The Acting Person*, 19–20.

28. Wojtyla, *The Acting Person*, 9.

29. Ibid., 10.

30. Ibid., 30.

31. Ibid.

32. Ibid., 30–31.

33. Ibid., 78–79.

concrete 'I act.'"[34] Insofar as I act, and act as *humanum*, my own efficacy is lived, and only because of agency is duty "already contained," for only as I am agent is "I ought" or "I ought not" comprehensible.[35] Further, morality, as opposed to the science about morality, "is an experiential fact . . . always given in such a way that its understanding can come about only through an understanding of those elements which constitute it in experience, i.e., in human lived experience"—all other modes resulting in a "certain *hetero-genization* of morality," a *"reductio in aliquid genus* [reduction to another genus]."[36] That is, only the experience of duty given in my efficacious act provides an experience of morality as personal fact rather than an abstraction from which we are alienated, which is why we ask questions such as "What ought *I* do?" or "What sort of person shall *I* become?"[37]

While intrinsically linked to the subjective experience, and incoherent without the subject-ivization of nature-as-person, the questions do not collapse into subjectivism, but that risk is not solved by theoretical articulations of morality. Universal principles based on abstract conceptions of the person are not, for Wojtyla, the source of normativity:[38]

> By choosing the experience of the person as a point of departure, Wojtyla is able to work out a philosophy which is a reflection on experience and which finds its criterion of truth in the recognition and in the confirmation which it brings to the experience of the other, of the reader as of every human being. It is, therefore, neither a reflection on the history of philosophy . . . nor the attempt to force assent through abstract argumentation . . . but, rather, an articulated discourse on the fundamental structure of the experience of life which solicits every person to reflect on his own self to confirm and to enrich the author's reflection.[39]

Not the metaphysics of soul or the logic of a science of ethics, but rather the concrete person "confronted with the possibility of acting, experiences that 'I can but I do not have to,'" since it is my choice, confronts me as the foundational access point to morality.[40]

34. Wojtyla, *Man in the Field of Responsibility*, 8.

35. Ibid., 8–9.

36. Ibid., 13–14.

37. Ibid., 21. See also Reimers, *Truth about the Good*, 117–22.

38. Ibid., 58–59.

39. Buttiglione, *Karol Wojtyla*, 122.

40. Reimers, *Truth about the Good*, 117–18.

In linking freedom and duty, John Paul II continues his highly differentiated project of subjectivity but refuses to hypostatize consciousness—there is no good absent the subject's apprehension, but there is also a truth about the good, counter to certain tendencies in contemporary moral theology holding that "one's moral judgment is true merely by the fact that it has its origin in the conscience."[41] Freedom is "not unlimited," but is "called to accept the moral law given by God," who alone has the power to decide what is good and evil.[42] Yet, there is no conflict between freedom and law, for John Paul II reaffirms "the interior character of the ethical requirements deriving from that law, requirements which create an obligation for the will only because such an obligation was previously acknowledged by human reason and, concretely, by personal conscience."[43] Yes, but reason depends on revelation, for man does not lay law for himself law "in an autonomous manner," even though "*man himself* has been *entrusted to his own care and responsibility*."[44]

The tensions and nuances here are intricate. The human is free and entrusted to their own care through reason and the natural law, and their own judgment and conscience genuinely bind, yet reason does not create or constitute norms from nowhere. As expressed in *Veritatis Splendor*, "*moral law has its origin in God and always finds its source in him:* at the same time, by virtue of natural reason, which derives from divine wisdom, it is *a properly human law*," for man "possesses in himself his own law, received from the Creator."[45] God does not compete with humans, and "obedience to God is not, as some would believe, a *heteronomy*, as if the moral life were subject to the will of something all-powerful, absolute, extraneous to man. . . . Such heteronomy would be nothing but a form of alienation. . . ."[46] Instead, human freedom is "*participated theonomy*"; our will and reason participate in

---

41. John Paul II, *Veritatis Splendor*, 32.

42. Ibid., 35.

43. Ibid., 36; cf. *Dignitatis Humanae*, 1: "A sense of the dignity of the human person has been impressing itself more and more deeply on the consciousness of contemporary man. And the demand is increasingly made that man should act on their own judgment, enjoying and making use of a responsible freedom, not driven by coercion but motivated by a sense of duty" (Second Vatican Ecumenical Council, "Declaration on Religious Freedom *Dignitatis Humanae*").

44. Ibid., 36, 39.

45. Ibid., 40.

46. Ibid., 41.

God's, and the divine will and reason, while in no way reducible to our own, are not alienating or entirely foreign either.[47]

This balance, states the encyclical, *is* natural law, for God's directing providence does not happen to us "'from without' through the laws of physical nature, but 'from within,' through reason" because God governs persons, the only creature willed for its own sake, differently than all others.[48] Persons have an interior law, and thus follow their own counsel, which in no way is a creative norm unto itself even as it remains free and self-governing.

These distinctions serve to correct "the more or less obvious influence of currents of thought which end by detaching human freedom from its essential and constitutive relationship to truth," particularly as those currents influence "certain theological positions."[49] Truth is not constituted by consciousness, but neither is truth about the good alien to the person; the starting point is not nature as instinct, or regularity, or physical order, or what is present to the human in light of their birth, or even what is present to the human in light of their universal human essence *alone*, but rather as personal: "no other nature has any real (that is, individual) existence as a person—for this pertains to man alone."[50]

Anthropology, understood as experiencing and apprehending the person *as* person, as actor, has "fundamental significance" to grasping the natural law:[51]

> . . . the natural law . . . is not some kind of rigid and closed system. It is a "flexible" system of its own. The flexibility of that system is entirely based on values as a content, on the one hand objective and transcendent—and on the other hand, subjectively knowable and experienced.[52]

Thus, when *Veritatis Splendor* articulates the basis of intrinsically evil acts against moral revisionists, it does so not by appealing to universal abstraction. Acts "contrary to the commandments of the divine and natural law" are intrinsically evil, but the morality and meaning "*of the human act depends primarily and fundamentally on the 'object' rationally chosen by the*

47. Ibid., 41.
48. Ibid., 43.
49. Ibid., 4.
50. Wojtyla, *The Acting Person*, 84.
51. Wojtyla, *Man in the Field of Responsibility*, 68.
52. Ibid., 70.

deliberate will," knowledge of which requires placing "oneself *in the perspective of the acting person*."[53]

ETHICS WITH A POINT: MARTIN RHONHEIMER

How precisely to interpret the perspective of the acting person and the object of the will is contestable, and we turn to Martin Rhonheimer's reading, not because his is the only possibility but because it so clearly embraces the mode of interiority and reveals the implications of doing so. My intention is not a conclusive reading of Wojtyla/John Paul II, but only the more minimal task of summarizing a significant thinker who self-consciously articulated his project as (1) in deep continuity with the metaphysical and theoretical controls of meaning found in the Thomistic tradition of natural law, but who (2) found that mode of meaning not fully adequate for articulating a sufficient anthropology of the human, and thus also insufficient on its own to express the reality of natural law. Wojtyla does not turn *away from* the tradition, nor against metaphysical theory, but *toward* the subject and the mode of interiority to complete the tradition in apprehending the *actus humanum*. That turn has detractors, or certainly those wishing to wrestle the turn into the controls of theory, but others pushed deeply into interiority. I do not adjudicate that dispute, but in turning to Rhonheimer we discover a thinker obviously conscious of interiority.[54]

Consequentialism as Imperfectly Human

Veritatis Splendor addresses intrinsically evil acts because of a revisionist thread within Catholic theology *"which holds that it is impossible to qualify as morally evil according to its species—its 'object'*—the deliberate choice of certain kinds of behavior or specific acts, apart from a consideration of the intention for which the choice is made or the totality of the foreseeable consequences of that act for all persons concerned."[55] Advocates for such consequentialism or proportionalism often distinguish between the *rightness* and *goodness* of actions, holding that the rightness or wrongness of an

53. Pope John Paul II, *Veritatis Splendor*, 78.

54. Rhonheimer's interpretation has many, voluble critics. See McCormick, "Some Early Reactions to *Veritatis Splendor*," 481–506; Long, "A Brief Disquisition," 45–71; Long, *Teleological Grammar of the Moral Act*; Jensen, "Thomistic Perspectives?," 135–59.

55. John Paul II, *Veritatis Splendor*, 79.

action concerns norms governing actions, while goodness and evil concern "the intentions, the attitudes, and inner disposition of the agent, to qualities of his will and his heart."[56] A right action can be done with evil intentions, but so too can a wrong action be done with good intentions, for evil intent does not thereby make an action wrong.

Since "good" and "evil" describe the intentions, attitudes, and dispositions of the agent rather than the action, and it is the action which is right or wrong, it follows that actions are neither good nor evil, and thus "intrinsically *evil* actions" is a category mistake, particularly because the action, no matter how right or wrong, has no necessary relationship to the agent's will.[57] That is, an egregiously wrong act tells us nothing of the agent's intentions, which may have intended to bring about a greater good, as when Paul Touvier claimed that his direct collaboration with Nazis to kill seven Jews resulted in saving ninety-seven, and thus he was morally good for willing to save ninety-seven Jews.[58] Willing to produce the best state of affairs makes the will good, or so say consequentialists.

Rhonheimer, on the other hand, suggests that one "might speak about earthquakes in a similar way: we consider it to be better (more desirable) that an earthquake kill only one person rather than a hundred," as the outcome is better, but humans aren't earthquakes, or birds, and thus our actions are *our* actions.[59] This distinction is very close to that made by Wojtyla between the *actus humanus* and the *actus hominis*, between a person's voluntary and willed choice and something which happens to, in, or by means of the person even though not chosen. A bird building a nest, says Rhonheimer, does not perform the action of building because it does not purpose to build, as opposed to a person who when pulling the trigger intends the death of the other has as the object of choice the death of the other, not merely the pulling of the trigger.[60] The "intentional content is what we call the *object* of a human act," and we can judge this as right or wrong by judging whether it is good or evil to will the object.[61] That is, the action is not simply the external behavior so much as it is the willed object.

56. Rhonheimer, *Perspective of the Acting Person*, 22.

57. Ibid., 23.

58. Ibid., 78–89

59. Ibid., 25.

60. Ibid., 26.

61. Ibid.

In this, Rhonheimer explicitly appeals to *Veritatis Splendor,* where morality depends on object and the "object of the act of willing is in fact a freely chosen kind of behavior" and not "a process or an event of the merely physical order, to be assessed on the basis of its ability to bring about a given state of affairs in the outside world."[62] Act depends on object, and the morality of the act is determined by whether that object is ordered "to God . . . in conformity with the good of the person with respect for the goods morally relevant for him."[63]

The consequentialist could object that consideration of the best possible state of affairs is objective, or at least more objective than determining what the object of choice is, for in willing the best state of affairs we can appeal to the calculable consequences in the world. As plausible as that might appear, Rhonheimer suggests that this kind of objectivity is possible only if we "talk about human action from the standpoint of an outside observer (the 'third person')," and if actions are thought of "not as intentional and properly human actions, but more like simple events or natural processes."[64] Such objectivity is a "view from nowhere," and "speaks about actions as performances of a 'third person,' but not as *my* actions."[65] It really would not matter if it was I who did the action or someone else, since the only relevant matter for the *action,* according to this account, is the state of the world and not the state of my will. But the tradition has emphasized the first person perspective, for a human action "implies a will whose intentional content forms part of what we traditionally call the *object* of this act . . . and it determines this appetite as a good or an evil one. So it determines whether the person becomes a good or a bad person. The acting subject changes while acting . . . he or she shapes himself or herself. He or she becomes good or evil precisely by choosing."[66]

The Perspective of Practical Reason

Rhonheimer follows *Veritatis Splendor* in holding that one cannot understand the background of intrinsically evil acts without grasping the moral

---

62. John Paul II, *Veritatis Splendor,* 78; cf. Rhonheimer, *Perspective of the Acting Person,* 39, 73–75.

63. Ibid.

64. Rhonheimer, *Perspective of the Acting Person,* 25.

65. Ibid., 28.

66. Ibid., 30.

object, and that one cannot grasp the moral object without taking the first person point of view, or the perspective of the acting person.[67] For Rhonheimer, John Paul II's explicit turn to this perspective is essential, for while Aquinas's own ethics was first personal, his account was largely implicit and "vulnerable to distortion," particularly by an ethics of decisionism understood in "casuistic presuppositions that morality should be understood primarily in terms of obligation."[68] Not only did this tend towards legalism, but also understood intention as coming not from the perspective of the acting person but as "inherent in the physical performance of the bodily behavior"—with a meaning obvious and accessible to any external, third person observer, and with objective judgment of the act given over to the objective observer—placing moral order in "our 'pre-rational nature.'"[69] That is, moral meaning existed in the order of nature (*ordo naturae*), as discussed in previous chapters, and was handed over to those who could look "out there" at behavior and meaning, but stripped away and alienated from the person who acted.

For Rhonheimer, the object is the chosen action (or intelligible purpose) and not a physical thing or object-as-physical-entity. This suggests, as in Aquinas, that the will chooses a "good understood and ordered by reason" (*bonum apprehensum et ordinatum per rationem*), for human acts are determined by intelligence and not by physical things.[70] Human action, insofar as it is human, is "the object of the practical reason which orders and regulates, the fundamental rule or measure of which is the natural law."[71] Not nature but practical reason, and practical reason regulated by natural law, is implied by the perspective of the acting person—but what does it mean, precisely? "What is the importance of the practical reason for the constitution of the *lex naturalis*?"[72]

For revisionists, the major objection to the tradition is its supposed derivation of ethical norms from the pre-moral and pre-rational order of

---

67. While the details are not necessary for my taxonomic project here, Rhonheimer's interpretation of the object is highly contested by both revisionists and neo-Thomists. For a helpful overview, see Murphy, "Aquinas on the Object and Evaluation of the Moral Act," 205–42. Also Rhonheimer, *Perspective of the Acting Person*, 68–94, 195–249.

68. Murphy, "Aquinas on the Object and Evaluation of the Moral Act," 209. For a developed history, see Servais Pinckaers, *Sources of Christian Ethics*, 240–79.

69. Ibid., 210.

70. Rhonheimer, *Perspective of the Acting Person*, 40–41.

71. Ibid., 41.

72. Rhonheimer, *Natural Law and Practical Reason*, 3.

nature, especially from biology, which fails to grasp that morality cannot be inferred from the physical nor an ought from an is.[73] Rather than grasping the constitutive role of practical reason, revisionists continue to picture law "as an object of knowledge that lies, somehow, in the nature of things, over against the practical reason"—as "out there," or "in things," "discovered" and "read off" reality rather than constituted by reason which is itself the law-giver.[74] On this picture, practical reason is nothing more than theoretical apprehension of metaphysics plus the will, with theory grasping the natural order underneath things (*ordo naturalis*). While rejecting the validity of such "readings" from nature, revisionists retain the divide between reason and nature, merely privileging an autonomous and creative reason over against being/nature/ontic order, but also determining moral rightness in terms of consequentialism's insistence on the "best state of affairs" or "maximization of benefits" determined by reference to pre-moral goods. Proportionalism rejects the naturalism of physicalism, but then sneaks natural and pre-moral goods as the ultimate arbiter of right/wrong "through the back door."[75] Rather than freeing themselves from the order of nature, revisionists mimic physicalists, retaining the very same standard of moral meaning (the order of nature) but in a mirrored or reversed image:

> Physicalism or naturalism, whether in its traditional form or in newer variants, depends on the failure to realize the constitutive function of the practical reason as the *evaluating factor* of human behavior. This morally evaluating reason is what must be rediscovered today; an understanding of it is closely connected with the reason's most basic function: the establishment of an order, since "*it is the task of the reason to put into order*" (*rationis est ordinare*). Unless this function of the reason is first understood, it will be difficult to conceive that the natural law is an *ordering of the reason* (*ordinatio rationis*), or that moral virtue is an *order of the reason* (*ordo rationis*).[76]

Hoping to free themselves from nature, revisionists posit conscience as creative and emancipatory (and thereby revert to the natural, pre-moral goods of utility) failing to realize "that the same law, to which the conscience is obliged, has its cognitive origin precisely in the human person as moral

73. Ibid., 5.
74. Ibid.
75. Ibid., 6.
76. Ibid.

subject."[77] Natural law is never brought in "from outside" but emerges from a "*person's own insight* into the moral 'ought,'" for the person, "*bears in himself*" the eternal law which "truly belongs to man" through participation.[78] For Rhonheimer, reason is both subjective and objective in its rule, because reason is not merely the "*application* of a measure" but "the *measure itself*, and thereby the norm of morality."[79] This may be so, but the neo-Thomistic, or theoretical/metaphysical mode of natural law, also claims that natural law is "internal," in the sense of an inner nature, but Rhonheimer's distinction goes farther in distinguishing practical from theoretical reason.

If an ought is based on an is, with being apprehended by theoretical reason and then applied practically, reason seems alien to our experience of freedom, for while our being and nature are coterminous, freedom could never be derived from nature and still be free.[80] Human freedom is *human* rather than divine or angelic or animal, and yet is not a logical conclusion derived from our nature. Voluntary action, and practical reason operating in action, is not "an insight into an essence, but rather a matter of practical experience," just as the "ought" of our action is not a metaphysical derivation but measured by practical reason.[81] The question "How should I be?" is not equivalent to "What am I?"

A confusion arises, claims Rhonheimer, in conflating speculative with theoretical reason. For Aquinas, there is only one reason however distinct the various powers and operations of that unity. Intelligent agents are oriented to the apprehension and judgment of truth, but apprehension, while speculative in kind, is not thereby theoretical since the kinds of judgments we perform differ in purpose—theoretical and practical judgments, while both oriented to truth, are oriented to truth with two distinct goals or ends, namely being and good.[82] Theoretical reason judges the apprehension of the truth of being, while practical reason is oriented towards the intelligible good achievable by action, although still governed by truth. There is, then, one reason (speculative) operating in two ways with two distinct and non-reducible goods, the truth of being (what is) and the truth of action (what is to be)—a distinction clearly articulated in the opening lines

77. Ibid., 14.
78. Ibid.
79. Ibid., 15.
80. Ibid., 21.
81. Ibid., 22.
82. Ibid., 25.

of the *Nicomachean Ethics*, where ethics is identified by its directedness or goal-intentionality: "Every art and every inquiry, and likewise every action and every decision, appears to aim after some good, so that the good has been aptly named to be that toward which all things aim."[83]

Practical Reason and Inclination

Practical reason is situated within a seeking after the desirable or *appetibile* and is meaningful only in that goal-situatedness rather than as a metaphysical given which cannot be otherwise than it is—practical reason seeks those goods which may or may not be attained in freedom, but which we desire to have. Further, and reminiscent of Wojtyla, these are appetites not only of disembodied reason but of the person, the psychosomatic unity of body-soul, and thus occur within the context of inclinations.[84] Such inclinations, the sexual urge as an example, are practical in the sense of aiming to some goal or good toward which they prod the agent, and the satisfaction of those desires is the good of that inclination, but the question of practical reason is not how to satisfy those inclinations but the good and end of the person.[85] Determining whether the goods natural to the desires are good for the person is the domain of the natural law, but not as if the person (a) stands before the law as heteronymous and superior, and (b) not as if the law is read-off the physical state of affairs in nature, and (c) not as if the law is read-off a prior metaphysical apprehension of human essence.

Ultimately, says Rhonheimer, without the divine the natural law would be non-operative, but it is not as though one need know this explicitly or derive the natural law from divine pronouncement, for natural law really does operate in the human through practical reason. The practical principles manifest themselves in the immediate, non-derived grasp of the primary "experience of 'good' as a correlate and formal content of our tendencies," or inclinations, for having experienced our inclinations, we have experienced the practical striving or seeking of these goods.[86] From this experience we apprehend the first practical principle, namely, the first

83. Ibid., 22.

84. Rhonheimer, *Perspective of the Acting Person*, 111–22, 170–75; cf. *Natural Law and Practical Reason*, 27–30, 284–87; *The Perspective of Morality*, 95–101.

85. Ibid., 173.

86. Ibid., 176.

principle of the natural law: good is to be done and pursued but evil avoided (*bonum est faciendum et prosequendum, et malum vitandum*).

Not only is the first principle not derived from theory, it is not derived from anything; it is not a logical entailment so much as the basis for meaningful action, which is meaningful insofar as it pursues something apprehended as a good, as something to be sought. This is why practical judgments are of the form "seek *x*" or "avoid *y*" or "*z* is to done," for these judgments take the form of goal-directedness given in our experience as conscious, embodied, persons of inclination and appetite who are also aware of those appetites insofar as we act voluntarily (as *humanum*).

Since we begin from an "inclinational environment," practical reason has as its conditions our inclinations and seekings, and reason operates to judge what is to be done to attain not this or that good but the good of the human person in their entirety: "the natural law is a conjunction of the natural judgments of practical reason, which in a preceptive or imperative way express the good to be done and the evil to be avoided in the sphere of the ends indicated by the natural inclinations."[87] The *ordo*, then, is not that of metaphysics or theoretical judgments, neither is it merely a blind following of inclinations, but is the order of reason itself as reason judges and integrates the proper place of the various goods "in relation to one another and toward an end," namely, happiness or well-being.[88] Natural law is not human nature or even *ordo naturae*, but "is specifically practical reason, and in more precise terms, the set of determined judgments of practical reason."[89] As judgments, they articulate a truth of what is to be done, what good is to be sought, although the various goods are manifested through our inclinations, and subsequently ordered by reason (*praescriptio rationis* or *ordinatio rationis*). Reason is not nature or natural regularity, but it is a law "that 'by nature' has the character of a law, that is, of an ordering of reason towards the good," with good first experienced in inclination:[90]

> . . . in the context of a purely philosophical ethics, the term "law," at least in this connection, is redundant when understood precisely. The category of the *lex naturalis* really involves nothing new that would need to be added to the doctrine of the standard-giving-role of reason; rather, it leads, for Thomas, back to the doctrine

87. Ibid., 181.

88. Rhonheimer, *Natural Law and Practical Reason*, 33.

89. Rhonheimer, *Perspective of the Acting Person*, 164.

90. Rhonheimer, *The Perspective of Morality*, 262.

of the practical reason, to the doctrine of human actions, and of the determination of good and bad through reason. . . . The only thing that is new here is just the integration of this doctrine into the context of a Christian theology of law . . . and the integration of human reason to the divine reason. . . . [91]

Natural law just *is* reason in its practical ordering of naturally apprehended goods. As a measure it is also measured by the eternal law, but it is *our* measure, and certainly not the measure provided by nature or theory or metaphysics. In this way, for Rhonheimer, natural law is a rational virtue theory, since the virtues provide the proper rational ordering to inclinations, although the reason by which this is done is ours as our reason participates in eternal law; it is a "participated theonomy."[92]

He goes farther. Not only is practical reason the foundation for natural law, and not only is theoretical anthropology not first, but he inverts or reverses the theoretical impulse, arguing that practical reason is the *basis for theory*: "Knowledge of human nature is not the point of departure for ethics, and even less for the practical reason of each acting subject: it is, rather, its result."[93] Moreover, it is by means of practical reason that metaphysics gains "an understanding of the dynamic aspect of being," without which nature is static and flat.[94] How does this happen?

Rather than beginning with self-evident propositions or a theory of nature, we begin from our own strivings, and within this context of striving "we make judgments or commands about our strivings—Seek this! Do that! Avoid this!—and while very often those commands do not rise to the level of linguistic utterance, operating more as conscious seeking or desire, we can *experience* ourselves commanding and seeking, and then cognitively objectify that experience and the precepts of practical reason."[95] We do so through reflexivity, whereby the intellect returns (*reditio*) to its own act, notes our inclinations and judgments, and makes statements about what we have already done. The propositions are not the natural law but an account of the law as it is already operative in our judgments: "every act of the intellect provokes, as it were spontaneously, a reflection of the same intellect upon its own action, by which we become conscious of the act itself as well

---

91. Ibid., 263.

92. Rhonheimer, *Natural Law and Practical Reason*, 64–68.

93. Rhonheimer, *The Perspective of Morality*, 162.

94. Rhonheimer, *Natural Law and Practical Reason*, 23.

95. Snell, "Saving Natural Law from Itself," para. 10.

as of its object and, finally, of the power that is the basis of the act. In this way we reach, more or less explicitly, the nature of the human soul."[96]

As we'll see again in the next chapter, this insistence upon the Thomistic account of how essence is known requires an epistemological primacy for the operations of our practical reason, and subsequent reflection upon them, as the basis for a philosophical anthropology. It is a basic Thomistic principle that the essence of a thing is not known to us directly: "We know it by knowing the specific faculties of each nature. The faculties are known by their acts, but we know the acts by their objects. The object of human freedom—which lies in reason and the will as *appetitus in ratione*—is specifically good in the multiple forms of its self-expression."[97] We begin with objects—goals or goods of practical reason—reflection upon which allows us to know the acts whereby the goods appeared and were apprehended by us, thus revealing our faculties (or potencies), the differentiation of which allows us to know our essence as distinct from other entities. In the end, therefore, the intelligibility of our nature depends on "the very subjectivity of the moral agent," for it is "precisely the intellectual acts . . . that open the human subject to an understanding of the human good according to the truth of his 'being a person.'"[98]

This is a tidy reversal of the default model; ethics is not a branch of metaphysics or theory, neither is a knowledge of human nature foundational for deriving the natural law. Instead, we begin in our concrete situatedness as actual and individual subjects finding ourselves oriented by desire to this or that good, but also freely measuring and ruling our actions toward the accomplishment of those goods through the measuring power of our practical reason. Having performed this rule, we are capable of reflecting—noetic exegesis—on that performance, of noting what we are doing, and so discovering who and what we are. We start as strangers, in a sense, to our being, and discover what we are insofar as we are practically oriented.

This is not the mode of theory but interiority: "the natural law shows that it is located specifically on the side of the subject and, as a result, that it is really 'subjective.' Its objectivity—and thus the objectivity of the moral norms based upon it—consists in the fact that in this natural knowledge of human good the truth of subjectivity is expressed."[99] And natural order,

96. Rhonheimer, *Natural Law and Practical Reason*, 29.

97. Rhonheimer, *The Perspective of Morality*, 161–62.

98. Ibid., 161.

99. Ibid., 160.

if by this we mean being or physics or regularity or biology, is not what is meant by the truth of subjectivity, nor is this truth derived from nature (*ordo naturae*) but from reason (*ordo rationalis*) insofar as reason operates in a concrete subject.

SOME CONCLUDING THOUGHTS

In this chapter, we've traced a transition in how meaning operates, and thus also the *performance* of natural law. While *common sense* looks to inclination, proverb, or physicalism, *theory*, at least in its classical sense, looked to the essence of things as necessary and unchanging, but *interiority* looked to the performance and operations of the concrete subject, paying attention to the intelligibility of what we had already done. Karol Wojtyla/John Paul II retains the best of theory and interiority, complementing and perfecting one mode by the other. Martin Rhonheimer privileges interiority, although he means by this the exercise of practical reason in its intentional striving.[100] And yet, each begins with the concrete subject, thus positioning natural law within the truth of subjectivity, access to which requires first my subjectivity and its acts and subsequent reflection on those acts, that is, the objectification of my subjectivity and its operations through noetic exegesis. Natural law is not quite the same as for theory.

As concrete subjects, we operate in bodies, in place, in time, with desires; we are not static unchanging essences, but rather agents and actors; we are not necessary causes, but free; not pure consciousness or pure essence, but persons. Given this enrichment of personhood, it should hardly surprise us to find that Wojtyla/John Paul II and Rhonheimer (1) point to the perspective of the acting person, (2) recognize reason as linked to God in a "participated theonomy," (3) note the role of vice and sin in impairing natural law[101] and (4) the capacity of the human to recognize the naturally reasonable,[102] (5) point to the positive aspect of faith in healing reason, and

---

100. Rhonheimer explicitly distinguishes his account from the phenomenological mode of reflexivity, arguing that only in reflecting on the "act of the practical reason" would we "find ourselves in the area of moral philosophy." See *Natural Law and Practical Reason*, 29–30.

101. Rhonheimer, *Perspective of the Acting Person*, 16–17; John Paul II, *Veritatis Splendor*, 1: "Man's capacity to know the truth is also darkened, and his will to submit to it is weakened."

102. Rhonheimer, *Perspective of the Acting Person*, 1–17.

(6) the uniquely central role of Christ in doing so.[103] I do not interpret this enrichment as merely the adding on of content, but rather the difference of how meaning is controlled, for in common sense and theory these six aspects are not especially relevant to how natural law is understood, while interiority finds them directly at the center of the conversation. This is not, I suggest, the same account with more detail, but rather, the detail is present because the account and its control is significantly distinct in its exigence.

These claims will be explored and defended with more attention in future chapters, but another major school of thought rooted in interiority remains to be investigated, namely, the so-called "new natural law theory" of Germain Grisez, John Finnis, and Joseph Boyle.

---

103. Ibid., 17; Rhonheimer, *Perspective of Morality*, 24–30; John Paul II, *Veritatis Splendor*, 1–3, 6–27: "Consequently the decisive answer to every one of man's questions, his religious and moral questions in particular, is given by Jesus Christ, or rather is Jesus Christ himself . . ." (2).

5

Contemporary Natural Law

Grisez, Finnis, Boyle, and Company

One of the most influential and controversial developments has been the so-called "new natural law" theory (NNL) associated with Germain Grisez, John Finnis, Joseph Boyle, and their students.[1] Like Rhonheimer, they eschew ethics derived from metaphysics, not only because they accept Hume's is-ought critique but also because natural law does not derive its first principles from anything, let alone from metaphysics. As a result, and also because of their sustained and nuanced work on the principle of double effect, nuclear deterrence, abortion, homosexuality, contraception, medical ethics, and political theory, the group has created a school of thought competing with, and drawing the severe criticisms of, more traditional accounts.[2]

As in previous chapters, I do not adjudicate the disputes so much as position them within an account of meaning. NNL, or as its adherents would prefer, Contemporary Natural Law (CNL), operates within *interiority*. Again, I'm attempting to position these differences in such a way that the chapter provides an introduction to CNL, differentiates it from other

1. For helpful introductions to the school, see Gómez-Lobo, *Morality and the Human Goods*; May, *An Introduction to Moral Theology*, 93–119.

2. For just three influential critics, see Long, "Natural Law or Autonomous Practical Reason," 165–93; Hittinger *A Critique of the New Natural Law Theory*; McInerny, "The Principles of Natural Law," 1–15.

accounts, and opens the way to articulating why the usual Protestant objections are insufficiently differentiated.

The First Principle of Practical Reason

A foundational text of CNL is Germain Grisez's 1965 essay, "The First Principle of Practical Reason," a commentary on the plurality of precepts in natural law.[3] According to Grisez, many readers of Aquinas are mistaken in thinking that the first principle of practical reason—*Do good and avoid evil*—is a command found in the conscience, "written there by the hand of God," which receives content when "man consults his nature to see what is good and what is evil."[4] This metaphysical derivation entails that a person "examines an action in comparison with his essence to see whether the action fits human nature or not. . . . All specific commandments of natural law are derived this way," or so says theoretical natural law.[5] But the first principle of practical reason—which is also the first principle of natural law—is not a command of morality, says Grisez. Rather than "Do good and avoid evil," Thomas actually says "Good is to be done and pursued, and evil is to be avoided" (*Bonum est faciendum et prosequendum, et malum vitandum*), and these statements "differ considerably in meaning and . . . belong in different . . . contexts."[6]

The question articulated in I-II 94.2 is "Whether the Natural Law Contains Several Precepts, or One only?", a genuine problem for unity of law, nature, and reason in the human. Aquinas's solution, suggests Grisez, is that "the precepts are many because the different inclinations' objects, viewed by reason as ends for rationally guided efforts, lead to distinct norms of action," since practical reason begins with, and exercises judgments over, objects viewed as reasons for acting.[7]

Aquinas makes an analogy—not a derivation—between the first principles of theoretical reason and practical reason: "the precepts of the natural law are to the practical reason, what the first principles of demonstrations are to the speculative reason. . . ."[8] The principles of both are plural, and,

3. Grisez, "The First Principle of Practical Reason," 168–201; cf. Aquinas ST I-II 94.2.
4. Ibid., 168.
5. Ibid.
6. Ibid.
7. Ibid., 171.
8. ST I-II 94.2.

moreover, self-evident, although he follows the usual distinction between that which is self-evident in itself and self-evident to us. Something can be perfectly self-evident and not recognized as such. The point is not whether the principles are innate or obvious or known by everyone, but that the principles of theory and natural law are underived. If one understands that the "predicate is contained in the notion of the subject," which is the objective or "in itself" aspect of self-evidency, one knows it to be impossible to ground or derive the intelligibility of the predicate from the subject.[9] Of course, a given person *might not* understand, for while some self-evident propositions may be known to all, others are known only to the wise, to those who understand. Furthermore, continuing the analogy, being is that which is first apprehended in theoretical reason, such that the principle of non-contradiction is the first indemonstrable principle of theory, and "on this principle all others are based," although not derived.[10] As theory apprehends being, "so *good* is the first thing that falls under the apprehension of the practical reason, which is directed to action: since every agent acts for an end under the aspect of good. Consequently the first principle in the practical reason is one founded on the notion of good, viz., that *good is that which all things seek after. . . .*"[11]

The analogy is crucial. Aquinas clearly distinguishes theoretical reason, grounded upon an apprehension of being, from practical reason, grounded upon an apprehension of good, and never reduces practical reason to theory. The precept, "good is to be done and pursued, and evil is to be avoided," is a principle of action rather than deduction; one does not define the good and then deduce instances thereof so much as one *desires* or *seeks* the good as an *object*.

> Now what is practical reason? Is it simply knowledge sought for practical purposes? No, Aquinas considers practical reason to be the mind playing a certain role, or functioning in a certain capacity, the capacity in which it is "directed to a work." Direction to work is intrinsic to the mind in this capacity; direction qualifies the very functioning of the mind. Practical reason is the mind working as a principle of action, not simply as a recipient of objective reality.

9. Ibid; cf. Grisez, "First Principle of Practical Reason," 172–75.

10. ST I-II 94.2.

11. Ibid.

> It is the mind charting what is to be, not merely recording what already *is*.[12]

In a reversal of theory which knows what is, practical reason knows *what is to be*, beginning with an intention or goal. In theory, we grasp "a dimension of reality already lying beyond the data," but the practical mind "bears gifts into the realm of being" through action and brings being "into conformity with reason."[13] This is not what Rommen had in mind at all.

The object brought into being through action is the good, for good is that which practical reason presupposes as its "object of tendency."[14] Good is intelligible only as *what each thing tends toward*, and practical reason's task is directing work (action) toward an end, and such directedness or intentionality is the condition for practical reason. This is *not yet* morality, just intelligibility, "it simply determines that whatever [practical reason] thinks about must at least be set on the way *to something*—as it must be if reason is to be able to think of it practically."[15] Practical reason entails only "that there shall be direction," with multiple possible directions, such that the "primary precepts of practical reason . . . concern the things-to-be-done that practical reason naturally grasp as human goods, and the things-to-be-avoided that are opposed to those goods."[16]

If we lacked reason, we would still have tendencies and inclinations seeking satisfaction; in practical reason the "object of a tendency becomes an objective," as reason directs.[17] But one should not immediately judge such direction as morality, for the first precept was merely the intelligibility of action—*to something* rather than *to nothing*—not the command "do good but avoid evil!" Conflating intelligibility of action with the morality of action leads to the mistaken notion that "law is essentially a curb to action . . . a command set over against even those actions performed in obedience to it," whereas law "rather, is a source of actions. Law makes human life possible."[18] Even non-contradiction operates in false theoretical judgments, practical reason operates in false practical judgments, or the actions would not be voluntary—they would be *happenings* but not human acts

12. Grisez, "First Principle of Practical Reason," 175.

13. Ibid., 176.

14. Ibid., 178.

15. Ibid., 179.

16. Ibid.

17. Ibid., 180.

18. Ibid., 186, 188.

(*humanum*).[19] Actions are human insofar as directed by practical reason toward objectives, even if wrong—thus, the law is the source of action and not an external constraint upon action, since the first precept is not about what we *ought* to do.

With respect to prescriptions—the *ought*—Grisez reiterates that the default view considers precepts as imperatives. When Aquinas runs through the precepts following from our substantiality, animality, and reason, the temptation is very strong to interpret this as a perhaps-not-exhaustive list of "do what supports existence, life, reason," even though such reasoning makes it difficult to know why you could counter some natural processes but not others, as in haircuts and contraception. Instead, according to Grisez, we should understand the precepts do *prescribe*, inasmuch as they direct and ordain actions toward the realization of a known good, but this is not an imperative of morality.[20]

An imperative, it would seem, is a dictate of will—do this!—but for Aquinas the will depends upon a rational apprehension of the good, and so willing the goods (even as an imperative) is consequent to the prior apprehension and directedness toward them. Thus, practical reason's prescriptive ordering towards intelligibility is a condition of subsequent imperatives (and of all human acts). Law does not make an imperative for practical reason to obey but depends on practical reason to be intelligible.[21] This also preserves the self-evident aspect of the precepts, for they are not derived from theory and mandated by will; they are not derived at all, but are first in the practical reason's directionality *to something*:

> Aquinas's position is not: we conclude that certain kinds of acts should be done because they would satisfy our inclinations or fulfill divine commands. His position is: we are capable of thinking for ourselves in the practical domain because we naturally form a set of principles that make possible all our actions.[22]

19. Ibid., 187–88.
20. Ibid., 191.
21. Ibid., 191–93.
22. Ibid., 195.

THE FIRST PERSON POINT OF VIEW

While not the fullest or most recent account of the CNL project, this early article discloses the commitment to subjectivity and interiority. According to Christopher Tollefsen, a prominent member of the CNL school, Grisez, along with Finnis and Boyle, are properly identified as providing a "basic goods" ethics for which "the foundations of human action lie in an agent's practical recognition that certain goods give basic, non-instrumental reasons for action."[23] As basic, the goods are self-evident, or underived, and as non-instrumental the goods are reasons for action and not instruments to other, more basic goods. Further, as goods, they are grasped as *something to* seek. Against other basic good accounts, CNL holds that "the relevant standpoint for understanding intention, and hence for understanding human action in the proper sense, is exclusively the standpoint of the acting person, or . . . the first person standpoint."[24] Or, as I would describe it, CNL operates within interiority.

Tollefsen explains, with particular reference to the principle of double effect, the core of the first person account as "what I intentionally do, that is, what is strictly a matter of my intention, is a matter of what I have chosen to do in order to bring about some benefits I seek."[25] That is, there is some benefit sought, the state of affairs required by that benefit, and the means or instruments chosen to that desired state. Taking medicine to reduce blood pressure has the intention of "the taking of medicine for the reduction of blood pressure for the sake of health," but if the medicine happens to cause nausea and impotence, I accept but do not choose them.[26]

Unlike common sense or physicalism, the first person account does not imagine actions as out-there waiting for me:

> . . . the first person approach denies that actions lie before one, like bronze, in such a way that one can then choose to do something with, or take an attitude to, those actions. . . . What constitutes an action . . . is itself a function of the agent's choice. . . . It is not a physical, or contextual or social description that determines the nature of the act, but the agent's intention; and that intention is a purely first person reality.[27]

23. Tollefsen, "First Person Account of Human Action," 441.

24. Ibid., 442.

25. Ibid., 444.

26. Ibid., 445–46.

27. Ibid., 447.

Causal closeness does not entail that an agent has chosen that which is caused. For instance, while leaping from a burning skyscraper to avoid the fire means that one will die from the fall, and under normal conditions the leap is inseparable from causing one's death, one has not chosen suicide, for the intention is to avoid the flames by leaping from the building. The person may know the action will result in death, they may accept those consequences, and may even bear moral responsibility for unintended consequences, but, says Tollefsen, in no way can it be reasonably judged that the person has intended (chosen) their death, although the distinction would be difficult to maintain from a third person standpoint. From the first person standpoint, morality is a "matter of the heart," requiring "an upright will," although this "does not mean an idle retreat from the world into the life of subjectivity; an intention is an intention to act. But it does indicate a truth in Kant's great claim that there is nothing of unconditional worth save the good will."[28]

Now, it is my impression that these claims are surprising; certainly a wide range of thinkers in the broadly neo-Thomistic tradition find them startling.[29] They just don't seem like the natural law we expect as more "objective" than this. That may be, and the disruption intensifies if we ask further questions about law.

LAW AND THE INTERNAL POINT OF VIEW

In his classic *Concept of Law*, H. L. A. Hart, articulates how odd it is that the problem of law's nature persists:

> No vast literature is dedicated to answering the questions "What is chemistry?" or "What is medicine?," as it is to the question "What is law?" . . . No one has thought it illuminating or important to insist that medicine is "what doctors do about illness," or "a pre-diction of what doctors will do," . . . [y]et in the case of law, things . . . as strange as these have often been said, and not only said but urged with eloquence and passion, as if they were revelations of truths about law, long obscured by gross misrepresentations of its essential nature.[30]

---

28. Ibid., 458–59.
29. For CNL, a flash point has been craniotomy; for Rhonheimer, contraception.
30. Hart, *The Concept of Law*, 1.

Despite a long tradition, it is still difficult to adequately explain the difference between law, command, and habit, and the method to distinguish these is even more obscure.

For instance, is it habit or rule (in Britain in the 1960s) "that the male head is to be bared on entering a church," and how would we know?[31] According to Hart, (1) rules do more than predict but also claim that divergence is a fault, (2) with failure to keep the rule thought sufficient grounds for criticism, and (3) only from within an internal point of view can rules be grasped as more than habits with social compulsion.[32] To view a law as a scholar might, say someone cataloguing the laws of a community to which they do not belong, is not to experience the law *as* law but merely as a list of predictors which others seem to habitually follow. From the internal point of view, however—for those within the system of law—the rule acts as a reason to follow and sufficient grounds from which to criticize (even punish) those who deviate from the rule.[33]

Hart's student and interlocutor, John Finnis, objects that Hart's account, "rather obviously, . . . is unstable and unsatisfactory," unable to distinguish central from peripheral cases.[34] Defining from the central case, *pros hen*, requires practical reasonableness, he suggests, but some accounts of practical reasonableness are more reasonable than others, so determining the central case requires "the viewpoint of those who not only appeal to practical reasonableness but also *are* practically reasonable," or, following Aristotle, to grasp the essence of law requires not only a theory of law but "the *spoudaios* (the mature man of practical reasonableness) . . . in other words, the concerns and understanding of the mature and reasonable man provide a better *empirical* basis for the reflective account of human affairs."[35] That is, the judgment of the judger cannot be jettisoned—it is not that kind of objectivity, the kind which acts as if there is no person judging:

> Does this mean that descriptive jurisprudence . . . is inevitably subject to every theorist's conceptions and prejudices about what is good and practically reasonable? Yes and no. "Yes," in so far as there is no escaping the theoretical requirement that a judgment of *significance* and *importance* must be made. . . . "No," in so far as the

31. Ibid., 55.
32. Ibid., 55–56.
33. Ibid., 87–91.
34. Finnis, *Natural Law and Natural Rights*, 13; hereafter *NLNR*.
35. Ibid., 15 n. 37.

> disciplined acquisition of accurate knowledge about human affairs
> . . . is an important help to the reflective and critical theorist in his
> effort to convert his own (and his culture's) practical "prejudices"
> into truly reasonable judgments. . . .[36]

Such "conversion" is not a matter "of deriving one's basic judgments about human values . . . by some inference from the facts of the human situation," or simply enshrining "one's ethical or political judgments," but is rather a "critically justified" account of natural law which "with full awareness of the methodological situation" is "attainable by one in whom wise knowledge of the data, and penetrating understanding . . . are allied to a sound judgment about all aspects of genuine human flourishing and authentic practical reasonableness."[37]

Note the standard for defining law is found "by one in whom"—or *is one whom* (the *spoudaios*)—has converted their biases rather than a theoretical deduction.[38] Objectivity looks more like genuine subjectivity than classical theory; in fact, Finnis posits no objection to the supposedly "decisive" fact/value objection to natural law, claiming that natural lawyers "have not, nor do they need to, nor did the classical exponents of the theory dream of attempting such a derivation."[39] The "most popular objection to all theories of natural law has to be abandoned, too, and the whole question of natural law thought through afresh by many"—including, if Finnis is correct, a good many Thomists.[40]

Agreeing with Grisez, Finnis suggests that Aquinas makes it quite clear that the first principles are *per se nota*, or self-evident, which is to say underived and underivable: "They are not inferred from speculative principles. They are not inferred from facts. They are not inferred from metaphysical propositions about human nature, or about the nature of good and evil, or about 'the function of a human being', nor are they inferred from a teleological conception of nature. . . . They are not inferred or derived from anything."[41] As such, the natural lawyer has no need to answer Hume but can move right along into natural law reasoning, which

---

36. Ibid., 17.

37. Ibid., 17–18.

38. Finnis, as I have argued elsewhere, creatively uses Bernard Lonergan a good deal in his methodology and cognitional theory, see my "Performing Differently."

39. Ibid., 33.

40. Ibid.

41. Ibid., 33–34.

is self-evident and used by everyone, without worrying about the usual counter-examples based on absurdities implied in the so-called perverted faculty accounts—such as cutting one's fingernails or abstaining from food or sex—and, so we might expect, can change the way sin is understood within the natural law tradition. Natural law is not what people think, and they attack a straw man.

Further, Finnis explains that the natural law, which is a set of basic practical principles and a methodological requirement, is not a theory: "A first essential distinction is that between a theory, doctrine, or account and the subject-matter of that theory, doctrine, or account. There can be a history of theories . . . of matters that have no history. And principles of natural law . . . have no history."[42] That is, while one can provide a history of what Plato, Aristotle, the Stoics, Aquinas, or Grotius wrote and thought about the natural law, such history, and even the accounts it would summarize is *not* the natural law. Natural law *is* the very principles of practical reasoning—the principles are plural, and yet the variegated and non-reducible principles are *the* (singular) natural law—"which would hold good, as principles, however extensively they were overlooked, misapplied, or defied in practical thinking, and however little they were recognized by those who reflectively theorize about human thinking."[43] These principles are the basis of all practical judging, always and everywhere, and theorizing *about* them is not them, for they provide the basis upon which practical thought is intelligible for the person operating as practical. The performance is the thing, not the account of the performance, however important such accounts may be, for the account, if done critically, will be noetic exegesis, but the performance precedes and makes meaningful such exegesis.

Knowing the Basic Human Goods

As with Rhonheimer and Grisez, Finnis emphasizes the practical aspect of ethics, not only the perhaps obvious claim that ethics is about action, but also the methodological point, namely, that access to the principles of ethics depends upon the concrete and individual human subject *doing something*: ". . . one does ethics properly, adequately, reasonably, if and only if one is questioning and reflecting *in order to be able to act.*"[44] Only from

42. Ibid., 24.

43. Ibid.

44. Finnis, *Fundamentals of Ethics*, 1.

the first personal standpoint, and only insofar as the person is seek-*ing* or striv-*ing*, question-*ing* or reflect-*ing*, can ethics be reasonable. The performance whereby one is *doing something* is foundation; even, in a sense, the do-*ing* must be current, ongoing, present now, and not something done once but no longer accessible: "primary understanding of human good . . . is attained when one is considering what it would be good, worthwhile to do . . . by definition, when one is thinking practically."[45]

To clarify the performative element of ethics, Finnis articulates his account of objectification, or paying attention to those performances of intentionality which allow the world of meaning to appear but which generally remain in the background, inchoate: "Ethics is genuinely reflexive. It can advance its understanding of the full human good by attending to the sort of good which leads one to engage in the pursuit of ethics. It can refute certain ethical or 'meta-ethical' claims by showing how they refute themselves. . . . if one is doing ethics with awareness of what one is doing, one will reflect on the condition under which the goods directly at stake in ethical inquiry are reasonably (appropriately) pursued."[46] We do ethics when we pursue, as we also do ethics when we reflect on how we pursue, but without the pursuing we have nothing about which to reflect.

Furthering this point, Finnis explicates the many passages in the *Nicomachean Ethics* where Aristotle appears to settle contested points by appealing to what "everyone would say," which is not an appeal to consensus but to intelligibility.[47] The point is not "parroting common opinions . . . but by attending to precisely those aspect of our experience . . . of which our language serves as a reminder and in which human good(s) became or can now become intelligible."[48] "No one would say . . ." indicates a reminder of the intelligible experience available to us in our own practical reasoning, and conveys the judgment that "no one could reasonably say." Of course, people *might* say all sorts of things, including those very statements Aristotle suggests no one *would* say, but they *cannot* say them in an intelligible way.

This turns to reason and not nature, and is methodologically fruitful. As with Rhonheimer, Finnis holds that human nature is not the foundation of ethics, but "rather, ethics is an indispensable preliminary to a full and

45. Ibid., 14.
46. Ibid., 9.
47. Ibid., 17–23.
48. Ibid., 18.

soundly based knowledge of human nature," for ethics is not deduced or inferred from metaphysics or anthropology."[49] Instead, "the *nature of X is* understood by understanding *X's capacities* or capabilities, those capacities or capabilities are understood by understanding their activations or *acts*, and those activations of acts are understood by understanding their *objects*."[50] One could read this, perhaps, as metaphysical baggage from an earlier age, but it can also be read performatively, whereby acts are understood by attending to their object(ive)s or ends, and object(ive)s grasped by asking the question *why*.[51]

We understand nature by working backwards, as it were, from our objects identified from the first person standpoint of practical reason, for the *"objects* of human life . . . are precisely the concern of practical reason, i.e., of our thinking about what to do and be."[52] In ordinary language, we might say that objects are what we *want* through our actions, so long as we distinguish the ethical meaning of want, "the things I want to get, to do, to have or to be" from "my present desires conceived of as states of my present being, my will, psyche or experience," and, further, identify the ethical *satisfaction* of wants not as that which "is satisfying or creates satisfactions," but as that which is intelligibly "suitable for a purpose."[53] The nexus of want/satisfaction concerns goodness or purpose, the intelligent grasp that some objectives are viewed as good.

The intelligent grasp of objectives as good implies that they are suitable for a purpose, that they provide an answer to the questions "Why?" or "What for?" Whenever an action is intelligible, it has some purpose in mind, a free and reasonable action in keeping with the precept of practical reason is one which has a point (whether moral or not is not yet the question) as acting for the sake of something which can provide an intelligible answer to "Why?" or "What for?"[54] Whenever one acts purposively, the question, "What are you doing?" is answered, ultimately, with reference to the *for something* for which one acts. "What are you doing? I'm typing"—

---

49. Ibid., 21–22.

50. Finnis, *Aquinas*, 29; cf. *Fundamentals of Ethics*, 21; *Moral Absolutes*, 41–43; *NLNR*, 61.

51. Ibid., 31. Cf. Grisez et al., "Practical Principles, Moral Truth and Ultimate Ends," 102–8.

52. Finnis, *Fundamentals of Ethics*, 21.

53. Ibid., 31

54. Ibid., 33.

this is not yet an articulation of *what* the action is, for typing is meaningful and intelligible only insofar as there is a reason or intention to the behavior. "I'm typing merely to see if the keys work" is a distinct act, even if the behavior might be similar, from "I'm typing in order to write a sentence." But this too is not fully intelligible. "Why are you writing a sentence?" may lead to the answer "to complete a suicide note" or "to finish a book chapter," answers which themselves are not fully explained unless I continue, "to avoid suffering" or "to protest a corrupt tyranny" or "to get tenure." And protest or tenure themselves are not yet resolved: "to guarantee employment," or "to get rich" or "to satisfy my desire to know" or "to become famous," are all quite distinct reasons, and thus distinct actions. Of course, feelings of satisfaction, or dissatisfaction, may very well accompany the action, or not, but the objective is determined by the reason for which I act.

Internal to this chain of reasons is the distinction between instrumental and final goods. "Moving my fingers to press the keys to form letters which construct a sentence" is merely instrumental, and "finishing the book" or "getting tenure," are not intelligible reasons, or at least not sufficient articulations, of acting.[55] An intelligible good is one having a point, a good, as something which, in itself, provides a sufficient practical reason to act, and such goods, which CNL terms "basic human goods," are those providing "a non-baffling answer to the question 'What for?'" That is, it would no longer be sensible to ask "Why?" since the answer is provided by the basic goods. Basic goods *are* the reasons for acting, and they are the reasons for acting rendering the wide array of actions intelligible:

> ... when one pursues the question "What for?" to the point where no further such question is intelligent, one arrives, not at a "contingent desire" or state of feeling ... to be explained in turn by the mechanics, biology and/or psychology of "human nature." Rather, one arrives at the perception (i.e., the understanding or intelligent discernment) of a basic form of human flourishing in which, not one human being on one occasion, but somehow all human beings in appropriate circumstances can participate.[56]

The basic human goods are not innate or read off human nature or biology, neither are they intuited, but are intelligently grasped by attending "to one's own inclinations" and grasping the intelligibility "[B]y an insight which is not an 'intuition' (because it is not made in the absence of data nor

55. Ibid., 36.
56. Ibid., 52.

by any 'noticeable' intellectual act). . . ."[57] Such attending occurs upon the condition of already engaging in practical reason, of already "wanting" and intending some good participating in some for-the-sake-of-which providing a point. Attending is not introspection as some sort of "attempt to peer inside oneself, or to catch oneself as it were in a mirror out of the corner of one's eye," but appeals to the data of one's own intending and then "understanding those acts by understanding their object(ive)s."[58]

The objects which answer the "What for?" question are thus basic, or self-evident (*per se nota*), since not derived or deduced from anything else. Neither are they instruments for another higher good upon which they depend for intelligibility. They are, in themselves, explanations of an action's coherence (which is not yet to say morality) and are basic—they are self-evident, although clearly they must be understood as such through the process of reflecting upon the directionality of our practical reason(s).

Further, while there is only one intelligence, only one "I" who is intelligent, we can distinguish theoretical from practical reason because of different objects or goods intended, just as we distinguish a plurality of object(ive)s within practical reason.[59] That is, actions are not explained by a singular good—*the* Good which is the ultimate for-the-sake-of-which of every act. Even happiness, or human flourishing, does not suffice, since it entails a variety of goods. I may type in order to gain knowledge. I may rest in order to play, and both knowledge and play provide coherent reasons for working or not, but knowledge and play are irreducible to each other. From this it follows, says CNL in one of their more contested claims, that basic human goods are variegated and irreducible, namely, there is more than one basic good and the various goods do not reduce to a solitary hyper-good. From this it also follows that the merely utilitarian calculus of determining the amount or quality of "the good" cannot be sufficient, for goods cannot be reduced to one kind.

While the list of basic human goods develops in the work of CNL, eight emerge. The first four are existential or reflexive in that choice is an aspect in the very meaning and instantiation of the goods: "(1) self integration or 'inner peace,' which consists in harmony among one's judgments, feelings, and choices; (2) 'peace of conscience and consistency between one's self and its expression,' . . . ; (3) 'peace with others, neighborliness, friendship,' . . . ;

57. Ibid., 51.
58. Ibid.
59. Ibid., 11.

(4) 'peace with God'. . . ."[60] In addition to these existential or reflexive goods are three *substantive* goods, so called because they fulfill aspects other than choice: (5) human life, including conditions such as health and physical integrity; (6) knowledge of truth and a proper appreciation of beauty; (7) play and skill. Additionally, (8) marriage is a basic human good, although unique in having aspects of both existential and substantive good.[61]

Of course, while the goods provide an explanation of action, they are not properly moral principles, for even a wicked action could be coherent, and being directed by the precept towards intelligent choice does not guide us in the right *way* to conduct or enact that choice. Consequently, the first principle of morality is not "do good and avoid evil"—for that operates in every coherent actions, even immoral ones—but rather "one ought to choose and otherwise will those and only those possibilities whose willing is compatible with a will toward integral human fulfillment."[62] That is, one ought to be the kind of person, and ought to act as such, for whom the real goods perfective of persons are embraced and sought but never violated: "the rightness of action is always intelligibly related to human good, indeed to the good of particular individuals or groups of individual persons. The upright heart, the will, the choice, is always a choice, will, heart which does and pursues that good and avoids what harms that good."[63] One ought always to act in keeping with human good, just as one ought never to act in such a way directly harming the participation in those goods, or in which one intends to harm, with intention playing a determinative role in the morality of an action.[64]

The Impossibility of Denial and Intellectual Conversion

As this project primarily treats the control of meaning and cognitional theory behind various accounts of natural law, I am not concerned to explore the concrete applications and implications of the various articulations. Suffice it to say that much more is needed to trace out how CNL reaches judgments about the morality of this or that contested proposal or act. But

60. May, *Introduction to Moral Theology*, 95.

61. Ibid., 95–96.

62. Ibid., 100; cf. Snell, "Understanding the Natural Law," paras. 20–21.

63. Finnis, *Moral Absolutes*, 11.

64. Ibid., 71.

we have enough of the methodology to follow out some interesting aspects of the argument.

Basic human goods are not derived from anything, but neither are they innate or intuited; that basic goods are self-evident or *per se nota* does not preclude *coming to understand* from the data of our own practical reason. Coming to understand is not a derivation but a grasp of intelligibility inherent in the data, in much the same way that one grasps the intelligibility of a joke or a diagram from the data without deducing the punch line or relations. Something can be self-evident, and even heuristically directive in practical reason, without being understood explicitly. One knows, as stated previously, by an insight into that which makes an intention intelligible, namely, the object(ive)s. This is understanding, not experiencing, says Finnis, and in ethics *everything* "depends on the distinction between the good as experienced and the good as intelligible."[65]

So vital is the distinction, that grasping it is akin to the intellectual conversion needed to overcome naive empiricism. To sense is not to understand, but still the world of common sense and its extroversion thinks that (1) knowing is somehow like taking a look, (2) objectivity is something like seeing what is there, and (3) the real is out there to be looked at.[66] Similarly, objectivity in ethics requires intellectual conversion by which we overcome the myth that knowing is like seeing, "com[ing] to understand how understanding grasps intelligibilities in experience and thus attains knowledge, by a process which is not like opening one's eyes or activating one's other senses."[67] Objectivity does not mean "opening one's eyes and taking a look" and yet the basic human goods "are objective; their validity is not a matter of convention, not is it relative to anybody's individual purposes," even though "they do not stand in need of demonstration."[68]

Of course, this makes the communication of basic human goods, as well as the defense of an account such as CNL, difficult if someone does not understand or agree, thus opening up charges that the account is intuitionist or relies on the "wicked or stupid" defense. If the goods are not derived but understood, and understood from the first person point of view *as* or *insofar* or *when* the person is engaged in practical reasoning, and if *per se*

---

65. Finnis, *Fundamentals of Ethics*, 42.

66. Snell, *Through a Glass Darkly*, 69–105.

67. Finnis, *Fundamentals of Ethics*, 42.

68. Finnis, *NLNR*, 69, 71.

nota does not mean obvious or innate, then how can the goods be defended against their deniers without an appeal to special privilege or intuition?

Much depends on intellectual conversion, which is not special pleading but a defense of the mode of knowing proper to the world mediated by meaning, including a refusal to smuggle the empiricism of common sense into the fully human knowing of practical reason. Even then, though, conversion merely sets the conditions whereby the first person standpoint would be accepted or understood, for conversion grasps how objectivity works but does not simultaneously provide conceptual knowledge of the basic human goods. Even if the cognitive myth of "opening one's eyes" is overcome, one could still deny the basic human goods.

But not coherently. Denying the basic human goods entails a performative contradiction, so while the goods cannot be proven, it can be shown that any rejection is self-defeating. Again, the analogy to the principles of theoretical reason are obvious, for non-contradiction cannot be proven or established without begging the question, but any denial of the principle is absurd, which is why it grounds all other thought: 'We can show that *any* argument raised by the sceptic is going to be self-defeating. To show this is not to show that the basic value . . . is self-evident or objective; it is only to show that counter-arguments are invalid."[69] Such is the method of *retorsion*, or refuting a statement with the statement's own self-refutation.

Some contradictions are propositional or directly self-refuting, such as "I know that I know nothing." A second type occurs when the utterance happens to refute the content of the statement, but not intrinsically, such as singing the line "I am not singing" happens to contradict only so long as one is singing, but not when speaking. A third version involves propositions "which cannot be coherently asserted, because they are *inevitably* falsified by any assertion of them," such as "I do not exist."[70] Denial of the basic goods is of this third type.

Take the denial of knowledge as a good. To make the statement "knowledge is not a basic good" in a serious way is to intend the statement as meaningful and worthwhile to make, also that it is true for oneself and others. Of course, this enacts a commitment to the goodness of knowledge, in this case stating "knowledge is not a basic good . . . not a good which is worth pursuing," is a performative contradiction. Instead of denying the goodness of knowledge, one has affirmed its goodness, and one has

69. Ibid., 73; cf. Finnis, *Collected Essays*, 1:62–91.
70. Ibid., 74.

affirmed it precisely as a basic good, namely, as an answer to "Why?" which makes the action directed, purposive, and intelligible in such a way that it would be a good for all others in a similar situation. This is to affirm its truth from the first person standpoint, and to make impossible its coherent denial from the first person standpoint.

CONCLUSION

While I've confined my discussion of CNL to the fairly abstract level of its methodological commitments rather than to the inner workings of its moral argumentation and conclusion—as with theorists in previous chapters—that methodology reveals a striking dissimilarity from the default model. Rather than agreeing with Rommen that natural law flourishes only in an age of metaphysics, CNL rejects the need or the validity for a theoretical basis for natural law, turning instead to practical reason and its first person point of view. While not equivalent to the thought of John Paul II or Martin Rhonheimer, serious and substantive methodological commitments are shared, especially the turn to the acting or practical person and subsequent reflexivity—but the articulation made possible by reflexivity is *not natural law*.[71] Natural law is in the operations of seeking and intending, and not in any theory or deduction either antecedent or consequent.

In the next chapter, I articulate the intentionality analysis of Bernard Lonergan, a thinker both highly praised and sharply criticized by CNL, but criticized insofar as he is judged unfaithful to his own intentionality analysis and the intellectual conversion effected by it.[72] While Lonergan is rarely considered a natural law thinker, perhaps quite the contrary, it would be better, I suggest, to think of him as not a thinker of *theoretical* natural law, but a significant, even seminal thinker of natural law in the mode of interiority.

71. Rhonheimer, "Practical Reason, Human Nature, and the Epistemology of Ethics," 873–87.

72. Finnis, *Fundamentals of Ethics*, 32, 42–45; *Collected Essays*, 5:139–62. See also Lawrence, "Finnis on Lonergan," 849–72.

6

Intentionality Analysis

The Achievement of Bernard Lonergan

 B ernard Lonergan (1904–1984) was a Jesuit philosopher-theologian most noted for his work on methodology. Hoping to continue upon a basis of Thomism while appropriating "features of the last seven centuries of thought" constitutes a dual problem, he thinks, since Thomas is largely ignored outside the Church, while Thomism internally has "not developed in proportion to the development of other fields of culture and in a measure consonant with what we feel to be its intrinsic resources."[1] Consequently, Lonergan's attempt is foreign "for those who hold [Aquinas] has already given all the answers [and] for those who would write him off as an error of seven centuries' duration."[2]

Rather than choosing one over the other form of thought, Lonergan attempts to raise his own mind to the level of Aquinas, "for, instead of pivoting between a world of Medieval physics and twentieth-century science, the disciple would pivot between operating mind and operating mind; and here, despite the difference in development, the basic laws of operation would seem to be discoverable in approximately the same terms."[3] In his historical scholarship, Lonergan attempted something more than a recount-

1. Crowe, *Appropriating the Lonergan Idea*, 21, 25.

2. Ibid., 25.

3. Ibid., 26.

ing of Aquinas's texts, but instead was (1) going "beyond the words and milieu to attempt to reach the mind of Aquinas," (2) by "a pivoting movement between his own developing rational self-consciousness and that of his master," and thus (3) from "that appropriation to develop Thomism in the manner required by seven centuries of thought."[4] A creative retrieval depends upon the noetic exegesis of one's own operating intellect, for Aquinas too was an operating intellect and its integral structure is invariant. At the same time, the texts of Aquinas, as achievements of an original genius, prompt a critical engagement and development of one's own mind and exegesis thereof.

In this chapter, I provide a brief summary of how Lonergan raises his intellect to the level of Aquinas, although some themes will be left to forthcoming chapters to avoid redundancy. I begin with an overview of his project, expand that in terms of knowing and acting, and articulate the first hints of his contribution for natural law, however unlikely that might appear to the default model of natural law.

The Lonerganian Project: Self-Appropriation

In *Insight*, Lonergan's magisterial exploration of human understanding, the project is envisioned as follows: "*Thoroughly understand what it is to understand, and not only will you understand the broad lines of all there is to be understood but also you will possess a fixed base, an invariant pattern, opening upon all further developments of understanding.*"[5] To accomplish this end, *Insight* explicates (1) "a study of human understanding," (2) an unfolding of "the philosophic implications of understanding," and (3) "a campaign against the flight from understanding."[6] As a study of understanding, the text seeks insight into insight, discovering there a "basic yet startling unity on the whole field of human inquiry and human opinion" which allows "a common ground on which men of intelligence might meet."[7]

While those "dynamic but formal structures" of intelligence are common to all persons, access requires self-appropriation through the noetic exegesis by which the concrete and intelligent subject reflexively utilizes the

---

4. Ibid., 27.

5. Lonergan, *Insight*, 22.

6. Ibid., 6–7; cf. Crowe, *Appropriating the Lonergan Idea*, 13–30.

7. Ibid., 3, 7.

dynamic and formal structures to know those very same structures. From this perspective, attempts at self-knowledge beginning anywhere other than reflexivity are strange and alien. If, however, we turn to ourselves as performing or doing human acts, we find that "[h]uman spirit is constituted as exigence, the exigence unfolds in a series of structured steps," and this integral structure allows us, through the acts of that very same structure, "to become aware of the standards intrinsic to their nature."[8] Further, in discovering the integral and normative structure of the operations, we find a totality, for human activity develops, with one act leading to another so long as desire and love are the operators of the dynamism of the spirit's structure: "Man wants to understand completely."[9]

Since Lonergan recognizes, as do Rhonheimer and Finnis, that "souls are distinguished by their potencies, potencies by their acts, acts by their objects," then grasping the integral structure of human spirit, the key to which is insight into insight, is not accomplished by an introspectively immediate grasp of our nature but by an examination of our objects.[10] Further, since the "final object of intellect is the real," then it is our intention of the real by which our acts are revealed, thus our potencies.[11] As discussed in earlier chapters, this intention can unfold in distinct exigencies—common sense, theory, interiority—and yet each intends the real, and the distinct anticipations of each distinguishes the modes of meaning.

In ordinary experience, we attend to the matters of our lives without really being aware of ourselves as attending. As we work, drive, play, or eat, the world is present to us, given through the data of sensation of which we are conscious, and yet our subjectivity (our consciousness) and our self-awareness (consciousness of consciousness) accompanies our everyday lives in a hidden, unobtrusive, unnoticed sort of way—there the whole time, of course, or we would not *be* subjects, and yet not an object of which we are aware; it's hidden. Like other objects, subjectivity only stands out when conspicuous, somehow an issue. One uses a pencil without really giving any thought to it until the lead breaks, at which point one looks at it *as* an object. (When missing a ball, the batter or tennis player glares at the bat or racquet as if suspicious that its substantiality is in doubt—the strings

---

8. Crowe, *Appropriating the Lonergan Idea*, 9.

9. Ibid., 11.

10. Lonergan, *Verbum*, 150; cf. *Method*, 8–9.

11. Ibid.

became non-existent for a moment, and yet here they are *now*!)[12] So, too, subjectivity—human spirit and its integral structures—are not attended to until they become conspicuous, until object-ified and intended.

Questions are the clue, the key to objectifying and understanding ourselves. In ordinary experience, we move along in our various projects, using the various *pragmata* in basically the same way as a clever animal. A new reality emerges when we ask "What is it?" about our experience. Our mode of being develops, and so does the world, no longer that which we experience, use, and perhaps enjoy in our projects, but something distinct from us. The world emerges as something distinct, as an object or problem, once conspicuous, when intelligence asks "*quid sit?*" Attention pivots and the world becomes something of which we seek intelligibility; we seek its nature, the *x* making it to be "this sort of thing."[13] But not only does the being of the world pivot as we attend, but *we* emerge in a new way as well, *as* intelligent; and we can attend to this emergent and intelligent self by asking of our own intelligence "What is it?", thereby becoming intelligent about intelligence, or having insight into insight.

Since we intend the real, a second question emerges from our dynamic orientation towards the real—"Is it?" Not every insight turns out to be productive or true. In fact, insights happen quickly and frequently in the intelligent, somewhat more slowly and infrequently in those less so, but a good many bright ideas or potential apprehensions are inadequate. We cannot intend the real without intending the intelligible, for the real is intelligible, and yet we intend more than a possible way of organizing the data into coherence, for we seek that *which is*. Of insights we query, "Is it?," thereby pivoting our attention anew, and in this new attending we expand both the world and our own subjectivity. We are not only intelligent, but *reasonable*, and the world is not only ordered but relates adequately to the data.[14]

When we *experience*, we have *data* or the *matter* of the world and our consciousness; as we ask "what?" we intend *intelligibility* or *form* and

12. See Heidegger's analysis of the "present-at-hand" in *Being and Time*, 111; cf. Snell and Cone, *Authentic Cosmopolitanism*, 44–54.

13. The operations of consciousness are transitive, that is, "the operations intend objects . . . as that by seeing there becomes present what is seen, by hearing there becomes present what is heard . . ." See Lonergan, *Method*, 7.

14. This polymorphism of consciousness and the various ways in which the invariant and integral structure of spirit operates receives hundreds of pages of analysis in *Insight* and *Method*; and, yet, the structure remains invariant.

understand; as we ask "is it?" we intend the *real* or *existence* and *judge*.
Because spirit is dynamic and total, this tripartite pattern of experience–
understanding–judgment recurs and progresses; we do not stop questioning but continue, and we do not accept just one direction to questions but
integrate our answers into systems, and then systems of systems, for we seek
to know everything about everything as we intend all reality. In principle,
there is no limit to the dynamism of our intellects, a claim confirmed not
only by the years spent by this or that person attempting to master a discipline, a language, the markets, a sport, or prayer, but also by the cumulative
experience of humanity as we move from one epoch and world-picture to
another:

> The level of experience we share in large part with animals, it is
> the level of data, or presentations, of the empirical, of the merely
> given. Understanding is the properly human; here occurs insight
> into data, the insight whose content is an idea, whose products
> are hypotheses, theories, definitions, concepts, formulations,
> systems; this is the level of thought. Insight is a new beginning
> . . . its possibility is the possibility of all that enormous develop-
> ment of intelligence that the human race has undergone in the
> course of millennia and that the individual attempts to appropri-
> ate for himself in a short lifetime. Yet thought is incomplete, it is
> not yet knowledge; we may think of centaurs and perform acts
> of understanding with regard to them but we do not know them.
> On the third level there is reflective understanding, the taking pos-
> session of the evidence, which issues in judgments, affirmations,
> the truths by which we know what is; it is the level of rationality,
> reasonableness, knowledge.[15]

Experience–understanding–judgment merely symbolizes an enormously complex nexus of recurring operations of our intellects, but the
articulation can be affirmed, for once the operations occur we can objectify
them and know them in the same way that we know other things. We can
(1) *experience* ourselves experiencing, understanding, and judging, (2)
understand the intelligibility of experiencing, understanding, and judging,
and (3) *judge* or affirm that we know the reality of experiencing, understanding, and judging.[16] Further, the symbolic articulation is not itself
the understanding but rather the formulation (external word) of an understanding (inner word or *verbum*), since understanding is the act of the

---

15. Crowe, *Appropriating the Lonergan Idea*, 16.

16. Lonergan, *Insight*, 343–62.

intellect to which the formulation refers and obtains its meaning. As such, Lonergan's goal is not to convince others of his arguments or articulations but to organize them in fruitful pedagogical order to "assist the reader in effecting a personal appropriation of the concrete dynamic structure immanent and recurrently operative in his own cognitional activities."[17] The concrete human subject is "the operator" of the operations, and while it is by the operations that the operator becomes aware of the objects, so too do the operations "make the operating subject present to himself," not through the mistaken idea of an inward look but by the "process of objectifying the contents of consciousness."[18] This is noetic exegesis, or what Lonergan terms "self-appropriation," "transcendental method," or "intentionality analysis."

Normativity and the Transcendental Precepts

The preceding description of Lonergan's cognitional theory stressed the self-referential consistency of his position. Unlike so many epistemologies which violate their own standards of knowing in presenting those standards, of which verificationism and falsificationism are perhaps the most famous instances, Lonergan's account consistently operates according to the patterns of operations presented. This is interesting in itself, but Lonergan's support goes beyond mere consistency.

First, the consistency of the position implies its accessibility to every human subject, and thus not an abstraction or an imposition of alien and alienating standards of knowing. Instead, the operations are available for any subject to discover as immanent and operative in themselves. The position claims universality; these operations are the operations of *human* spirit, and are invariant and transcultural. Cultural differences themselves, the wide variety of custom, meaning, ethics, and organization, presuppose "an original unity from which the differences developed," that is, the capacity and power of the human to understand and judge the world of their experience.[19]

Second, that may be true, but proving it would be quite the task, for obviously one cannot demonstrate the structure of every person, but it

17. Ibid., 12.

18. Ibid.

19. Crowe, *Appropriating the Lonergan Idea*, 34.

can be demonstrated that such a structure is consistent, possible, and performatively contradictory to deny. That is, an argument from retorsion is available here: Say a person wishes to deny Lonergan's account, on what basis would they do so? Perhaps they note that he's overlooked something of significance, some aspect of consciousness or the world that he ignored. In that case, they appeal to data which his theory failed to incorporate. Alternatively, they might find his data adequate but find fault in his formulation, but then they appeal to intelligence and understanding. Further, they might argue that his account has no relation, or at least an inadequate relation, to reality, but they then make a judgment. How could an argument be made against his position which did not appeal to some data, had some understanding, and made some judgment? Could this be done? Even asserting his wrongness is a judgment, and to give reasons is to judge based on data, and to claim that one's own account is true because it is more coherent is to understand and judge. In other words, his theory cannot be denied without making use of the theory—or at least the operations which the theory is based on—and any denial is a performative contradiction.

> . . . no one, unless some of his organs are deficient, is going to say that never in his life did he have the experience of seeing or of hearing, of touching or of tasting. . . . Again, how rare is the man that will preface his lectures by repeating his conviction that never did he have even a fleeting experience of intellectual curiosity, or inquiry, of striving and coming to understand, of expressing what he has grasped by understanding. Rare too is the man that begins his contributions to periodical literature by reminding his potential readers that never in his life did he experience anything that might be called critical reflection, that he never paused about the truth or falsity of any statement.[20]

Through retorsion, Lonergan's position is demonstrated as non-revisable and the very basis of all criticism; *just like* a first principle, human operations are the basis of all thought: "operations exist and anyone that cares to deny their existence is merely disqualifying himself as a non-responsible, non-reasonable, non-intelligent somnambulist."[21]

Third, not only is there a performative contradiction entailed when utilizing the very operations to deny the operations, but another contradiction

20. Or, if they did so, we would thereby be justified as using those admissions as good reasons against their declarations; Lonergan, *Method*, 16–17.

21. Lonergan, *Method*, 17.

entangles the subject themselves as the operator. For Lonergan, especially in *Insight*, the aspect of the subject impelling the structure forward, the dynamism of the operations, is the "eros of the mind, the desire and drive to understand. . . ."[22] More than anything, intellect is marked by the desire to know, and proper function is attained when the exigence of the intellect is followed. As Aristotle noted in the *Metaphysics*, by nature we desire to know, and thus "to put these questions is natural: it supposes no acquired habit, as does playing the violin; it supposes no gift of divine grace, as do faith and charity. Hence, since the questions are natural, the desire they manifest must also be natural. There exists, then, a desire that is natural to intellect, that arises from the mere fact that we possess intellects, that is defined by the basic questions, *an sit* and *quid sit*."[23] As such, denials of this account utilize the operations, and do so because of the dynamism of the desire to know. Not only is this desire natural, it is inextricably linked to our nature, even, perhaps, *is* our nature, for if we are rational animals, and if rationality *is* the integral structure identified by Lonergan, then denying this eros is a denial and deformation of human nature by that same nature.

The pure, disinterested, dynamic desire to know—the agent intellect—is that which renders our intellects what they are, enlivening and actuating them, and also *us* insofar as the different questions bring about also a new level of consciousness in which we are present and without which we do not exist *qua* subjects. This love, and its structured order—the *ordo amoris*—is a remarkable and powerful reality:

> Deep within us all, emergent when the noise of other appetites is stilled, there is a drive to understand, to see why, to discover the reason, to find the cause, to explain. Just what is wanted has many names. In what precisely it consists is a matter of dispute. But the matter of inquiry is beyond doubt. It can absorb a man. It can keep him for hours, day after day, year after year, in the narrow prison of his study or his laboratory. It can send him on dangerous voyages of exploration. It can withdraw him from other interest, other pursuits, other pleasures. . . . [24]

This is not idle curiosity, but rather the natural exigence of the intellect following itself to its culmination, with normativity contained within the desire to know, fidelity to which allows the directionality immanent to

22. Lonergan, *Insight*, 247.

23. Lonergan, *Collection*, 84.

24. Lonergan, *Insight*, 28.

the desire—the anticipation and intention of the intelligible real—to push ever onward into the further question as origin and finality of the intellect. We cannot ignore this direction "without, as it were, amputating our own moral personality, our own reasonableness, our own intelligence, our own sensitivity"—which is the worst sort of contradiction.[25]

It would seem to directly follow, fourth, that in objectifying the desire to know and its structures, we disclose normative intentionality. The desire to know is intentionally ordered to the real, and so the end or good of our desire to know is being. That may seem a bit thin, perhaps stating the truism *that* our desires are ordered to their fulfillment but not explaining *how* or *whether* this is to be accomplished. Of course, appeals to anything external to the integral structure itself will be abstract, alien, non-verified, revisable, and perhaps deniable, but appealing to the norms immanent in the structure will, like the structure itself, be non-revisable and irrefutable.

Since the operations are intentional and transitive, pointing beyond themselves to that which they anticipate, the operations contain an immanent law of their own satisfaction, namely, to allow their systematic exigence, an allowance which tends to its completion. Since the desire to know is the operator moving the integral structure in its dynamism, and since that dynamism tends to its accomplishment, the norm is the operator itself—the desire to know as operating through questions. So long as the desire to know is followed in further questions, the truth tends to be obtained when all the relevant questions have been asked and answered, and questions are asked so long as the desire to know is followed; Lonergan suggests that this will be accomplished "not in terms of principles and rules, but as a normative pattern of operations with cumulative and progressive results."[26] To make this somewhat more concrete, he identifies a transcendental precept, a "rule" of normativity proper to each level of the operations, adherence to which is adherence to the dynamic desire to know as it operates in the structure of consciousness. As we have experience, so the precept is "Be attentive"; as we ask questions for intelligence, so the precept is "Be intelligent"; as we ask reflective questions, so the precept is "Be reasonable"; and as we ask questions of value, an operation yet to be discussed in detail, so the precept is "Be responsible."[27] Normativity is not in the statements but has "a prior existence and reality in the spontaneous, structured

25. Lonergan, *Method*, 18.

26. Ibid., 14.

27. Ibid., 20.

dynamism of human consciousness"—the normativity resides in and as the desire to know, with any stated precepts referring to that desire.[28] Or, as Lonergan was fond of saying, "objectivity is simply the consequence of authentic subjectivity, of genuine attention, genuine intelligence, genuine reasonableness, genuine responsibility."[29]

Fifth, and last, since the structure is universal, verified, non-revisable, irrefutable, and normative, it also serves a critical function, as a "rock on which one can build," and from which one can identify deficiencies and errors in other positions, what Lonergan termed "reversing counter-positions."[30] A "position" is an account in keeping with integral structure, while a "counter-position" is incoherently related to the structure. For example, Hume's claim that anything other than analytic or synthetic statements should be consigned to the dustbin is utterly counter-positional, or incoherent, because knowing is a structured series of operations summarized as experience–understanding–judgment, as Hume *fully* followed in developing his theory. Hume was an intelligent and reasonable man, and his performance was much better than his quite obviously false theory; his performance was human, his theory out of step with what he actually did, and so his theory was counter-positional. Aquinas, on the other hand, described the process of abstraction by which the intellect worked discursively to grasp the form and exercise a judgment—in keeping with the actual performance of human intellect, and thus positional.

Consequently, turning to subjectivity does not lose itself in subjectivism, but instead reveals a universal and normative structure of human nature, although that structure is not derived from a theoretical anthropology appropriated by the subject from within, as it were.

THE FOURTH LEVEL OF CONSCIOUSNESS

While three levels of consciousness were uncovered, four precepts were indicated, with the fourth—"Be responsible"—suggesting something about action irreducible to the first three precepts. This apparent ambiguity reflects a development in Lonergan's work between *Insight* and *Method in*

---

28. Ibid.

29. Ibid., 265.

30. Ibid., 19, 251–54.

Theology, for while the basic thrust of the project remains, it becomes more differentiated.

In *Insight*, a kind of intellectualism is pervasive, with the basic structure formed around the dynamic desire to *know*, a version of the Thomistic account of the natural desire to see God. As the desire to know was unfolded in the account of structure as intending being, Lonergan considered that "as being is intelligible and one, so also it is good."[31] The good was considered under the aegis of the intelligible and reasonable, with particular emphasis on rational "self-consistency in knowing and doing."[32] Several decades later, in *Method*, the good was as much existentialist as intellectualist, and a fourth level of consciousness is acknowledged with the world of value emerging.[33] Consciousness is a four-level structure, with the level of responsibility completing the previous empirical, intelligent, and rational levels; so, too, a fourth precept. "Be reasonable" does not capture adequately the drama and agency required for a subject to "Be responsible."

Like the other three levels, *deliberation* is integrated into the structure of consciousness by the dynamism of intentionality, one we can access through attending to our own performance, for by the operation our consciousness develops and makes our subjectivity present to ourselves, in a fuller if inchoate way.[34] We are able to identify ourselves making judgments of fact (third level) as well as judgments of value (fourth level) about which we deliberate and choose and act, although in no way does this suggest that value judgments lack truth value; it is not as though judgments of fact can be true or false while judgments of value are just "valued," for deliberation occurs as a culmination of experience–understanding–judgment and not in some strange isolation, and, moreover, intends the good which is. Nothing about value judgments implies a lack of truth or wanton subjectivism, although, to be sure, on the fourth level our own subjectivity is existentially summoned: "At this fourth level consciousness truly becomes self-conscious—we not only take a stand on what is so, but we actually stand up for what we believe in and make ourselves through our decisions and actions. At the fourth level of consciousness my self-presence is accentuated, as I truly put myself on the line."[35] There "is a still further dimension to being

31. Lonergan, *Insight*, 619–22.
32. Ibid.
33. Crowe, *Appropriating the Lonergan Idea*, 52–54.
34. Lonergan, *Method*, 7–8.
35. Fitzpatrick, *Philosophical Encounters*, 31.

human, and there we emerge as persons," as we "discern between what truly is good and what only apparently is good."[36]

If we objectify the intentionality of deliberation, we find we intend good as an anticipation, a heuristic corresponding to the question. The question has a horizon, and what we intend in questions for deliberation— "What is to be done?" "What sort of person should I be?" "What is right to do?"—is the x which we call the good. Further, just as human knowing in its concreteness takes several forms, so too the human good. In its most elementary form, "the good is the object of desire" and experienced as "pleasant, enjoyable, satisfying."[37] But in addition to the world of satisfaction, there is *value*, which may in fact be disagreeable but "carries us towards self-transcendence and selects an object for the sake of whom or of which we transcend ourselves" and our satisfactions.[38]

> So we may distinguish vital, social, cultural, personal, and religious values in an ascending order. Vital values, such as health and strength, grace and vigor, normally are preferred to avoiding the work, privations, pains involved in acquiring, maintaining, restoring them. Social values, such as the good of order which conditions the vital values of the whole community, have to be preferred to the vital values of individual members of the community. Cultural values do not exist without the underpinning of vital and social values, but none the less they rank higher. Not on bread alone doth man live. Over and above mere living and operating, men have to find meaning and value in their living and operating. It is the function of culture to discover, express, validate, criticize, correct, develop, improve such meaning and value. Personal value is the person in his self-transcendence, as loving and being loved, as originator of values in himself and in his milieu, as an inspiration and invitation to others to do likewise. Religious values, finally, are at the heart of the meaning and value of man's living and man's world. . . .[39]

Judgments of value unite (1) our knowledge of reality, for this is about what is true and real and not merely preferred, (2) our intentional response

36. Lonergan, *Method*, 10–11.

37. Lonergan, *Insight*, 619; cf. *Method*, 31.

38. Lonergan, *Method*, 31. Lonergan's articulation of the human good develops; in *Method* value is a larger notion, including levels of the good which were distinguished from value in *Insight*.

39. Ibid., 31–32. That value is scaled for Lonergan is a distinction from CNL for which there can be no scale of goods.

to value, first apprehended, sometimes powerfully, in our feelings, and (3) the dynamic thrust toward self-transcendence, towards the existential attempt to be authentic, our end.[40] This end, while scaled, is variegated; the vital values remain distinct from social or cultural values and do not reduce to them even if they are related structurally, for the higher values could not emerge without the lower, even as the higher condition the recurrence of the lower.[41]

For instance, if there was no food or health, forms of social organization and polity would not emerge, and so vital values are a requirement for the emergence of the social, even as the good of order in social values allows forms of cooperation such as markets and contracts and infrastructure which allow the vital values to recur, for there to be not only breakfast but breakfast for everyone, every day. So, too, social institutions allow for the emergence of cultural values, even as cultural values condition the meaning and recurrence of the social. For example, the family is a requirement without which culture does not emerge, but if the cultural meaning of family alters significantly, families may have fewer or more children and assign different meanings to the having of children, for instance. And this pattern continues throughout, demonstrating that without vital and animal values no religion is possible, and yet, "when people lose all sense of higher purpose, they abandon their plows in the fields and stop eating."[42]

Subsequent chapters will explore Lonergan's account of value in more detail, particularly with reference to sin, grace, conversion, and the natural law, but this brief summary of value was needed to approach those questions. Before turning to sin and grace, some provisional claims about natural law from within Lonerganian interiority may be helpful to grasp the next chapters, while still needing considerable fleshing out.

Brief and Provisional Implications for Natural Law

First, in whatever mode, a feature common to the *lex naturalis* project is its claim to objectivity; natural law is knowable, known, and ought to be known, by everyone. Interiority and its reliance on subjectivity is not an obvious partner in the project if a foreign version of objectivity is maintained.

---

40. Ibid., 38.

41. In Byrne, "Which Scale of Value Preference?," 20–21.

42. Ibid., 21.

Objectivity in natural law is not (a) that of common sense modeled after taking a "good long look at what is there to be seen," (b) that of a classical law of nature with its necessity, or (c) that of physicalism pointing to that which is just "there" in its facticity. Instead, objectivity in natural law, as in all knowing, *is* the dynamic desire to know as the operator of knowing; insofar as we desire to know, we tend to objectivity in knowing in our attentiveness, intelligence, reasonability, and responsibility:

> Such is the objectivity of truth. But do not be fascinated by it. Intentionally it is independent of the subject, but ontologically it resides only in the subject: *veritas formaliter est in solu iudicio.* Intentionally it goes completely beyond the subject, yet it does so only because ontologically the subject is capable of an intentional self-transcendence, of going beyond what he feels, what he imagines, what he thinks, what seems to him, to something utterly different, to what is so. Moreover, before the subject can attain the self-transcendence of truth, there is the slow and laborious process of conception, gestation, parturition. But teaching and learning, investigating, coming to understand, marshalling and weighing the evidence, these are not independent of the subject.... The fruit of truth must grow and mature on the tree of the subject, before it can be plucked and placed in its absolute realm.[43]

Law, as reason, is not so objective as to exist without minds, for it is the *ordo rationalis.*

Second, reason operates within the integral structure of concrete human subjects. While the method of *abstraction* has its place, the excessive *abstractness* which often seems to follow has very little to do with the intelligence which I myself am and the insights I have into this or that intelligible reality: "the universal abstracts from the particular, but the intelligibility, grasped by insight, is immanent in the sensible...."[44] So, too, the Aristotelian version of science and its concerns for necessity and deduction risks overlooking the necessity of *understanding* and the "maieutic art of a Socrates, for intellectual conversion, for open-mindedness, striving, humility, perseverance."[45] Further, adverting to the intelligence of concrete human subjects accepts embodied, linguistic, communal, and historical subjects, not the "anti-historical immobilism" stalking a conceptualism

43. Lonergan, *Second Collection*, 70–71.
44. Ibid., 74–75.
45. Ibid., 72.

forgetful of the intelligence by which concepts are formed.[46] Reason has a place for the objective, and this is neither subjectivism nor "squishiness," but still reason will be hermeneutical, positioned, and placed within community and perspective.

Third, human nature, like reason, is not completely (and perhaps not best) understood through abstractness, for persons are not abstractions, and any account of humanity forgetful of personhood is hardly adequate.[47] Not only is nature "backed into" by first knowing intentions and subsequently arriving at nature, but intentions are not static or singular but dynamic and variegated. Consequently, while some accounts of human nature investigate the human using the same method as would apply for plants and animals, the study of the subject is unique:

> The study of the soul, then, is totally objective. One and the same method is applied to study of plants, animals, and men. The results are completely universal. We have souls whether we are awake or asleep, saints or sinner, geniuses or imbeciles.
>
> The study of the subject is quite different, for it is the study of oneself inasmuch as one is conscious. It prescinds from the soul, its essence, its potencies, its habits, for none of these is given in consciousness. It attends to operations and to their centre and source which is the self. . . . Subject and soul, then, are two quite different topics. To know one does not exclude the other in any way. But it very easily happens that the study of the soul leaves one with the feeling that one has no need to study the subject and, to that extent, leads to a neglect of the subject.[48]

Studies of human nature, often thought the *sine qua non* of natural law, often neglected what it really is to be a subject.

Fourth, for intentionality, the good is that which is desired, is *valued*. At least a few natural law accounts seem to place our existential reality (*Existenz*) very much in the background, with the good a metaphysical correlate to our potency. And yet our experience of the good is one of inclination, desire, purpose, love, directedness, and that experience is always one with a certain mood, feel, density, or stance. The deductive calculation of goods following from our nature in its third person objectivity cannot but

---

46. Ibid., 74.

47. See "The Subject," in Lonergan, *Collection*, 69–86.

48. Ibid., 72–73.

seem abstract, foreign, alien, and alienating to persons. Interiority turns to values and our existential trajectory toward value.

Subjectivity, hermeneutical reason, nature as dynamic structure, historicity, and values—these are not always the terms quick to mind when natural law is discussed; if anything, the opposite. And yet, if *lex naturalis* is to be genuinely human, these terms will play a central explanatory function. As Aquinas knew, the natural law is "nothing else than the rational creature's participation in the eternal law," and a participation precisely as rational, as both a measure and measured, but never just a passive thing measured.[49] Interiority does not contradict other modes of meaning, but it does operate in its own way, approaching the real along distinct tracks, and thus apprehending the real differently. Placed within subjectivity, history, and intentionality, it is not coldly abstract or rational, theoretical or conceptual, but is human, personal, and as such can be tainted by sin, healed and perfected by grace, elevated by the supernatural—but all this remains to be seen. Yet, something new is available.

49. Aquinas, *ST*, I-II 91.2.

Part Three

Natural Law for Humans

Transcendence

7

No Empty Optimism

Concrete Subjectivity and the Noetic Effects of Sin

Earlier, I claimed that for some Protestants, the trump card (or nuclear option) regarding natural law is the noetic effects of sin, with human nature and knowledge considered so impaired as to render natural law non-functional: "The chief reason for this theological hesitancy . . . is the problem of sin. Natural law seems to suggest that the order of being in the original creation has not been totally disrupted by the fall and sin."[1] And not just natural law, but Thomism in general is sometimes construed as overly optimistic, even Pelagian, about the human condition: "[c]ompared to Augustine, Luther, and Calvin, for example, Aquinas does epistemology as if in the Garden of Eden. . . ."[2]

Nor is this a uniquely Protestant position, although my claim is that it has become something of a *locus communis* or boundary marker within Protestantism and thus a prejudice or pre-judgment of the community. Catholic theologian Paul Griffiths, for instance, has this to say:

> . . . we must begin with the fact that human desire has been de-ranged. Our desires have moved from order to chaos; they have been opened to the damnable as well as the beautiful. . . . That's the

1. Braaten, "Protestants and Natural Law," para. 17.

2. Westphal, *Overcoming Onto-Theology*, 105. See also Moroney, *The Noetic Effects of Sin*; Snell, *Thomism and Noetic Sin*, 7–28; Snell, "Desires Natural and Unnatural"; Snell and Cone, *Authentic Cosmopolitanism*, 87–104.

way the human tale of desire begins—with blood and a hunger for taking from others what they have for no other reason than that they have it. And from this derangement comes, very rapidly, the evils of slavery, rape, genocide, and abortion, together with their many bloody cousins. We lack natural desire because our desires have been removed from their proper arrangement, their properly harmonious response to the fact that we are *created* beings. After the Fall, we suffer from derangement.[3]

In the end, I do not find these objections persuasive, but they are coherent or sensible, particularly when raised against the default model of natural law. I do not claim that they defeat the theoretical mode, but they are reasonable objections, and objections which the interior mode can incorporate given its understanding of reason and nature, as this chapter explains.

LOVERS OF DARKNESS

Human nature is, and is not, what it once was. On the one hand, a human is a human whether in the Garden or to its east; on the other hand, "the world is virtually inundated by sin," the intellect as well:[4]

Human reason is not an isolated faculty. A person's thinking cannot be completely dissociated from the rest of his or her life, including the "spiritual" aspects of his or her life. . . . Since we know that human beings have willfully turned from God, their rebellion has not only moral and spiritual but epistemological consequences." Apart from the freedom available in Jesus Christ, humans are in bondage to sin and all of its effects, including the noetic effects of sin. Human self-centeredness distorts human thinking. . . . It follows then that people's thinking is influenced by their relationship with God, specifically (1) whether or not they have been regenerated by the work of the Holy Spirit, and (2) to what degree they are sanctified.[5]

While the doctrine of original sin and its disastrous effects is maintained by all orthodox Christians, albeit with some divergence of explanation, the suspicion that Roman Catholicism, particularly its Thomistic inheritance, has the taint of Pelagianism remains among some Protestants. For instance,

3. Griffiths, "The Nature of Desire," paras. 8–9.

4. *Catechism of the Catholic Church*, 401.

5. Moroney, "How Sin Affects Scholarship," para. 27.

as mentioned in an earlier chapter, the influential Dooyeweerd suggested that Catholicism "did not accept the radical character of the fall into sin," and his epigone, Francis Schaeffer, claimed that Aquinas thought "only the will was fallen or corrupted but the intellect was not affected."[6]

Thinkers of interiority would have every chance to note the truth and effects of sin on subjectivity, and the authors examined in the recent chapters do so. John Paul II writes that "Man's capacity to know the truth is also darkened, and his will to submit to it is weakened."[7] Rhonheimer claims that original sin is "quite obvious" from the "anthropological, psychological, historical, sociological, and other data known to everybody," and without a salvation-morality the human good is not fully intelligible.[8] In keeping with the importance of intentionality for the act, both Finnis and Grisez highlight the reality of mendacity and self-deception: "analysis of chosen actions, to establish what one is and is not really intending, can be difficult and delicate. It affords much opportunity for rationalization and self-deception."[9] And Lonergan proclaims the "reign of sin" rendering intelligent progress impossible and from which there is no self-redemption.[10] My claim is that interiority exhibits a certain suppleness for incorporating the noetic effects of sin, and I'll use Lonergan to explain how this is so.

AQUINAS ON THE LOSS OF ORIGINAL JUSTICE

If one is not careful, Aquinas's explanation of original sin may seem to support the claims of Dooyeweerd and Schaeffer that the fall is not a depravity but a mere deprivation leaving nature fully intact. That's not what Thomas says, but it could be read as such, in part because of the limitations of articulating sin from the theoretical mode.

As a privation of a due good, sin can really only be understood in relation to things as they ought to be, for sin, strictly speaking, has no positive

6. Dooyeweerd, *In the Twilight of Western Thought*, 140; Schaeffer, *How Should We Then Live?*, 51–2.

7. John Paul II, *Veritatis Splendor*, 1.

8. Rhonheimer, *Perspective of the Acting Person*, 8.

9. Finnis and Fisher, "Theology and the Four Principles of Bioethics," para. 43. Although some critics protest that Finnis forgets his Nietzsche and thus has a "remarkably shallow treatment on the possibility of mendaciousness." See Kramer, "What Good is Truth?," 309; Bamforth and Richards, *Patriarchal Religion*, 136–39.

10. Lonergan, *Topics in Education*, 58–69.

reality. So, too, with original sin. Adam, says Aquinas, like all humans with created intellects, could not see God's essence without grace, without a "perfection of the intellect, strengthening it to see God."[11] For the saints who know God's essence in beatitude, this grace is the "light of glory," a grace which Adam did not possess, for humans cannot fall away from God once beatitude is attained. So while Adam had a relation and intimacy with God not possessed by post-lapsarian humans, he had neither a natural knowledge of God's essence nor beatitude; rather, God granted him a particular grace, that of rectitude or "original justice."[12]

This rectitude, while a supernatural endowment and not part of nature, brings with it a three-fold completion and harmonization of nature, "his reason being subject to God, the lower powers to reason, and the body to the soul. . . ."[13] Unlike God, Adam is not simple, but is composed of various "parts," powers, and principles, including soul, body, intellect, and will. Original justice allows Adam's perfect subjection to God and also his lower powers to the higher, particularly to reason, and thereby the avoidance of sin, although original justice does not provide beatitude. It's important to note, however, that unity of life is attained not by intellect but by will, for will, as rational appetite, has as its goal the good of the whole person, unlike other powers which seek their good but not the good of the whole agent.[14] Consequently, the harmony of original justice is effected through the will "which integrates all desires and appetites into the good and perfection of the agent," and insofar as the will is properly ordered the person will be as well.[15]

One consequence of original sin is the "privation of original justice, removing the subjection of man's mind to God" and with all the attendant wounds and consequences following.[16] The language of privation, however, coupled with the claim that original justice is a grace, an *addendum*, can make it appear that Adam's nature is constant throughout. Pre-lapsarian Adam has human nature *plus* rectitude, while post-lapsarian Adam is deprived of rectitude but possesses human nature in precisely the same way as

---

11. Aquinas, *ST*, I 12.5 ad. 2. See Snell, "Thomism and Noetic Sin," 11–13; Snell and Cone, *Authentic Cosmopolitanism*, 87–91.

12. See also the *Catechism of the Catholic Church*, 375–99.

13. Aquinas, *ST* I 95.1.

14. Ibid., I-II 9.1.

15. Snell, "Thomism and Noetic Sin," 14.

16. Aquinas, *ST*, I-II 82.1.

before the loss. Sin is thus a loss but not a depravity, with Aristotelian man constant throughout. But how is this a fall? And how is it sin? Doesn't this look very much as Schaeffer suspected, with sin not touching the core of the human, and if we are, by nature, rational animals, and nature is undamaged, then is rationality undamaged? How are we to reconcile the sense of mere loss with the destructiveness of sin identified by the *Catechism*?

> The harmony in which they had found themselves, thanks to original justice, is now destroyed: the control of the soul's spiritual faculties over the body is shattered; the union of man and woman becomes subject to tensions, their relations henceforth marked by lust and domination. Harmony with creation is broken: visible creation has become alien and hostile to man. . . . *Death makes its entrance into human history.*[17]

Answering these questions requires examining the will, for the loss of rectitude is not a non-essential accident, with nature remaining untouched, but rather the loss of an ordering principle affecting the whole:

> The whole order of original justice consists in man's will being subject to God: which subjection, first and chiefly, was in the will, whose function it is to move all the other parts to the end . . . , so that the will being turned away from God, all the other powers of the soul became inordinate. Accordingly the privation of original justice, whereby the will was made subject to God, is the formal element in original sin; while every other disorder of the soul's powers, is a kind of material element in respect of original sin.[18]

Nature cannot be destroyed without destruction of the human entirely, and we are not destroyed, yet it does not follow that a loss of original justice retains us as complete and functional; instead, with will no longer in harmony, the other powers—*all* the other powers—and their relations are disordered, with a resulting total disharmony: ". . . all the powers of the soul are left, as it were, destitute of their proper order. . . ."[19]

Reason also is destitute of its proper order, first in what Thomas calls "the wound of ignorance," which is not merely a lack of knowledge but a privation of that for which there is a "natural aptitude" (*aptus natus*) to know, such as the articles of faith, basic principles of morality and duty,

---

17. *Catechism of the Catholic Church*, 400.

18. Aquinas, *ST* I-II 82.3.

19. Ibid., I-II 85.3.

and matters of ordinary knowledge.[20] Now, the temptation is to construe natural knowledge as somehow innately known but now lost or obscured (and often natural law is presented as innate), but for Thomas there is *no* innate knowledge, not of God, morality, the world, or even ourselves. First principles are not innate either; even if the structure of our intellect or will is directed or intentional in a certain way, this is a heuristic anticipation rather than conceptual knowledge, a "reaching" rather than a "grasp."

Not innate knowledge but the fruits of natural *disposition* are impaired through the wound of ignorance, largely because of concupiscence, because of will's disorder:

> The answer seems to be because we do not want to, because we are in concupiscence. Quite simply, we do not want it. Since human nature is wounded, sin affects the *desire* for truth, even for those truths for which we are most apt, for which we are designed and made, because our desires are inordinate . . . we fail to will to know what we ought to know.[21]

For Lonergan, such an explanation makes sense, for we know at the culmination of a series of ordered operations making up an integral structure, but the operations occur and recur only on the condition of the desire to know; if the desire is truncated, limited, diverted, or squelched, then those items of knowledge most fitting the structure of operations would not be known. Just as the structure works when the operator works, the structure follows the operator in failure, and the absence of order from the will is not merely a loss but an impairment, a privation, and a distortion. To lose rectitude does not take us back to pure nature, it results in the disharmony proper to that nature—the wounds of sin.

Faculty Psychology and the Subject of Sin

According to Lonergan, one of the tasks facing Aquinas was "not merely in fitting an original Augustinian creation into an Aristotelian framework but also in attempting, however remotely and implicitly, to fuse together . . . a phenomenology of the subject with a psychology of the soul."[22] Augustine provides his existential self touched by sin and grace, while Aris-

20. Ibid., I-II 76.2; Snell, "Thomism and Noetic Sin," 16.

21. Snell, "Thomism and Noetic Sin," 17.

22. Lonergan, *Verbum*, 3.

totle provided science, and Aquinas's genius was preserving the insights of each in creative synthesis. One of the difficulties in accomplishing this, however, was that phenomenology, or interiority, was remote and implicit, merely inchoate, and not thematized or made objective. Lonergan thinks that Aquinas was too acute in his descriptions of the soul's powers to be unaware of his own operations, but the mode of communicating those insights and operations was the theoretical and metaphysical language of Aristotle. Consequently, a Rube Goldbergian apparatus of concepts emerges—potency, act, passive intellect, sensible species, intelligible species, habitual knowledge, active intellect, and etc.—all perfectly coherent, but if divorced from the acts of understanding (insights) behind them, the apparatus becomes reified, hypostatized, inert. But there was no other language to express the insights, and so the linguistic symbols must bear an enormous weight of intelligibility. Saturated with interiority while not thematized or articulated in the interior mode, *theoretical* discourse attempts to carry *interiority*, managing the task only when the terms are understood as referring to concrete operations and not things or parts.[23]

Time and again the temptation to reify the soul as a substance with parts rears up—the tripartite soul of Plato in the *Republic* is awfully static, as is Aristotle's account of the parts of the soul in *Nicomachean Ethics*, subdivided into the rational and irrational, the theoretical and practical, sensitive and vegetative. Neither can Aquinas leap out of his time; a genius, yes, but still a man of the thirteenth-century, and he appeals to *parts*-talk in explaining the soul:

> . . . when the harmony of a mixed *body* is destroyed, the *elements* have contrary local tendencies. In like manner, when the harmony of original justice is destroyed, the various powers of the soul have various opposite tendencies . . . Original sin infects the different *parts* of the soul, in so far as they are the *parts* of one whole . . . just as there is but one fever in one man, although the various *parts* of the *body* are affected.[24]

These are bad analogies: the soul is not much like a body since the soul has no parts, and its unity is not at all like composition or arrangement of elements. But as explained in the previous chapter, the classical (Aristotelian) method utilizes the same method for our soul as everything else. While there need be no contradiction between the soul and the subject, the *study*

23. Rhonheimer makes a similar point.

24. Aquinas, *ST* I-II 82.2 ad 2-3; emphasis added.

of each is quite different. The study of soul anticipates knowledge which is universal, essentialistic, deductive, static, whereas the anticipation for the subject is empirical, conscious, historical, operational, and dynamic; soul is known through metaphysics, subject through a hermeneutics of facticity.[25]

When it comes to sin and its noetic effects, the usual result of inadequate interiority is to render sin as an abstraction, as one more concept introduced in the nexus of concepts making up the soul. Concepts don't deal well with history or the dramatic existence of human reality, however, and so sin begins to look like an accidental property of a constant nature undergoing no substantial change:

> The medieval theology of original sin . . . is characteristic of theoretical theology. [But] [t]he reality they sought to explain— human alienation from God, sin—is experiential and empirical. Sin is manifest in the personal and systemic evils caused by human beings. But medieval theology described the experience of sin and alienation . . . abstractly . . . In a metaphysical theology, then, the technical explanation of religious realities is abstract. [But] . . . the metaphysical terms of medieval theology do not disclose the lived spiritual experience they attempt to explain. . . .[26]

To make sin concrete rather than abstract, something more than a concept in a system of analysis, Lonergan suggests a transposition of meaning, capturing what is true in Aquinas's account but articulated from interiority. First, rather than the "logical essence—'rational animal' in the sense of something common to infants, morons, geniuses and heroes," we turn to the concrete.[27] Second, from substance/soul to subject. Third, from faculty psychology to the integral structure of consciousness. The three hang together, with faculty psychology an explanation of how the logical essence of the soul is divided into various parts or "faculties," with each faculty responsible for a different function, distinguished by the distinct objects and acts intending those objects. The faculty of intellect, for instance, is distinct from that of will, leading to the familiar problems of how the two faculties integrate or conflict:

> A faculty psychology divides man up; it distinguishes intellect and will, sense perception and imagination, emotion and conation, only to leave us with unresolved problems of priority and rank. Is

25. Snell and Cone, *Authentic Cosmopolitanism*, 45–51.

26. Wiley, *Original Sin*, 180.

27. Lonergan, *Topics in Education*, 82–83.

sense to be preferred to intellect, or intellect to sense? Is intellect to be preferred to will, or will to intellect? Is one to be a sensist, an intellectualist, or a voluntarist?[28]

Rather than faculties, or distinct parts, the study of persons discloses an integral structure of operations unified within the dynamic flow of consciousness and not parts composing a body.

Consequently, the criticism that Aquinas confines sin to the will but leaves the intellect unscathed is possible *only* when approached from within the confines of faculty psychology, and even though Aquinas's own position is more sophisticated than the objection, handling it rather easily in fact, it remains that his position is expressed within faculty psychology. Given the limits of his vocabulary, the articulation of will, harmony, and concupiscence for intellect's function is remarkably supple, and yet faculty psychology "does not take us near enough to the concrete. You have to be in the concrete if you wish to study development. Abstractions do not move, do not develop, do not change."[29] Sin and its noetic effects, because they are concrete, operational, and within the flux and flow of the developing subject, are discussed in an oddly detached, third person sort of way, thus lacking the existential dimension and giving the impression that (a) the logical essence remains untouched in its static isolation, (b) sin affects some faculties more than others, and (c) not the revolt of human depravity but an abstraction within a system, a mere privation of a term within an analytical organizational chart. Of course, a few natural lawyers blissfully overlook sin in their commitment to the naturalness of moral knowledge, but I suspect more that the mode of discourse does not allow sin to be incorporated in a sensible way, and so it is overlooked.

Aquinas does not overlook sin, and recovering its role for natural law requires transposing meaning from the theoretical to the interior, articulating the intelligibility he uncovered within a method more adequate to persons.

THE NOETIC EFFECTS OF SIN, TRANSPOSED

The task is twofold, (1) to articulate the Thomistic account of the loss of rectitude and corresponding disharmony from interiority, and (2) to continue

28. Lonergan, *Philosophical and Theological Papers, 1965–1990*, 37.

29. Lonergan, *Topics in Education*, 83.

the exploration of Lonergan's integral structure of human consciousness. The two tasks are linked, and I use the précis of his theory from earlier chapters as the basis of transposing Thomas on the wound of ignorance.

Genuine objectivity is the fruit of genuine subjectivity, says Lonergan, with genuine subjectivity attained by following the transcendental precepts: be attentive, be intelligent, be reasonable, be responsible. Such a person is governed, at least in *Insight*, although this expands in *Method* as we'll explore in the final chapter, by the desire to know—by a kind of wonder, or love, fidelity to which *is* objectivity. Objectivity is attained, with the ensuing tendency towards knowing the real, when we really want to know and thus allow our structure of operations to follow out their intentional tendencies, governed by the operator of desire:

> The ground of normative objectivity lies in the unfolding of the unrestricted, detached, disinterested desire to know. Because it is unrestricted, it opposes the obscurantism that hides truths or blocks access to it in whole or in part. Because it is detached, it is opposed to the inhibitions of the cognitional process that arise from other human desires and drives. Because it is disinterested, it is opposed to the well-meaning by disastrous reinforcement that other desires lend cognitional process only to twist its orientation into the narrow confines. . . . Hence, to be objective, in the normative sense of the term, is to give free rein to the pure desire, to its questions for intelligence, and to its questions for reflection.[30]

In our "friendly universe," in which natural processes result in the emergence of new order, it follows that intelligence acts as an operator of progress *if* objectivity is followed, for "[p]rogress results from the natural development of human intelligence" working itself out in concrete situations and questions, with intelligence and reasonability allowing new and better insights and judgments in a loop of intelligence and progress.[31]

But we do not always want to know, for in addition to understanding, there is a flight from understanding, an inexplicable and utterly unreasonable refusal of intelligence, what Lonergan terms *basic sin*.[32] As in Aquinas, for whom concupiscence interfered with knowing because sinful humans did not really want to know, objectivity obtains when we want to know and allow the normative and directed structures of conscious intentionality to

30. Lonergan, *Insight*, 404.

31. Ibid.

32. Ibid., 689–90.

seek their good, a seeking occurring only to the extent that the operator of the dynamic process—the desire to know—governs. If we desire to know, we tend to know—sometimes after a long process of self-correction and progress. But if we do not want to know, we will not know. It would seem somewhat obvious, then, that the means by which sin causes noetic effects is through impairing or perverting desire:

> Just as insight can be desired, so too can it be unwanted. Besides the love of light, there can be a love of darkness. If prepossessions and prejudices notoriously vitiate theoretical investigations, much more easily can elementary passions bias understanding in practical and personal matters. Nor has such a bias merely some single and isolated effect. To exclude an insight is also to exclude the further questions that would arise from it, and the complementary insights that would carry it towards a rounded and balanced viewpoint.[33]

So sharp is the contrast between the recurrent and progressive operations of intelligence and those oversights precluding the further questions, that the desire to know and its absence become differentials of personal intellectual development and even of the human good and history.[34] There is progress when the recurrent structure is followed, and there is decline caused by sin. When we do not will what we ought—basic sin—we interfere with the operator of progress—the pure question, or desire to know—and the immanent law contained within the structures of consciousness is not followed, nor the good obtained. Instead of knowledge and subsequent policies and social ordering which would follow, thereby sustaining and extending an order in which intelligence and reason could flourish, and feed back into the recurrent cycle, there are interruptions and irrationalities, refusals and unintelligibility.

On one level, sin takes the form of actions, of crimes, of individuals failing to do what they ought. Crime is a matter of "passion, or moral failure, of bad will, of incomprehension," and is not unexpected, for the "annual crop of infants is a potential invasion of barbarians, and education may be conceived as the first line of defense."[35] While the consequences of such sin may be unpleasant, even severe, a reasonable society tends to be able to control the barbarism.

---

33. Ibid., 214.

34. Lonergan, *Topics in Education*, 49–78.

35. Ibid., 59.

On a second level, sin is an impediment or brake on civilizational order and its attainment of vital and social values, including the good of order
by which vital goods are coordinated, distributed, and expanded through
collaboration and cooperation.[36] Rather than achieving the common good,
civilization "develops under a bias in favor of the powerful, the rich, or the
most numerous class. . . . Thus in the very process of the development of
civilizational order, there result from sin a bias in favor of certain groups
and against other groups. . . ."[37] In such a situation, creativity is skewed, for
a good and new idea must be combined with power and interest rather than
the disinterest of the pure question and a commitment to the good. New
ideas do not develop through intelligence but are sped up or slowed down
to benefit some, or harm others, and creativity finds progressively fewer
avenues of development. Creativity leads, for some, to frivolity, sinking to
the bread and circus level; for others, retreats into the ivory tower with no
interest in contributing to social order; others revive archaism, a notion
that the ancient ways are necessary, even though those virtues are no longer
helpful; yet others turn to a vague future, a utopian hope lacking genuine
content:[38]

> . . . insight into oversight reveals the cumulative process of decline.
> For the flight from understanding blocks the insights that concrete
> situations demand. There follows unintelligent policies and inept
> courses of action. The situation deteriorates to demands still fur-
> ther insights, and as they are blocked, policies become more un-
> intelligent and action more inept. What is worse, the deteriorating
> situation seems to provide the uncritical, biased mind with factual
> evidence in which the bias is claimed to be verified. So in ever
> increasing measure human intelligence comes to be regarded as ir-
> relevant to practical living. Human activity settles down to a deca-
> dent routine, and initiative becomes the privilege of violence.[39]

Not only crime and civilizational impediment, but sin takes the third
form of *aberration*, an impediment to "cultural development."[40] Just as there
can be decline in the civilizational order of vital and social value, so too
the higher values and their symbolic representations. One culture may in-

36. Ibid., 60.
37. Ibid.
38. Ibid., 61–62.
39. Lonergan, *Insight*, 8.
40. Lonergan, *Topics in Education*, 62.

terpret vital values as necessary for leisure, the arts, and education, while another may interpret vital values as the main goal, with education supporting the indefinite extension of vitality. But if personal, cultural, and religious values are ignored, or bent to serve lower goods, the intentional directedness of the human spirit is closed off, blocked, and distorted, and so too human meaning. From this can follow false philosophies, degrading myths, inadequate visions of life, decadence, vileness, enervation, exhaustion, nihilism, violent political ideologies, and a culture of death: "As aberrant consciousness heads to neurosis and psychosis, similarly aberrant history heads to cataclysm."[41]

Articulated as a component of decline, I've provided something of Lonergan's understanding of the structural features of original sin, albeit in non-theological terms and without reference to our alienation from God. This is still rather general, and Lonergan thinks that sin is concrete, as is consciousness. Consequently, he moves from the broad differentials of history to articulate the ways in which the pure, disinterested desire to know is corrupted in *bias*, a failure of love, a disordering of the *ordo amoris*:

> Sinfulness similarly is distinct from moral evil; it is the privation of total loving; it is a radical dimension of lovelessness. That dimension can be hidden by sustained superficiality, by evading ultimate questions, by absorption in all that the world offers to challenge our resourcefulness, to relax our bodies, to distract our minds.[42]

First, *dramatic bias*. Without experience, no insights emerge, and relevant data must be noted and attended. In dramatic bias, data does not emerge to prompt inquiry and the dynamic process never begins. The aberration may occur as *scotosis*, a hardening of attention, which "arises, not in conscious acts, but in the censorship that governs the emergence of psychic contents."[43] Insights which could move the subject to knowledge are met with revulsion, suspicion, even horror, resulting in a troubled mind with "attacks and crises that generate in the mind a mist of obscurity and bewilderment . . . of doubt and rationalization. . . ."[44] When one wants to know, images (what Aquinas might call "phantasms") about which and into which we inquire multiply, and irrelevant or distracting images are censored, but if one does not care to know there is a *repression* of those images which

41. Ibid., 63.
42. Lonergan, *Method*, 242–43.
43. Lonergan, *Insight*, 215.
44. Ibid.

might give rise to thought, and we "prevent the emergence into consciousness of perspectives that would give rise to unwanted insights."[45] Not only images, but affects or feelings will be *inhibited* if the coupling of image and affect would result in the undesired insight. Either the affect will be detached from the relevant image, or associated with an irrelevant one, but in either case the stance or position we take toward the image will be severed from a proper care (*Sorge*) which would result in our *being attentive*. This controls of our neural networks, squelching the ordering tendency, so much that even the performance of our dreams will be distorted and without fecundity.

If dramatic bias impairs the rise of insights, *individual bias* reveals the egoism interfering with the natural spontaneity of intelligence's development, resulting in an incomplete development that "fails to pivot from the initial and preliminary motivation provided by desires and fears to the self-abnegations involved in allowing complete free play to intelligent inquiry."[46] In its failure of courage, egoism excludes correct understanding, satisfied too easily with inadequate or even improper apprehensions, and even though this occurs with an uneasy conscience and sense of unease, there is a decision, a "conscious self-orientation" to which the egoist "devotes his energies."[47]

Group bias, like individual bias, relates to other people, but while individual bias struggles against the usual feelings we have for others, "group bias finds itself supported by such feeling" and by the common sense operative in that community.[48] Sticking together, the group overlooks data and questions challenging the received consensus, particularly denying the relevance of questions and experiences presented by outsiders, thus distorting the development of intelligence toward a limited perspective. As an example, in his famous 2006 "Regensburg Address," Benedict XVI noted that the secular West "has long been endangered by an aversion to the questions which underlie its rationality, and can only suffer great harm thereby."[49] As such, its questions have been closed to those of faith, and its mind has become incomplete, non-catholic in comprehensiveness. Such harm contributes to the *shorter cycle of decline*, where the very activities

45. Ibid., 216.
46. Ibid., 245–46.
47. Ibid., 246.
48. Ibid., 247.
49. Benedict XVI, "Regensburg Address," para. 16.

required by the community for sound policy and action are precluded and breakdowns occur. Good ideas are not championed, and irrationality rather than reasonableness dictates the wide range of action, with predictable results.

Distinct from the shorter cycle of decline, the *longer cycle* originates with *general bias*, which is a sort of impractical practicality.[50] The pure question does not always have an immediate payoff, and the only demand for its asking arises from wonder itself, with little apparent relevance or benefit. General, or practical bias, limits questioning to what is foreseen as useful, thus prescinding from unproductive questions; however, the foreseeable is quite limited, and when circumstances change the group which poured all resources into the useful finds itself equipped to thrive in a world no longer existing, while the community which allowed questions of leisure finds unexpected windfalls, and not merely in practical benefits but also cultural and personal. Limiting the pure question interferes with the cumulative, self-correcting, and progressive dynamism of intelligence, and such interference creates lacunae of insight, gaps of incoherence where the process stalls out or thrashes about, often at those moments of crisis or confusion when the dynamism is most needed.

Three consequences follow from the cumulative "disregard of fruitful ideas" and the further ideas dependent on them.[51] First, the social situation worsens, and the worsening snowballs. Progress entails a scheme of recurrence in which ideas coalesce and develop over time and with collaboration, but when that same personal and social dynamic departs from coherence, it has only "arbitrary fragments" and so "social functions and enterprises begin to conflict; some atrophy and others grow like tumors; the objective situation becomes penetrated with anomalies; it loses its power to suggest new ideas and, once they are implemented, to respond with still further and better suggestions. The dynamic of progress is replaced by sluggishness and then by stagnation."[52]

Second, in a self-fulfilling prophecy, the pure question is disregarded and self-enclosed. When it does voice itself, no one listens, and so it disappears and concerns itself with itself in a decadent self-regard: "Culture retreats into an ivory tower. Religion becomes an inward affair of the heart.

---

50. Lonergan, *Insight*, 252.

51. Ibid., 254.

52. Ibid.

Philosophy glitters like a gem with endless facets and no practical purpose."[53] In addition to this irrelevance, there is, third, intelligence's surrender, on both a minor and major level. The minor surrender entails the quaintness in which culture, religion, and philosophy serve as entertainments, respites from life, but not voices or engagements which ultimately matter. Major surrender occurs when reason is judged as non-normative, merely tasked to study the data of reality as they are, but providing no normative or critical role in telling us what ought to be. From this evacuation, an entirely new culture emerges, one rejecting the critical capacity of reason but embracing the empirical and descriptive, thus possessing "no standpoint from which it can distinguish between social achievement and the social surd."[54] Confined to scientism, either social or natural, it is remarkably inept at dealing with humans, even while creating a "new culture, religion, philosophy" upon this ineptness.[55] Here, the really human things are lost, and so, in a sense, is the natural law resisted, dampened, and muffled.

Sin and the Natural Law

Sin thoroughly and viciously impairs human life and accomplishment, and interiority heightens rather than denies these effects. Here I provide some initial thoughts, all addressed in more detail in subsequent chapters.

First, conflict between the gospel and the natural law is impossible, for both are from God. The suspicion of some that one must choose gospel or natural law is, I judge, based on a deeply incoherent picture of what the natural law is, and also, perhaps, how God relates to creation. Natural law is not, as some seem to think, based upon a Pelagian commitment to a pristine or untainted aspect of human nature operating as if in Eden. Or, to be fair, while it is possible, *but by no means necessary*, to read theoretical versions of the natural law as inadequately aware of sin, the interior mode can hardly be charged with this.

Second, interiority is concrete, starting with concrete subjects and their concrete operations, and if original sin is at all real it is not a placeholder in a systematic account of human nature, God, and salvation history, but a privation of the proper functioning of the operations of real persons.

---

53. Ibid., 254–55.
54. Ibid., 256.
55. Ibid.

The tradition has long held that sin was inordinate desire, a disordering of will and love, and so too does interiority judge, although interiority is better able to explain what this means in a non-abstract way than even systematics. Sin is the failure and disordering of the will which works itself out in the lovelessness and privation of total loving of the concrete subject. In some ways, human nature, understood as interiority, just is love as love is structurally integrated in consciousness—we are not first and foremost thinking things or substances, but lovers—and the loss of grace and ensuing deprivation of order is, for interiority, a totality of depravity by which human nature is thoroughly in decline.[56]

Third, understood this way, it is quite obvious that sin has noetic effects; in fact, interiority not only makes the noetic effects non-abstract, but radicalizes its effects. A good many proponents of the noetic effects of sin confine it to an impairment of our knowledge of God while remaining remarkably sanguine about ordinary knowledge. Interiority allows the totality of depravity in a way that a surprising number of adherents of total depravity do not![57]

Fourth, for interiority there is "a law immanent and operative in cognitional process" directing us toward truth, in both its theoretical and practical kinds.[58] This law functions in practical reason as first principles function for theory, namely, as self-evident or *per se nota*, but not innate, obvious, or given. First principles are not propositions or statements but "the dynamic structure of the mind, not a set of statements purporting to express such first principles."[59] To put it in another, somewhat stressed form, if I am my consciousness (although not just that), and if consciousness is the integral structures of operations, and if those structures have their directionality from the loving operator which I myself am, then the first principles of the natural law are not distinct from me. They are certainly not something operative in the physical world, but rather *are me*, or, *I am them*—I *am* the natural law and its first principles. And since I am effected noetically by sin in a total way, so too is the natural law.

---

56. Our nature as lovers is the primary thesis of Snell and Cone, *Authentic Cosmopolitanism*, 1–12.

57. Steven Moroney makes this claim about Reformed Epistemology, wondering why knowledge of the world is considered differently than knowledge of God. See his *Noetic Effects of Sin.*

58. Lonergan, *Insight*, 309.

59. Barden, "Insight and Mirrors," 99.

Fifth, since sin impairs but does not destroy nature, a claim which cannot be denied without a deeply incoherent performative self-contradiction, there are no grounds upon which to claim that sin vitiates natural law. None. Anyone can verify through interiority analysis that they operate according to the systemic operations of experience, understanding, and judgment, and anyone can verify, through retorsion, that this structure is non-revisable, referentially consistent, operative, universal, normative, critical, and irrefutable. Here we have a rock upon which to build, and anyone denying its foundations does so by those very foundations—thus demonstrating the irrationality of their denial and the rationality of that which they deny—or is merely asserting a claim without intelligence, reasonability, or data, and such claims need not be taken seriously. To make the argument that the noetic effects of sin either damage or render non-functional the capacity of reason to know the truth confirms the power of reason to know the truth and the self-evident goodness of truth, for there could be no other reason to make the argument than a commitment to the goodness of truth. Only someone who is an utter stranger to themselves would deny the natural law understood in the interior mode.

Sixth, if it is I who am redeemed and perfected by grace, rather than some abstraction, and if, properly understood, I am the natural law's first principles, then there is nothing innately hostile or competitive between natural law and redemption. Not only can natural law include redemption as part of its coherence, but it can do so without reducing redemption to the natural law. Natural law can function, and be impaired and redeemed, as natural because occurring in and as me. But more on that in the upcoming chapters.

8

The Spirit's Work

Value, Conversion, Authenticity

This chapter utilizes Lonergan's account of subjectivity to explore redemption as it relates to the first principle which I myself am. In doing so, his account of subjectivity remains to be fleshed out a bit more, for while earlier chapters introduced the distinction between the three level model of consciousness found in *Insight* and the four levels of *Method in Theology*, including the expansion of the transcendental precepts to include responsibility, more remains to the expanded commitment to value, love, emotion, and conversion which follows from the fourth level. While nothing in this chapter negates or denies preceding chapters, the integral structure of the human spirit outlined so far has remained thin on Lonergan's understanding of agency, attending mainly to his account of cognition. Here we expand that, noting the emergence of love to augment the disinterested desire to know as operator and the corresponding existentiality and responsibility of the fourth level. Further, including love and redemption in the account begins to enrich interiority with transcendence, and this chapter begins to transition natural law into the fourth mode of meaning, not in a way that leaves the subject behind, else we would no longer have natural law, but as perfecting and completing the trajectory of interiority.

The Fourth Level and Value

There is only one intellect, but we distinguish its operations by noting the various objectives of that unified reason. For instance, we distinguished understanding and judging by noting the intentionality of the questions *quid sit* and *an sit*, the first intending intelligibility and the second the real, or existence. As the questions intend, they anticipate the heuristic, or notion, intended. Also the self which asks the questions becomes present to itself in an expanded way: "it is a fuller self of which we are aware and the awareness itself is different."[1] While *Insight* tended to describe the good *as* the intelligible and reasonable, in *Method* Lonergan grasps a distinct notion and a fuller self in the fourth level of responsibility. *Value* and the *person* emerge in a more robust way.[2]

When we ask questions of understanding, we emerge *as* intelligent subjects through the questioning and intelligibility emerges as the transcendental notion intended. Notions are not categories. Categories give "determinative answers" to "determinative questions," as concepts, as when my question "What is this substance?" receives the answer "a brick made from clay." This answer refers to determinative intelligibility, to concepts which have their meaning from concrete instances of insight into this or that data set. Notions are different: "contained in questions prior to the answers. They are the radical intending that moves us from ignorance to knowledge. They are *a priori* because they go beyond what we know to seek what we do not know yet."[3] The notion of intelligibility is the condition of possibility of my asking about the brick, for if I did not have a horizon of meaning in which concrete intelligible substances would mean, I would never ask; but I do ask, and things mean for me because of the notion I intend.

In a similar way, *responsibility* has its own distinct intending, although because the levels are cumulative and sublimating this is not bereft of intelligibility or reasonableness. The transcendental notion is that *a priori* dynamism moving me beyond understanding to the truth, and beyond "factual knowledge to responsible action."[4] I do not make judgments of fact in an utterly detached mode as if the world existed separate from my agency and

1. Lonergan, *Method*, 9.
2. Ibid., 10. See also Lonergan, *Second Collection*, 277.
3. Lonergan, *Method*, 10.
4. Ibid., 12.

causality; I am involved with the world, entangled with it, and for me the world is always *engaging* because of dynamic directionality.[5] In light of the transcendental notions we could identify the transcendental *concepts* of intelligibility and being insofar as we objectify the questions *quid sit* and *an sit*. So too we "objectify the content of responsible intending [and] get the transcendental concept of value, of the truly good."[6] In other words, because we spontaneously engage with the world as agents who seek and desire the good, we can perform noetic exegesis, objectify that dynamism, and posit the heuristic of good, or value, as that which is intended by *questions for deliberation*:

> Value is a transcendental notion. It is what is intended in questions for deliberation, just as the intelligible is what is intended in questions for intelligence, and just as truth and being are what are intended in questions for reflection. Such intending is not knowing. When I ask what, or why, or how, or what for, I do not know the answers, but already I am intending what would be known if I knew the answers. . . . So when I ask whether this is truly and not merely apparently good, whether that is or is not worth while, I do not yet know value but I am intending value.[7]

Value, as the other notions, provides the dynamism of consciousness by which our questions continue—not only from level to level but also recurrently within a level as we ask and ask in the cumulative and correcting process—and by which our subjectivity expands. Like the other notions, value is a normative standard, for as the drive to understand was satisfied when understanding was attained, and the drive for reasonability satisfied when the evidence was deemed sufficient, so to the "drive to value rewards success in self-transcendence with a happy conscience and saddens failures with an unhappy conscience."[8] Also, like the other notions, value is not abstract but concrete, the source of each and every of *my* questions, and so the good I seek is always concrete, always the answer to particular questions by concrete subjects with actual objectives in real moments.[9]

---

5. Snell and Cone, *Authentic Cosmopolitanism*, 44–65. See also the work of Charles Taylor on engaged agency.

6. Lonergan, *Method*, 12.

7. Ibid., 34.

8. Ibid., 35.

9. Ibid., 36.

The notion of value, thus, is the *a priori* dynamism allowing and pushing my questions for deliberation—"What ought I do? Is this good? Which is more worthwhile? What is my duty?"—and the transcendental concept is the fruit of noetic exegesis about my intending, yet neither the notion or the concept are the concrete goods known through actual judgments of value which affirm or deny that "some *x* is truly or only apparently good" or that some *x* is "better or more important, or more urgent than the other."[10] Such judgments are not merely subjective, and certainly do not intend to be so, since the notion seeks the "truly" good. Neither are they detached from the lower levels of consciousness as if deliberation followed its own autonomous criteria in isolation.[11] Just as there is no intelligibility without data and no truth without intelligibility, so to "know the good, it must know the real."[12]

If we were pure intellects, responsibility would be folded into reasonability. We would deliberate, understand the good, and choose and perform the action. But this is not our reality, even if a good many theorists present the moral life in such a way. Consciousness is not so paper-thin, so detached and calculated, but is instead existential, mooded, involved—"intermediate between judgments of fact and judgments of value lie apprehensions of value. Such apprehensions are given in feelings."[13] We are not pure intellects transitioning seamlessly from judgments of fact to those of value. We are affective persons.

Drawing on Dietrich von Hildebrand, Lonergan differentiates feelings as non-intentional or intentional. Waking up on the proverbial wrong side of the bed with a general feeling of irritability and melancholy, or experiencing a feeling of hunger or sexual desire are instances of non-intentional states and trends. The feelings have causes—lack of sleep or food, an excess of sugar, the endocrine system—and goals which would accomplish or satisfy that which the feeling indicates. But the feeling happens to us and from the feeling one discovers the state or trend rather than the feeling emerging from our own conscious intentionality. For instance, I find myself feeling grumpy and realize that I have not eaten or need a nap; or I am bumped in the store, feel irritation, and realize the situation in which I find myself. With intentional responses, however, feelings have more than

10. Ibid.
11. Lonergan is not guilty of the creative autonomy vilified by Rhonheimer.
12. Ibid., 13.
13. Ibid., 37.

causes or ends but have *objects*, and feeling arises or relates to that which is "intended, apprehended, represented" because we "are oriented massively and dynamically in a world mediated by meaning."[14]

Take the following example: during the Eucharist, my two-year-old pointed at the Host, loudly said "the body of Christ," and indicated she wanted the Host placed in her mouth. I was *pleased*. Why? Not out of biological sympathy for the pleasure of eating bread but because I believe the Eucharist is the culmination of Christian worship and hope my children will embrace the faith. I know, of course, that at twenty-four months she's unlikely to understand, but the feeling arose because of my understanding, because of the meaning I ascribe to the event.

Or another example, I was displeased to learn that an older daughter and her playmate had an argument and that my son, fearing the playmate would not like him, sided against his sister. This displeased me because I value family, and think disputes should be settled justly rather than from self-preservation, and my displeasure arose because of meaning, just as the feeling made obvious what I value. There's a pivoting here, for I had the feeling in intentional response to my values, but having the feeling allowed an apprehension of what my values were (religion, family, justice), prompting me to ask whether I was correct about them (should allegiance to family always trump the neighbor? Why did I think that? Should I?). Feelings come from value, illuminating my apprehension of the values I have.

Intentional feelings, as opposed to non-intentional states and trends, are of two types, namely, those regarding the agreeable/disagreeable and those regarding values. The second concerns us here. While feelings are, quite obviously, subjective, there is an objectivity to the scale of values feelings apprehend. Further, on the side of the subject there can be development, refinement, coarsening, or immaturity, not only in particular moments, say when one's feelings get the better of reason, but also in the channels of attention, the horizons of the person, for feeling can shape subjectivity beyond the mere happenstances of today's mood.[15] Horizons, or stances of attention and connation, can be developed or aberrant, and "a distortion of the whole scale of values can spread through a whole social class, a whole people, a whole epoch."[16]

14. Ibid., 30–31.
15. Ibid., 34.
16. Ibid., 35.

Feelings play an important role in ethics, lying between judgments of fact on the third level of consciousness and judgments of value on the fourth, and while feelings *apprehend* value they are not yet moral *knowledge* since knowledge always occurs on the level of judging.[17] But as desire moves us from experience through judgments of fact, so the intentional apprehension of value fosters "the stirring of our very being when we glimpse the possibility or the actuality of moral self-transcendence."[18] Judgments of value, then, unite cognitive knowledge of reality, feelings, and the impetus or tendency towards moral self-transcendence, and if any of these three element is missing or distorted, so too will moral knowledge be affected, for knowledge alone is insufficient, feelings alone can be haphazard, and moral self-transcendence must be authentic rather than inauthentic. Incidentally, since there is only one subjectivity, the noetic affects of sin could not be merely cognitive or noetic, but, given the harmony or disharmony of the whole subject's will/love, affect moral knowledge insofar as knowledge of reality was affected, feelings were aberrant, and moral self-transcendence dampened or inauthentic.

Growth requires development in all three aspects of value judgments: (1) knowledge of reality, or adequate judgments of fact, (2) development of intentional responses "from the agreeable to vital values, from vital to social, from social to cultural, from cultural to personal, from personal to religious," and (3) being in love:[19]

> But continuous growth seems to be rare. There are the deviations occasioned by neurotic need. There are the refusals to keep on taking the plunge from settled routines to an as yet unexperienced by richer more of living. There are the mistaken endeavors to quieten an uneasy conscience by ignoring, belittling, denying, rejecting higher values. Preference scales become distorted. Feelings soured. Bias creeps into one's outlook, rationalization into one's morals, ideology into one's thought. So one may come to hate the truly good, and love the really evil. Not is that calamity limited to individuals. It can happen to groups, to nations, to blocks of nations, to mankind.[20]

17. John Finnis, I believe, misunderstands Lonergan on this point, reading apprehensions as somehow self-justified knowledge claims of a utilitarian kind, *Fundamentals of Ethics*, 42.

18. Ibid., 38.

19. Ibid., 39.

20. Ibid., 39–40.

Of these elements of development/growth and inauthenticity, the most obscure but essential is that of being in love, the ordered thrust of moral self-transcendence, or *vertical liberty* where one is explicitly and knowingly "responding to the transcendental notion of value, by determining what it would be worth while for one to make of oneself, and what it would be worth while for one to do for one's fellow men."[21]

In the first three levels, we desire to know, and it is that desire operating behind the tension of inquiry, that sense that we have not yet fully understood and so thus have further questions awaiting us. The experience is odd, for of course we respond to an intention, a heuristic, an anticipation of fullness which is, as yet, non-explicit and so not really known except as *notion*, as a tendency for an objective; this is the horizon of knowing, itself formed not as a particular object but as the space or clearing in which all particular objects appear. While the desire is not equivalent to knowing, the cognitional process by which knowing is accomplished would never begin without the desire, and, moreover, the desire is itself a measure of objectivity "against" which judgments occur. Whatever naïve realism holds, we do not have our ideas in one view and reality in another to compare in some sort of super-intuition, and if we did the ideas would be redundant and extraneous anyway; instead, we have the process of cognition itself, driven by dynamism as a cumulative and self-corrective endeavor. Of course we consult data—but from where does data come if not from those who explore or develop techniques or equipment with which to uncover new data—and the canons of a discipline—but from where do those come except as principles of intelligence—and we consult with others who are competent, but in the end intelligence comes to rest when the person of sound judgment comes to rest. Those who are rash, or dull, rest too soon; those who are scrupulous or hyperbolic in their doubts, never judge; those whose dynamism is tempered come to rest when the further relevant questions have been asked and answered to their satisfaction. Obviously this is not a recipe to be followed like a technique, but dynamism *is itself* the test of objectivity.

So, too, in the moral life—as the desire for intellectual self-transcendence results in the dynamism of asking yet more questions rather than taking "good enough," moral self-transcendence goes beyond the mere satisfactions of pleasure toward the truly and really good, truly and really in keeping with the scale of values. As in cognition, this thrust to transcendence

21. Ibid., 40.

keeps the process moving, keeps it "in gear," just as it operates as a standard against which to judge completion. In a fundamental sense, this means that if "one's love of God is complete, then values are whatever one loves . . . *Ama Dei, et fac quod vis.*"[22] Good moral judgment "is ever the work of a fully developed, self-transcending subject, or, as Aristotle would put it, of a virtuous man"—the *spoudaios.*[23]

As it operates within the world of meaning and the experience and judgment of many others, this is not solipsistic. Nor is it emotivism, since feelings apprehend and move us to continue acting but are not themselves judgments or knowledge, although they can be reasons, even good ones, if a person is developed enough. Nor is this mere wish, as if our strong desire for authenticity somehow makes us so. Instead, the factors include sufficient and relevant knowledge of reality, properly ordered feelings, and the thrust to self-transcendence as these unite in judgments of value. Of course, like judgments of fact, these judgments are not true merely because made, or earnestly held, but they *tend* towards truth insofar as the virtuous person engages in the critical, cumulative, and self-correcting process of deliberation. "Is this the right decision? Have I understood what's at stake? Have I considered other relevant parties or views? What values is this based on? Are they the proper values? Am I biased? Have my feelings helped or swamped my critical faculties? Have I consulted others who might know? What are the conditions in which I operate? What is my intention?" and so forth. Knowledge is not obtained in the absence of intelligence and insight, in this case *deliberative insight*, and insights do not occur in the absence of data. Neither are insights grounded unless judged adequate to the data and against the dynamic desire which is objectivity, and moral knowledge of this desire includes the desire to be fully in love with God! No formula to mindlessly follow exists, for objectivity is not so objective as to exist without minds, or feelings, or bodies, or languages, or histories, or contexts— and yet, there is objectivity, and not all judgments are equally intelligent, reasonable, or responsible:

> Such judgments are objective or merely subjective inasmuch as they proceed or do not proceed from a self-transcending subject. Their truth or falsity, accordingly, has its criterion in the authenticity or inauthenticity of the subject's being. . . . Judgments of value differ in content but not in structure from judgments of fact.

22. Ibid., 39.
23. Ibid., 41.

> They differ in content, for one can approve of what does not exist, and one disapprove of what does. They do not differ in structure, inasmuch as in both there is a distinction between criterion and meaning. In both, the criterion is the self-transcendence of the subject ... In both, the meaning is or claims to be independent of the subject: judgments of fact state or purport to state what is or is not so; judgments of values state or purport to state what is or is not truly good or really better.[24]

There is moral knowledge, and not every judgment counts as true, and yet we must come to know, and this is accomplished only through the discursivity of human reason.

AUTHENTICITY AND CONVERSION

The thrust toward self-transcendence is a condition of possibility for human authenticity and the personal and social progress which can follow, so long as subjects observe the transcendental precepts, but "development is not inevitable, and so the results vary. There are human failures."[25] Precepts can be violated, with judgments "biased by an egoistic disregard of others, by a loyalty to one's own group matched by hostility to other groups, by concentrating on short-term benefits and overlooking long-term costs. Moreover, such aberrations are easy to maintain and difficult to correct," for individuals, groups, societies, civilizations, and whole cultures.[26] Insofar as we are inauthentic, we are alienated from the human good, including, it turns out, from ourselves and our self-transcending tendencies. While the thrust toward self-transcendence is not sufficient for authenticity it is necessary, but the inauthentic person, the one lacking the fullness of self-transcendence, is alienated from the good as if it were something distinct from them and strangers to themselves and the process by which they might progress and develop. The odd irrationality of inauthenticity is not only that one judges, chooses, and acts wrongly, but also that one judges, chooses, and acts wrongly with respect to one's capacity to judge, choose, and act. Just as there is a performative referentiality in the process by which one comes to know and affirm the levels of consciousness such that the search for self-knowledge is simultaneously a means by which the self

24. Ibid., 37.
25. Ibid., 51.
26. Ibid., 53.

develops, so too alienation rejects itself, and the performative aberration is disastrous:

> Decline has a still deeper level. Not only does it compromise and distort progress. Not only do inattention, obtuseness, unreasonableness, irresponsibility produce objectively absurd situations. Not only do ideologies corrupt minds. But compromise and distortion discredit progress. Objectively absurd situations do not yield to treatment. Corrupt minds have a flair for picking the mistaken solution and insisting that it alone is intelligent, reasonable, good. Imperceptibly the corruption spreads from the harsh sphere of material advantage and power to the mass media, the stylish journals, the literary movements, the educational process, the reigning philosophies. A civilization in decline digs its own grave with a relentless consistency.[27]

Such is the *reign of sin*, and the problem "is radical, for it is a problem in the very dynamic structure of cognitional, volitional, and social activity," and thus an entire orientation toward evil, leading to disharmony in "every use of the dynamic structure."[28] This is a "despotism of darkness; and men are its slaves," and incapable of escape, for the very normative structures by which to do so are imprisoned, alienated, and in love with darkness rather than light. Reason no longer operates but grinds its own gears into rubble.[29] "A leap from unreason, from the unreasonableness of sin, to reason," is needed, but the subject, the operator, is profoundly incapable of this leap.[30] The redemption of love is necessary "inasmuch as such love can undo the mischief of decline and restore the cumulative process of progress."[31]

The Way Up, the Way Down—Achievement and Heritage

In *Topics in Education*, Lonergan identifies three differentials of the human good—development, sin, and redemption—or what could also be summarized as progress, decline, and redemption as these work themselves out in the histories of individuals and groups alike. Progress or development

---

27. Ibid., 54–55.
28. Lonergan, *Insight*, 653.
29. Ibid., 714.
30. Lonergan, *Topics in Education*, 64.
31. Lonergan, *Method*, 55.

follows from authenticity, decline from the alienation and inauthenticity of the reign of sin, but redemption needs discussion.

Following Lonergan, let's distinguish *achievement*, or development "from below upwards," from *heritage*, or development "from above downwards," with the up-down image garnered from the ascending levels of consciousness in experience, understanding, judging, and choosing:

> For human development is of two quite different kinds. There is development from below upwards, from experience to growing understanding, from growing understanding to balanced judgments, from balanced judgment to fruitful courses of action, and from fruitful courses of action to the new situations that call forth further understanding, profounder judgments, richer courses of action.
>
> But there is also development from above downwards. There is the transformation of falling in love: the domestic love of the family; the human love of one's tribe, one's city, one's country, mankind; the divine love that orientates man in his cosmos and expresses itself it his worship. Where hatred only sees evil, love reveals values. At once it commands commitment and joyfully carries it out, no matter what the sacrifice involved. Where hatred reinforces bias, love dissolves it, whether it be the bias of unconscious motivation, the bias of individual or group egoism, or the bias of omnicompetent, short-sighted common sense. Where hatred plods around in every narrower vicious circles, love breaks the bonds of psychological and social determinism with the conviction of faith and the power of hope.[32]

Ordinarily, self-transcendence is an achievement of human spirit following the immanent law of our integral structure. Our capacity for sensation takes us beyond ourselves and into the universe we contact bodily, but we go beyond mere environment to a world mediated by meaning when we ask questions of intelligence and move into a truth independent of the subject when we reflect and seek what is reasonable. Finally, we can go beyond our mere comfort as we seek objective value, becoming a person who is fully authentic and thereby fully objective. We achieve this because of the dynamism operative in the transcendental notions, our own capacity for self-transcendence.

But the reign of sin makes achievement chaotic, impermanent, unlikely, and even, in the end, impossible if we become deeply inauthentic

---

32. Lonergan, *Third Collection*, 106. See also Crowe, *Old Things and New*, 1–29.

and alienated from the self-transcending capacity. We become inattentive, unintelligent, unreasonable, irresponsible in our many biases and hatreds trapping us in whims, satisfactions, vices, and fears. Only redemption, the third differential, allows escape, attained, says Lonergan, by a *faith* which is the "fundamental answer to the problem of sin," and which liberates intelligence and reason, by a *hope* which liberates us socially, and by a *love* which frees us from hatred and allows us to repay evil with good.[33]

True, but still abstract, and for Lonergan abstraction incapable of grounding in our own performance is an alienation; just as achievement was knowable and affirmable through the referentially consistent, concrete, and non-revisable method of interiority analysis, so too should redemption, development "from above downwards," be concrete. Human nature is concrete, sin is concrete, and grace is concrete.

Redemption operates when the capacity for self-transcendence "becomes an actuality when one falls in love"—marriage or sociality, for instance—but redemptive love is "God's love flooding our hearts through the Holy Spirit given to us (Rom. 5, 5)."[34] While the agent of this love is God who gives it to us, being in love with God is the "basic fulfillment of our conscious intentionality," for "as unrestricted questioning is our capacity for self-transcendence, so being in love in an unrestricted fashion is the proper fulfillment of that capacity."[35] As fulfillment of intentionality, being in love operates at the fourth level of consciousness, at the existential level of persons and values, remaking the horizons of what matters to us.[36] Being in love is thus not the consciousness accompanying experience, or inquiry, or reflection, but "the type of consciousness that deliberates, makes judgments of value, decides, acts responsibly and freely. . . . the gift of God's love occupies the ground and root of the fourth and highest level of man's intentional consciousness. It takes over the peak of the soul, the *apex animae*."[37] Most fundamentally, being in love, as a gift of God, is a conversion which "dismantles and abolishes the horizon in which our knowing and choosing

---

33. Lonergan, *Topics in Education*, 67. See also Rhonheimer, *Perspective of the Acting Person*, 1–17, and Finnis, *Moral Absolutes*, 12–20.

34. Lonergan, *Method*, 105.

35. Ibid., 105–6.

36. I here prescind from the question of whether Lonergan introduced a fifth level of consciousness in his later work. For recent scholarship, see Blackwood, "Love and Lonergan's Cognitional-Intentional Anthropology."

37. Ibid., 107.

went on and it sets up a new horizon in which the love of God will trans-value our values and the eyes of that love will transform our knowing."[38]

Understood theoretically, being-in-love is sanctifying grace, or the in-fusion of God's own life into the human soul; understood from interiority, being-in-love is first an experience of having one's values radically remade, the horizons of engagement, care, and good altered, and only after the ex-perience remaking horizons of value could the experience be objectified in a non-abstract way. Understood from interiority, the religious experience of God's love flooding our hearts is the gift of faith, or "knowledge born of religious love."[39] Faith, Lonergan suggests, is the knowledge available when God's love floods our hearts, allowing an apprehension of transcendent or religious value distinct from achievement. That which we seek in desire is now given in love and the light of faith links to all other values to "trans-form, magnify, and glorify them" as we are absorbed in "an all-encompass-ing good."[40] Pope Francis describes something very similar in *Lumen Fidei*:

> The light of faith is unique, since it is capable of illuminating *ev-ery aspect* of human existence. A light this powerful cannot come from ourselves but from a more primordial source: in a word, it must come from God. Faith is born of an encounter with the liv-ing God who calls us and reveals his love, a love which precedes us and upon which we can lean for security and for building our lives. Transformed by this love, we gain fresh vision, new eyes to see; we realize that it contains a great promise of fulfillment, and that a vision of the future opens up before us.[41]

Having remade the horizons of the fourth level of consciousness, de-velopment from above downwards transforms our values and correspond-ing affectivity.[42] On those values rests *belief*, or knowledge handed to us by others—the way of *heritage*—functioning at the level of judgment. The Creed, say, is something I believe. Neither the Creed nor my belief in it are my achievements, as I inherited both from the legacy of the tradition and its members. But because I have God's love, I believe it, and judge it to be true—the fourth level has worked downwards to the third. Further, from those judgments can arise growth and development in understanding

38. Ibid., 106.
39. Ibid., 115.
40. Ibid., 116.
41. Francis, *Lumen Fidei*, 4.
42. For a succinct summary and explanation, see Lonergan, *Third Collection*, 181.

on the second level, for because I believe I can understand, in large part because I want to—*fides quarens intellectum*. Finally, my developed understanding alters my experience; from the fourth level to the first.

As a simple example, I decided to enter the Church right around the Feast of the Assumption. A friend asked me if I believed the doctrine of the Assumption, which I affirmed, but only because the Church taught it, and I accepted this authority, but I certainly didn't understand the Assumption and wished the doctrine had not been defined. A year later I'm at Mass on the Feast of the Assumption full of eagerness and delight. I had accepted the doctrine (judgment), which I came to understand as an articulation of the fullness of grace and participation in Christ's resurrection, which resulted in an experience of delight (and some contrition for my previous attitude.) This is not an unusual or particularly recondite experience, and I suspect anyone who's ever fallen in love with anyone or anything can attest to its reality—love changes the way we see, and know, and encounter the world.

Grace develops us as concrete subjects from above downwards, and like achievement allows progress, for although we are inhibited and bent by sin, faith reverses decline.

> So faith is linked with human progress and it has to meet the challenge of human decline. For faith and progress have a common root in man's cognitional and moral self-transcendence. To promote either is to promote the other indirectly. Faith places human efforts in a friendly universe; it reveals an ultimate significance in human achievement; it strengthens new undertakings with confidence. Inversely, progress realizes the potentialities of man and of nature; it reveals that man exists to bring about an ever fuller achievement in this world; and that achievement because it is man's good also is God's glory. Most of all, faith has the power of undoing decline. . . . If human progress is not to be ever distorted and destroyed by the inattention, oversights, irrationality, irresponsibility of decline, men have to be reminded of their sinfulness. They have to acknowledge their real guilt and amend their ways. They have to learn with humility that religious development is dialectical, that the task of repentance and conversion is life-long.[43]

---

43. Lonergan, *Method*, 115–16.

Conversion(s)

This last quotation indicates the life-long task of conversion, an important category for Lonergan and one needing more attention. In the previous paragraphs, *religious conversion* has been discussed, by which Lonergan means something broader than the acceptance of this or that doctrine or membership in this or that group, although religious conversion often brings with it tradition, sociality, and belief. Primarily, though, religious conversion is being-in-love with God, the "total and permanent self-surrender without conditions, qualifications, reservations. . . . For Christians it is God's love flooding our hearts through the Holy Spirit given to us. It is the gift of grace . . . the replacement of the heart of stone by a heart of flesh."[44] Religious conversion as a mode of self-transcendence is total loving, just as the reign of sin was lovelessness, with love as the "efficacious ground or all self-transcendence, whether in the pursuit of the truth, or in the realization of human values, or in the orientation man adopts to the universe, its ground, and its goal."[45]

While religious conversion is the ground of self-transcendence (a development from the more intellectualist position of *Insight* in which it was the "pure question" rather than love), it is not the sole category of conversion, joining intellectual and moral. *Moral conversion* is to the world of value from the domain of satisfactions, an exercise in vertical liberty by which we opt "for the truly good, even for value against satisfaction when value and satisfaction conflict," although deciding for the good is not yet to *do* it, let alone with firm character.[46] *Intellectual conversion* is the rejection of the myth that knowing is like seeing, that objectivity is something like a good look, or that reality is out there to be seen, instead accepting that (1) fully human knowing is a dynamic structure, (2) objectivity is the disinterested desire to know, and (3) reality is that which can be intelligently conceived and rationally affirmed, whether a body or not.[47] Intellectual conversion, normally, as achievement, occurs as the fruit of noetic exegesis whereby one discovers what one has been doing whatever one's epistemology declares, and affirms that what one is actually doing is human knowing, with

44. Ibid., 240–41.

45. Ibid., 241.

46. Ibid., 240.

47. Snell, *Through a Glass Darkly*, 69, 105; Snell and Cone, *Authentic Cosmopolitanism*, 81–84, 105–27. For my analysis of the three conversions in Augustine, see "Teaching for Cosmopolis," 95–112.

standards of objectivity and normativity in keeping with the performance (a position) rather than an abstract theory (a counterposition).

Intellectual conversion's self-transcendence takes us from mere perception, however sublime, to the world of meaning intended in fully human knowing. Moral conversion is self-transcendent, taking us beyond mere satisfaction to value. Religious conversion is self-transcendent, orienting us to ultimate concern, the universal good. In one way, we can consider the conversions as patterned, with intellectual conversion occupying the ground and religious conversion the heights, and with moral conversion sublating intellectual and religious sublating moral conversion, putting everything in a new light but not interfering with or destroying the preceding.[48] For instance, moral conversion is not just intellectual conversion with value added; instead, moral conversion places us into a new horizon of meaning where we are new subjects with distinct concerns and engagements, but if not intellectually converted we will think that the real is reducible to that which can be seen, making it quite difficult to move beyond satisfaction. So, too, religious conversion without moral conversion would be a deformed thing, likely a warm heart unconcerned for reversing decline (and thus an instance of decline), and religious conversion without intellectual conversion would find it a considerable challenge to grasp God as something immaterial and transcendent.[49]

So the conversions go beyond the lower levels without thereby discounting the proper functions of the lower, but adding something new. Religious conversion, for instance, adds knowledge born of religious love to the knowing attained in intellectual conversion; such knowledge of the heart does not replace reason, nor is it irrational, but it cannot be reduced either. Further, while the sublations would seem to require the preceding conversions, it is not the case that the lower cause the higher; in fact, "from a causal viewpoint, one would say that first there is God's gift of his love. Next, the eye of this love reveals values in their splendor, while the strength of this love brings about their realization, and that is moral conversion. Finally, among the vales discerned by the eye of love is the value of believing the truths taught by the religious tradition, and in such tradition and belief

---

48. Lonergan, *Method*, 241.

49. As Augustine in the *Confessions*, who struggles mightily to overcome his image of a corporeal God. When he does so, understanding that truth is a relation and God immaterial, he posits his famous position on the unreality of evil and is then capable to respond to moment of religious conversion in the garden.

are the seeds of intellectual conversion."[50] Thus it is that development from above downwards is not merely religious love allowing decision to be freed-up from bias or cognition to escape scotosis, but, even more fundamentally, religious conversion grounds both intellectual and moral conversion, although, of course, the experience and self-understanding of this might not be so neat, tidy, or systematic.

Since authenticity is attained in self-transcendence, and self-transcendence in conversion, it follows that to be authentic is to be thoroughly converted such that development from above downwards allows the subject to operate freely and without alienation from below upwards as well—*heritage* allows for *achievement*—which is why decline can be reversed and progress re-started through grace as we are again made fully human. Grace does not swamp autonomy but, rather, perfects, elevates, and frees nature to be nature. Because of grace, the authentic subject is not trapped by sin and can operate on the path of ordinary human achievement again. Faith allows progress by allowing achievement.

PROVISIONAL CONCLUSIONS

There is nothing about interiority which precludes or overlooks the noetic effects of sin; if anything, interiority incorporates the reign of sin more fully than most accounts, even if it does not articulate them in the familiar categories. There is also nothing about interiority claiming autonomy from grace, instead developing an account of human development cooperating with grace. Further, while the method here is philosophical rather than theological, there is nothing about interiority hostile to Christocentrism if we assume, as I would, that grace is given because of the work of Christ, and incorporate that gift of *heritage* into reflection and understanding.

While the various threads remain in need of weaving together, I think all the ground work is present to answer the usual objections of Protestant Prejudice. Interiority incorporates sin; interiority claims human autonomy as a kind of participated theonomy without thereby denying autonomy or theonomy; interiority welcomes the work and grace of Christ as essential to interiority's own self-interpretation. Further, this chapter set the framework for the mode of transcendence, certainly a transition of relevance for

---

50. Ibid., 243.

responding to the objections. But while the framework is there, the explanation is not yet developed.

Further, it is, perhaps, not fully clear whether and how transcendence is law. Certainly John Paul II, Rhonheimer, and contemporary natural law theorists articulate natural law using the interior mode, but Lonergan is doing something distinct, I'd suggest, maintaining interiority to provide the structure of human nature, but incorporating a new operator—sanctifying grace, or the love of God—into that structure. An exploration of how Lonergan might present natural law will show, I suggest, just how distinct interiority modified by transcendence is from theory and common sense— and thus how comfortable with the usual Protestant concerns—and flesh out the source of law operative in the human person in a more formalized manner.

9

Natural Law from the Heart

Lonergan is not obviously a natural law thinker; if anything, some might judge that he obviously is not. Certainly natural law is not a subject he wrote on widely, and in turning to the subject many suspect a corresponding turn against the realism necessary for the natural law to flourish, let alone that Lonergan accepts historicity, the empirical, and pluralism of communications.[1] And as a hermeneutical thinker in the vein of Gadamer, Lonergan appears more concerned with the educative function of ethics and the practice of self-understanding than with any sort of deductive casuistry, and the tone, the "feel," seems quite distinct, more postmodern than the natural law might be able to bear.[2] Further, one does not find in Lonergan's students much in the way of natural law thought, and even some reticence.[3]

Certainly I do not wish to force Lonergan into something, or forge alliances where there are genuinely dialectical differences, and yet distinguishing the modes of meaning clarifies some of the differences between thinkers such as Rommen, Budziszewksi, and Lisska, on the one hand, and

1. Etienne Gilson, for instance, suspected that a turn to consciousness meant being trapped in a labyrinth from which there was no return to the real, see his *Methodical Realism*, 17–36. In addition to his worries that Lonergan falls into utilitarianism in his later work, Finnis sharply rejects the classical-empirical distinction made by Lonergan, claiming that such historicity fails to escape historicism and cannot but result in the revisionism of Rahnerians, see *Collected Essays*, 5:139–62.

2. See Lawrence, "Finnis on Lonergan," 852, see also 849–87.

3. See Crysdale, "Revisioning Natural Law," 464–84 for the tensions.

Rhonheimer, Grisez, Finnis, and Boyle, on the other. Both sets of thinkers are enormously sophisticated, both reject revisionist theologians and an ethics of proportionalism, and both hold to the natural and universal access of basic moral knowledge. Having distinguished the modes of meaning, I find in the thinkers of interiority a certain suppleness, or at least a potential for such, in dealing with the objections J. Daryl Charles has termed the "Protestant Prejudice," even though those objections are shared in part by Catholics such as Hittinger and Rowland. Having expanded the horizon of natural law beyond common sense and theory—which is not to deny the achievements, perhaps lasting, of those modes—to include interiority and transcendence, Lonergan has much to offer through his foundational methodology to natural law in its third and fourth modes. Some of those offerings have been articulated in a provisional way throughout the text thus far, and in this in this chapter I attempt to bring them together, although certainly this is still metatheory and not a developed ethics.

FOUNDATIONAL PRINCIPLES

"Foundations," Lonergan says, "may be conceived in two quite distinct manners."[4] The first "conceive[s] foundations as a set of premises, of logically first propositions," while the second "move[s] out of the static, deductivist style—which admits no conclusions that are not implicit in premises—and into the methodical style—which aims at decreasing darkness and increasing light and keeps adding discovery to discovery."[5] For the first, the content of self-evident propositions and validity of deduction is paramount, while the exigence of the dynamic process governs the second. Given this statement, Lonergan's version of law would be less a science of logic and more hermeneutical, concerned with understanding the good always already operative as people live and work together, and giving less attention to logical inference than to practical judgment.[6] Further, the default model considers first principles, in theory at least, as available to anyone, saints and scoundrels alike, while interiority and transcendence suggests natural law is known and measured best by the authentic person,

---

4. Lonergan, *Method*, 269.

5. Ibid., 270.

6. Lawrence, "Finnis on Lonergan," 852.

the *spoudaios*, and it is this morally serious person who is the measured-measure, or best judge of natural law.[7]

At least in its Aristotelian form, logic organizes the relations of concepts, including the relations of first premises, but Lonergan believes that unless attention is given to the source of concepts, the ensuing mistake of *conceptualism* is likely. If by concepts we mean either the formulation of an inner word (*verbum*), or act of understanding by which intelligibility is grasped, then concepts are formulations of an already grasped intelligibility, with the concept referring to intelligibility through the insight. If there is no insight, the concept does not, strictly speaking, have an adequate relation to the intelligible, or at least not for the person using the concept without an insight. A teacher, say, who understands, may provide concepts for students quite capable of organizing and manipulating the concepts in the "correct" way, and yet those concepts might not mean much to students lacking the corresponding insight; for them, the concepts may be jabberwocky, but still they demonstrate the proper, or nominal, use of the terms. Perfect logic is not understanding if the originating insights are absent.

From the perspective of conceptualism, a hermeneutical approach to natural law is odd, even incoherent, since the hermeneutical approach tends to think that the questions "*What* should be done? Should *I* do it?" begin not from clear-cut definitions of the good, or concepts of human nature, but with less definite, although perhaps more meaningful, anticipations of the worthwhile or valuable. We operate in a world radically drenched with meaning and value, and pre-conceptual anticipations are not unintelligent because not conceptualized, especially since much of our moral sense is given to us by community as heritage. Of course, this basic directionality to value is not necessarily intelligible either, for not only can common sense turn out to be common nonsense, but the broad thrust toward value requires "many additional insights into and . . . concrete judgments regarding each new situation as it arises" in order to judge and choose what *I* should do *now*.[8] This is not, incidentally, anything like situation ethics, nor does it deny that some actions are intrinsically illicit, but it does acknowledge, as did Aristotle, that action is concrete and requires *phronesis* or practical wisdom about what to do, and what to do is always what I (or we) are going

---

7. I'm thoroughly indebted to Fred Lawrence for this insight, from his own example, teaching, articles, and from the essay mentioned in the previous footnote.

8. Ibid., 857.

to do here and now, and thus I (or we) require insight into the intelligible good of *this* action. As Newman put it:

> Thus in concrete reasonings we are in great measure thrown back into that condition from which logic proposed to rescue us. We judge for ourselves, by our own lights, and on our own principles; and our criterion of truth is not so much the manipulation of our propositions, as the intellectual and moral character of the person maintaining them, and the ultimate silent effect of his arguments or conclusions upon our minds.[9]

If natural law is understood as a conceptualistic rationalism, such claims cannot seem as anything other than a denial of the natural law, although perhaps a virtue theory; even natural lawyers operating in a theoretical mode as non-rationalists would find this without rigor, and certainly all forms of physicalism or biologism would, I suspect, reject this. But there is more than one type of foundation, and the real question, I take it, is not only whether natural law proceeds from universally known propositions, but where those propositions come from, and they cannot be meaningful or present to the human subject without the process by which human cognition always and everywhere must operate. Even if there are universally known first moral principles, they are not strictly foundational since the subject and their conscious operations are the means by which they could be understood and known at all.

Before every moral formulation, there is an "*inner law*. It precedes, and asks to measure, all else that might come later, including especially what we do in the name of the law. The law of any community . . . is what is generated by and only by human operators faithful to the foundational operator that is inner law. For that desire, rather than anything external to us, is our 'natural law.'"[10] That natural law, the inner law serving as "*the final criterion for all our judging, deciding, and doing is that we satisfy the unrestricted desire to know that constitutes who we are*," and such a law is not out in the world but rather "in" the transcendental notions forming the dynamic intentionality of our conscious subjectivity.[11] However much the default model and its proponents "who crave a univocal definition of law will cringe at the suggestion that the human *eros* to know the real, and to know and do the valuable, is—for crying out loud—*law, natural law*," such law is

9. Quoted in Lawrence, "Finnis on Lonergan," 859.

10. Brennan, "Asking the Right Questions," 3.

11. Ibid.

not "a (static) cosmic law."[12] Always prior to any meaningful and intelligible formulation is the criterion of our own desire to know, operational in the four levels of consciousness, and governed normatively by the transcendental precepts. The first responsibility is to genuine authenticity, and such is the natural law for humans.

This last paragraph is correct, as far as it goes, and adequately represents natural law as *achievement*, or as attained from below upwards. And yet there is also natural law, which is the same natural law, as *heritage*, both in the sense of moral formation provided by a community, but also, more radically, as enabled and actualized by *caritas*, by the gift of God's love flooding our hearts on the fourth level of consciousness, radically remaking our horizons, thus our judgments, understandings, and experiences in turn.[13]

So while it always remains the case that the inner law, the natural law, just *is* the dynamic desire as it operates and moves up the levels of consciousness toward intelligently conceived, reasonably affirmed, and responsibly chosen, that very same inner law functions as it ought in the *thoroughly converted subject*, in the person who is intellectually, morally, and religiously converted—the *spoudaios*. By our very nature, we have a thrust to self-transcendence which includes a thrust towards the scale of values—vital, social, cultural, personal, and religious—and yet the existential joker in the deck, as Lonergan somewhere puts it, entails the possibility of choosing evil, of fleeing from understanding, of loving darkness rather than light, and so our natural and inner law is fully actualized insofar as the person is genuinely authentic, and authenticity requires self-transcendence, and self-transcendence requires conversion.

The foundation of law—the natural law—*is the dynamism of the thoroughly converted person*. When tracing the history of natural law accounts, it is customary to note that "it was the sheer multiplicity and diversity of the practices and beliefs of the peoples of the earth" that led the ancients to speculate on the distinction between convention and nature—animals had nature, humans seemed to have convention, but was there something natural underlying the pluralism of human life?[14] The tradition decided there was, that "underneath the manifold . . . there existed a component or factor

12. Ibid., 21.

13. Ibid., 37–38.

14. Lonergan, *Third Collection*, 171–72.

that possessed the claims to universality and permanence of nature itself."[15] The permanent could be, and often was, considered as foundational in the first sense noted above, naturally known certitudes, but it could also "be placed in nature itself, in nature not as abstractly conceived, but as concretely operating."[16] Aristotle defines nature as the "immanent principle of movement and of rest," which, for the human, is the human spirit's integral structure, and it is the *question*, the pure question or desire to know (transcendental notions), which governs movement, just as the immanent law of the question posited the principle(s) of rest (transcendental precepts). When we are attentive, intelligent, reasonable, responsible, which is to say, when we are intellectually, morally, and religiously converted such that the way of achievement is actualized, we have our nature, our principle of motion or rest.[17]

So, too, did Aquinas argue that the person, of all creation the only thing willed for its own sake, possessed their own light of intellect; not in isolation from God, for as a creature there is no such possibility, and yet God's providence for us included our own providential care for ourselves. Natural law is the way that rational creatures participate in the eternal law—the participated theonomy of John Paul II and Martin Rhonheimer—which they do *by nature, as their nature*. Further, since everything acts for its own perfection and seeks its own end, human nature does as well, as evidenced in our intentionality or directedness, our acting for purpose—natural law as articulated by Grisez, Finnis, and Boyle—as seeking good(s) or object(ive)s. Prior to every judgment, moral or otherwise, *is* the natural law. *Lex naturalis* is *not* moral propositions and concepts but rather the thrust for meaning and value expressed in propositions, concepts, laws, systems, polities: "The source of natural right lies in the norms immanent in human intelligence, human judgment, human evaluation, human affectivity."[18]

Natural Law as Universal and Naturally Known

Natural law, we are sometimes told, cannot not be known, is known by every functioning rational agent, and anyone who does not know is either

15. Ibid., 172.
16. Ibid.
17. Ibid.
18. Ibid., 176.

mistaken or utterly dysfunctional, even bestial. The plurality of laws, moral codes, and moral judgments indicates the universal law working itself out in diverse communities, or reveals that some laws are unjust, perhaps not even laws at all but merely edicts of power or wicked customs.

If natural law is considered in the first model of foundations, this would seem to indicate that the precepts are naturally known and knowable, whether through innate knowledge, inclinations, intuition, a metaphysics of the person, or some other means. Consequently, judgments and human laws out of keeping with these precepts indicate either a mistake or injustice, but in either event the agents were culpable. They could have known better, they should have known better, and they could be critiqued, educated, and reformed according to a pattern they already knew. Some communities do throw widows on their deceased husband's funeral pyre, but no external or foreign standard should be needed to assist them in grasping the apparent injustice. Even sin could not completely destroy this knowledge, however much impaired, for the knowledge was a human inheritance impossible to completely excise from the human heart so long as it remained human. They were culpable for their ignorance, or they were bestial. QED.

Is this natural law from the heart? Yes, and no. For contemporary natural law, as in Finnis, the claim is very clearly yes, for Rhonheimer also, although perhaps slightly more muted of an affirmation. For Lonergan, the "no" accompanies the yes rather closely. First, there is "neither Jew nor Greek, but One Human Nature and Operation in All."[19] Behind and before every judgment and every community and tradition of judgments is that human activity which makes the judgments possible, namely, the integral structure of the human spirit, moved to operate by the dynamism of human eros, and healed by divine *caritas*. The four levels of consciousness is the principle of motion and rest comprising human nature, and it is universal. There is only one structure, only one immanent law to that structure, and only one set of transcendental notions and transcendental precepts articulating that immanent law. To be human is to be a person, a concrete subject, and there is no human absent potentiality for subjectivity.[20] The structure is universal.

19. The title of an essay in Crowe, *Appropriating the Lonergan Idea*, 31–50.

20. The usual questions of the incapacitated person or the person with some impairment is one I will not here address, but my answer would be the usual one of natural lawyers, namely, that that these indicate a material impediment but not a formal one, and analogous arguments can be made regarding the unborn and like cases.

Second, the structure is naturally knowable, and self-evidently so. Since self-evidency does not mean obviousness or that which is universally acknowledged, I need not claim that every subject in fact does explicitly know and affirm integral human structure as articulated, but only that intentionality analysis and subsequent self-affirmation is possible for every conscious operator if experienced, understood, judged and chosen. It is self evident in that it is not derived, but still must be understood by the referentially consistent process by which it can be affirmed. Further, because intentionality analysis, self-appropriation, and self-affirmation is referentially consistent, the structure is naturally known in that the very same principle of motion and rest—human nature operating dynamically in the integral structure—is known in the very same way that any knowledge is known. Rather than appealing to anything extrinsic, and thereby non-natural (to us), we know development from below upwards by experiencing experience, understanding, judging, and choosing; understanding experience, understanding, judging, and choosing; judging experience, understanding, judging, and choosing; and choosing experience, understanding, judging, and choosing. Since, by nature, this is what it is to know and choose, it is natural to know and choose by the very same means. It need not be explicitly affirmed by everyone for this argument to be true universally.

Third, the structure is non-revisable and impossible to deny without performative contradiction. In attempting to revise the structure, one must appeal to some data or experience it overlooks, something it has misunderstood or missed, some judgment it has incorrectly made, or some aspect of deliberation and choice made based on false judgments of fact, aberrant values apprehended in feelings, some scale of values distorted or misconstrued, or some thrust towards self-transcendence violated. One *could* not even wish to challenge the structure without performatively demonstrating its bases, and one cannot amend it except by it, and thus it cannot be denied. Like the first principles of theory, the structure cannot be proven without using the principles, and this does not beg the question but demonstrates the principles to be *first* and *underived* (*per se nota*). Retorsion, or arguments from performative contradiction, cannot prove the position, but they can defend it by showing the impossibility of coherently denying it. It is normative and universal, and also naturally known.

Fourth, at the same time, there is the reign of sin, oversight, a flight from understanding, bias, willful disregard, a love of darkness, inattentiveness, unintelligence, unreasonableness, and irresponsibility—decline, or sin, is one of the differentials of the human good and human history. As such, there may be some, even many, who reject the structure and its normative implications. Not only ignorance, but wickedness is a real human possibility, one occurring with statistical frequency, especially because of what Christian theology refers to as original sin and the concomitant loss of original justice or rectitude. While theoretical versions of natural law suggest that human nature cannot be lost because it is the formal principle of our substance, interior modes suggest that the structure and operations of human nature can be impaired, rejected, inhibited, repressed, and become largely sclerotic and bizarre. Even then, the structure cannot be vitiated, for the most evil of persons will have experiences, will have insights, make judgments, and seek what they find valuable, they just do so in those inauthentic ways which violate the transcendental precepts. Their experiences are truncated, irrationally limited, skewed, and censored wrongly; their understandings are misunderstandings; their judgments are erroneous; their choices evil—but still they *do* these things. And persons can be so utterly alienated as to unconsciously or consciously be strangers to themselves, even intentionally attempting to be so, and yet they are strangers to the subjects which they in every case are and cannot not be.

Fifth, consciousness is polymorphic and takes many forms. Not only is common sense not theory or interiority or transcendence, but the control of meaning within each mode differs, for the proverbs of common sense are not the canons of reason governing contemporary science. Further, we operate in a variety of patterns of experience, sometimes organizing our attention and connation along biological concerns, sometimes aesthetic, sometimes dramatic or existential, sometimes intellectual, and in each the world for us changes as our stance toward it alters. Again, we can be converted, thoroughly or not, and in a wide variety of combinations, perhaps intellectually converted but not religiously, perhaps morally but not intellectually, and conversions can suffer breakdowns or regressions and need not be permanent accomplishments. Because subjects are not static, neither are their horizons or worlds, and whole systems of meaning can ebb and flow as subjects change from one mode of engagement to another, including developing and breaking down, and we should not anticipate the world to be the same for the person of common sense and the scientist, the converted and the unconverted, the sinner and the saint, the authentic and inauthentic person, and each of us can be all of these at different moments. The conclusions, the judgments, the meanings are not constant or universal, but the integral structure is, for common sense and science both follow the structure in distinct ways, as does the person who is converted or not, a saint or not, authentic or not. Consciousness is structured, but it is not frozen.

Sixth, and closely related to the fifth point, we are historical.[21] In addition to the permanent and abiding nature of our structure, there is historicity, and so deeply are these two aspects conjoined in us that any "contemporary ontology would distinguish two components in concrete human reality: on the one hand, a constant human nature; on the other hand, a variable, human historicity."[22] We are not pure intellects, or pure structures, but embodied, linguistic, and communal. Social institutions, cultures, religions, literature, arts, sciences, languages can all change or evolve, sometimes quite radically, and their change brings with it changes of meaning. As just one obvious example, the meaning of family, marriage, and human sexuality is undergoing a massive and rapid change of meaning, and to understand these meanings history is necessary. Nor does development from above downwards—religious conversion—fundamentally alter this, for the way of *heritage* is not only the way of faith—knowledge born of religious love—but also of belief which codifies and articulates that faith as affections, judgments, understandings, and experiences handed on to other members of the community as tradition. To use the same example, many religious groups are undergoing revisions at every level of development with respect to marriage and family meanings and experiences. The transcendental notions are universal, natural, non-revisable and irrefutable, but categories of meaning, whether linguistic or affective or enacted, exist in history. Natural law does not preclude or end history; in fact, there is history precisely because of the dynamic desire and its many manifestations, some the mark of progress and others of decline, but in either event the prior, inner law immanent to subjectivity deals with the meanings in which humans are embedded and world-ed. Whether there are natural *meanings* is a question of real dispute, but natural law articulates how there is meaning at all, and the most coherent and authentic meanings and values in history are a matter which we must come to understand and judge, not a matter which we can simply remember, intuit, or find out there in nature.[23]

21. Lonergan, *Third Collection*, 169–71.

22. Ibid., 170.

23. I'm certainly not denying that some meanings can best fit the data, or intelligibility and so on, claiming instead that we come to understand and judge those meanings

Seventh, history is a dialectic of progress/development, decline/sin, and redemption, and human subjects, their horizons, categories, and meanings exist within a similar dialectic. Sometimes natural law is presented as if it could prescind from all these, escaping to a realm of pure, untainted meaning, but there is no meaning absent subjects—truth is not so objective as to exist without subjects, after all—and no subjects exist without being thoroughly embedded in culture, community, social practices, institutions, languages, and bodies. Natural law is not found in universal propositions, even if those are articulated by persons, but rather in the dynamic eros of the person thoroughly converted—redeemed, in other words. And even the redeemed can form a legitimate and sensible plurality of judgments and understandings. That is, natural law as grasped by interiority is actualized by transcendence.

Natural Law as Normative and Critical

But, if natural law is found in the eros of the redeemed, and if even the redeemed can have a plurality of legitimate judgments, how can natural law be normative? How can it be the basis from which to criticize injustice and ground justice? Hasn't interiority eviscerated the *law-ness* of natural law?

Pluralism is a fact, but distinguishing legitimate diversity from genuine incompatibility is not always easily accomplished, for differences take a variety of forms, some complementary, some genetic, and others dialectical because of the polymorphism of consciousness and the dialectics of the subject. Some differences may very well be bridged with the uncovering of new data or the advent of new insights.[24] In such an instance, natural law works itself out as the various parties inquire, explore, and argue out the positions, for even to engage in argument is to demonstrate the authority of the inner law and to assert its good for others as well. Still other differences are complementary, as when the specialization and division of labor within an organization or society results in different languages, systems, and expectations befitting the difference in interests, needs, and histories, even though none are self-sufficient in themselves. Other differences are genetic, as when a tradition develops, carrying along its past even as moving past it, although those differences can be understood in a kind of narrative

---

rather than simply derive them from human nature or biology. As an example of such disputes, see John Finnis's work on contraception or John Paul II's *Theology of the Body.*

24. Lonergan, *Method*, 235.

unity. Still other differences are dialectical, those "fundamental conflicts stemming from an explicit or implicit cognitional theory, an ethical stance, a religious outlook. . . . They are to be overcome only through an intellectual, moral, religious conversion."[25] Grasping this theory of difference is an achievement of our inner law, for it demonstrates the coherence and knowability even of difference, showing that not every difference threatens the coherence or universality of the inner law. Sometimes difference is just difference, sometimes not, and understanding the difference is an accomplishment.

Of these, the most serious challenge is dialectical difference representing incompatible horizons: "As fields of vision vary with one's standpoint, so too the scope of one's knowledge and the range of one's interests vary. . . . So there has arisen a metaphorical . . . meaning of the word, horizon. In this sense what lies beyond one's horizon is simply outside the range of one's knowledge and interests. . . ."[26] In dialectically related horizons, what "in one is found intelligible, in another is unintelligible. What for one is true, for another is false. What for one is good, for another is evil."[27] This incomprehension is true not only for the content of the horizon but of the horizon itself, as, for example, I do not merely think the content of the daily horoscope silly but find astrology as a whole ridiculous and bizarre, and these worlds cannot be bridged. The solution to such differences, however, is not more argument, the sort of engagement often productive in other types of differences, but conversion, for it is the basic stance or world of meaning which is at stake here and not merely this or that belief within its space. Such differences

> are not merely perspectival, for perspectivism results from the individuality of the historian, but these gross differences occur between opposed and even hostile classes. . . . They are not ordinarily to be removed by uncovering further data, for the further data, in all probability, will be as susceptible of opposed interpretations as the data at present available. The cause of the gross differences is a gross difference of horizon, the proportionate remedy is nothing less than a conversion.[28]

25. Ibid.
26. Ibid., 236.
27. Ibid.
28. Ibid., 246.

Dialectics as Converting Difference

Each of the horizons considers rejecting the others as in keeping with the inner law, even articulating coherent and complicated accounts of how they follow the transcendental precepts while the others do not. Appealing to data or arguments only confirms the various self-interpretations and there "results a babel," the solution to which occurs as *dialectics* functions to "develop positions; reverse counter-positions."[29] Positions, as articulated earlier in the text, are statements or theories about epistemology, metaphysics, and ethics compatible with the authenticity of thorough intellectual, moral, and religious conversion, while counter-positions are incompatible with the same, and are reversed when conversion is understood and effected. What might be termed the *basic position* is the understanding and affirmation that (1) knowing is a cumulative process involving the operations of four levels of consciousness, (2) objectivity is the fruit of genuine subjectivity, (3) the real is that which can be intelligently conceived and reasonably affirmed, (4) value and satisfaction are distinct, and values are structured in a set of objectives.

While dialectic has an objective structure, it matters whether the dialectician is themselves converted or not, as this is a critical-existential enterprise. For the converted, there is already experience and knowledge of positions and counter-positions, as well as the prerequisites thereof, such as intentionality analysis, noetic exegesis, and the conversions themselves. For the unconverted, or only partially converted, dialectics will seem "a very foggy procedure," and they tend to invert positions and counter-positions.[30] Further, as a person's character is so do they judge the adequacy of reasons; dialectics is not a formalized procedure but rather an engagement of persons and their horizons. Reversing a position, then, is not merely bringing to light the inadequacy of a theory but also the inauthenticity of a person, since dialectics is about horizons more than it is about data or arguments, and the horizons relevant to dialectics are those of conversion or non-conversion. To develop a position is to develop the conversion of a person, to reverse a counter-position is to reverse inauthenticity.

Dialectics occurs through the same method Lonergan presents throughout, else it would not be coherent, and requires the objectification of subjectivity as well as a revelation of "the selves that did the research, offered

29. Ibid., 247, 249.
30. Ibid., 251.

the interpretations, studied the history, passed the judgments of value."[31] That is, not only does the investigator come to know themselves, and know themselves as the self expands through the various levels of conscious-ness, but dialectics cannot occur without the revelation of conversions and breakdowns, self-affirmations, authenticity and inauthenticity, and so is an intrinsically personal engagement between persons. Dialectics is an I-Thou encounter (including my encounter with myself), not a syllogistic war; the war of syllogisms, after all, is really retained between and amongst those who occupy the same—or at least not dialectically opposed—horizons. Of course, this "crucial experiment," of the objectification of subjectivity, "will not be automatically efficacious, it will provide the open-minded, the serious, the sincere with the occasion to ask themselves some basic ques-tions, first, about others but eventually, even about themselves."[32] In a sense, dialectics just is the cumulative and self-corrective process of learning as one subject utilizing that process engages another subject doing the same, but where lack of conversion makes the engagement across horizons dia-lectical. Because the integral structure is *self-correcting*, there really is no method other than the structure itself by which to correct and engage.

In-Between Horizons

To put this another way, all sorts of moral and legal disagreements exist about a great variety of issues, some of which are prudential disagreements and others genuinely moral disputes. One picture of the natural law suggests that those disputes are resolved by appealing to a set of basic premises—the first principles of the natural law—showing how one side of the dispute violates them while the other follows consistently. Such a procedure may be helpful when the disputants both accept the same account of the natural law and disagree about a course of action, but in most moral disputes ap-peals to the natural law are not particularly persuasive, either because one party doesn't grant the natural law or because both happen to think they follow it, but mean something quite distinct and thus do not recognize the other's version. In a good many moral disputes, understanding requires the disputants appeal to data, augment hypotheses, refine arguments, modify judgments, appeal to texts, find counter-examples, pose dilemmas, and so on—the normal business of argumentation and intellectual give-and-take.

31. Ibid., 253.
32. Ibid.

Not much is gained by saying "the natural law is on my side," as if that bypassed the data, hypotheses, arguments, and so on, for all that remains to be done.[33] John Finnis, for instance, doesn't "resolve" arguments about homosexual marriage by asserting the natural law, but rather exercises the natural law by arguing, just as his opponents exercise the natural law by arguing, and while some of the arguments may be strong, others weak, some rooted in good understanding and others not, the natural law works itself out though the offering of justifications and the making of arguments; that is, through the integral structure of the human spirit and its eros. It is the natural law which corrects failures of the natural law—what else is there?

However, for those unpersuaded about the natural law itself, doubtful of its existence or knowability, it is not arguments of the usual sort but dialectics which is helpful. Again, appeals to the natural law as a series of naturally knowable propositions to prove the existence of those same propositions to one who denies them is largely a failure, and asserting that they *must* be known cannot but seem like an assertion of one horizon against another. But dialectics does not assert one horizon or even a set of arguments so much as it engages in the self-corrective process of learning to push against inauthenticity and move towards authenticity. But, this too is the natural law working itself out. Again, it is the natural law, properly understood, which corrects failures to believe the natural law—what else is there?

It must be remembered that this is an exercise in metaethics or metatheory. There are a good many disputes about this or that moral issue that cannot be immediately resolved by appealing to the natural law as I understand it. Whereas natural lawyers operating in the theoretical mode may move in a short deductive path from the first principles of natural law to a conclusion about issue x or y, my claim is that the first principles to which they refer are, in fact, not really the foundations of natural law but, insofar as those principles are intelligent, reasonable, true, and valuable, *result* from the natural law, and not as a product from a cause but from an inner *verbum*. Natural law is the foundational source of all meaning, and insofar as we follow the natural law, it is the transcendental notions driving the process of knowing and choosing, governed by the transcendental precepts, which is the immanent and normative functioning of the process, and is foundational to all meaning. From that foundational performative

33. For the natural law as exhibited in the giving of justifications, see Arkes, *First Things*, 11–30, 51–84.

source, which may need to be redeemed and healed from above downwards to function, we discover intelligibility and make judgments which can be articulated in concepts, proverbs, maxims, or even propositions of morality. Some of those propositions may very well be intelligible in a way admitting of no reasonable exceptions, while others may be rules of thumb true for the most part; some of these propositions may be self-evident in the sense that they are grasped by insight but not derived from other propositions, while others may occur farther down a chain of reasoning; some of these propositions may very well be found in one form or another in most legal systems, while others may be idiosyncratic. That may be, and I have no interest in denying a rigorous moral objectivity, but if there are propositions which are exceptionless, self-evident, and empirically universal, those propositions *still are not the natural law but the result of the natural law.*

This is not to suggest that the inner law of nature is silent and useless about controverted issues, but one does not deduce conclusions from the natural law. Instead one *follows* the natural law as a principle of motion (the thrust towards self-transcendence in thought and action) until one comes to rest (in a well-founded judgment and choice, the kind made by the *spoudaios*). Still we use this process normatively to evaluate every judgment of fact and value, every system and law, every institution and authority. The only adequate legitimization of a fact or value, system or law, institution or authority is its authenticity, and not codes or principles "that would express the eternal verities for all times and places."[34] By this I am *not* claiming that there are not articulations of code or principles which do say something true for all places and times—Kant's formula of the end in itself, or the First Commandment seem plausible candidates—but I *am* claiming that the grounding of those claims rests, ultimately, not in the propositions but on the authentic intellect coming to rest in the intelligibility they convey. I *am* claiming that some things really are true and right and good and others really are false and wrong and bad, and the difference is known to the operating subject, not in a concept or proposition, not in a theoretical anthropology, not in a physicalism, and not in a code of laws.

Perhaps this is why the natural law's relation to politics and social action is not what some think it is. In the back-and-forth of argumentation and organization which is the messy business of the polity, there are at times explicit appeals to moral principles to justify policies, or at least appeals to principles treated as somehow normative. So Lincoln and Martin

---

34. Lonergan, *Third Collection*, 11.

Luther King, Jr., appeal to the *Declaration*, just as MLK appeals to the Augustinian and Thomistic claim that an unjust law is no law at all in "Letter from a Birmingham Jail." In my reading, these are only indirect appeals to the natural law inasmuch as those principles are true, right, and good, but the truth, rightness, and goodness is ascertained by the intellect at work, and it is that work which is the natural law, not the explicit principles to which these thinkers appeal. Consequently, when thinkers wish to deliver the knock-out punch in some controversial moral dispute by appealing to a first principle of morality, they may in fact be correct that this is a true and binding principle upon all men and women of good conscience, but this, too, is only an indirect appeal to the natural law. Appealing directly to the natural law appeals to authenticity and to the thoroughly converted subject who is thereby authentic. Perhaps this is why, when Lonergan considers social renewal, and when I think about the real disorders plaguing our own time, the solution which occurs to us is not really appealing to these explicit principles of morality but to attempt to become, and assist others in becoming, authentic persons:

> There is bound to be formed a solid right that is determined to live in a world that no longer exists. There is bound to be formed a scattered left, captivated by now this, now that new development, exploring now this and now that new possibility. But what will count is a perhaps not numerous center, big enough to be at home in both the old and the new, painstaking enough to work out one by one the transitions to be made, strong enough to refuse half measures and insist on complete solutions even though it has to wait.[35]

Natural Law as Natural and Transcendent

In addition to wondering if this account provides law, it's also possible to wonder if it is at all *natural* given the prominent role of development from above downwards, or transcendence. Of all its features, perhaps the most central claim of the *lex naturalis* tradition is its accessibility to unaided human reason, precisely why the noetic effects of sin are thought so problematic, and I've accepted the noetic effects of sin ungrudgingly, even claiming that the reign of sin makes the proper exercise of reason unlikely without

35. Lonergan, *The Lonergan Reader*, 401.

the gift of God's love flooding our hearts. Since authenticity is the fruits of self-transcendence, and self-transcendence requires conversion, and religious conversion—total loving—becomes the operator by which even the way of achievement is open, how is natural law accessible to unaided reason? Perhaps I've granted too much to Protestant Prejudice.

In Thomism, the universe is hierarchical, with "gradations" of actuality. God alone is infinite act, without potency in any respect, and we can posit as a kind of place-holder a pure potency, matter, which has no act but which can become in-formed and actualized by anything which can inform it. In between, finite creatures are "restricted by the potency constituted by finite essence; yet they participate in . . . perfection simply by existing and operating, for to exist and to operate is to be in act."[36] Creatures have a measure of perfection as they have a measure of act, but not infinite act given their potency. The degree of perfection for a creature is proportionate to its finitude, its essence, and since essence grounds the acts, operations, and objects possible to that degree of perfection, the natural is that which is proportionate to a thing's actuality—not only the essence but also the acts, operations, and objects are proportionate, or natural, to the level of an entity's act.[37]

If the natural is proportionate, the supernatural is defined with reference to natural and is that which exceeds the proportion of a nature.[38] The supernatural, then, in the hierarchy of beings, is "any higher order . . . beyond the proportion of lower orders and so . . . relatively supernatural to them."[39] The relatively supernatural could be any higher integration not proportionate to a lower integration, as organic life is relatively supernatural to the organic chemical compounds which make it up but to which it does not reduce.[40] God, however, is not relatively supernatural but absolutely or infinitely so because his perfection is transcendent.[41] While nature is not proportionate to the supernatural, it is not self-enclosed or separated from it either, for nature can receive the supernatural which does not lift nature out of itself and deposit it on a higher storey, like an elevator, but

---

36. Stebbins, *Divine Initiative*, 43.

37. Ibid., 44.

38. Ibid., 55.

39. Lonergan, *Third Collection*, 25.

40. Stebbins, *Divine Initiative*, 55.

41. Lonergan, *Third Collection*, 25–26.

perfects nature, for the supernatural harmonizes nature and within created world order, for grace, too, is created, or given to us.

For Lonergan, of course, metaphysical accounts are transposed into categories of interiority, and the question is posed in those "terms of human consciousness" in which there is "the transition from the natural to the supernatural," that is, as *vertical finality*.[42] Horizontal finality is proportionate, a relation to the end which follows from the operation and intention of the perfection, and is thereby natural. Vertical finality, however, "is to an end higher than the proportionate end" which sublates the lower end, allowing the lower to participate in the higher without thereby replacing or jettisoning the horizontal finality proportionate to the lower. The proportionate end of the chemical compounds remain, for example, even when they participate in organic life, but organic life is not proportionate to the compounds. Carbon is still carbon and maintains the properties of carbon (horizontal finality) even when participating in the organic system of my body (vertical finality), and while conscious intentionality is arguably not proportionate to my organic bodily system, my mind sublates the body such that my body participates in the single *person* which I am even as my body maintains its own bodily functions which, while personal (vertical), are still bodily (horizontal).

Vertical finality is evident in the four levels of consciousness, for questions of intelligence, reasonableness, and deliberation are operators of self-transcendence by which a new level of subjectivity, of personhood, emerges even as a new intention to the world does, which is a sublation. Intelligence is not experience, and yet experience participates in intelligence; intelligence is not reasonableness, and yet intelligence participates in reasonableness; reasonableness is not responsibility, and yet reasonableness participates in responsibility. The operator allows for self-transcendence, and thus for vertical finality, because of the thrust toward self-transcendence, the dynamism, or as Lonergan later terms it, "the passionateness of being."[43]

So, too, does sanctifying grace—the gift of the Holy Spirit flooding our hearts with God's love—sublate that which is proportionate to us, but this supernatural gift does not deposit us in some new "supernatural land" or "storey," for higher orders "sublate the lower, preserving them indeed in their proper perfection and significance, but also using them, endowing

42. Ibid., 23.
43. Ibid., 29.

them with a new and fuller and higher significance, and so promoting them to ends beyond their proper scope."[44] Grace perfects nature.

Since sublation has already occurred within the subject because of our own achievement, religious conversion can be understood in terms drawn from our own achievement, and while there is a certain ontological priority to religious conversion, this loses the rigidity of conceptualist accounts. For conceptualism, nature is a concept referring to an entity, and the supernatural is also a concept conceived as something like an entity, a being, and concepts can relate but not participate, just like entities can be in proximity but not really participate—a kind of extrinsicism. But in conscious operations, we know what it means for a higher order to sublate the lower with the lower preserved and yet incorporated into the higher end, and we already know that it is the passionateness of being which allows for this.

Religious love is harmonious with the passionateness of being, although it sublates and perfects it. In the way of achievement, we accumulate experience, attain understanding, issue a judgment, and achieve real values; in the way of heritage our values are transformed and given to us in a way that radically remakes our horizons, we can reflect on those values and receive belief, understand those beliefs, and attain mature and perceptive experience, all of which allows the way of achievement to operate anew. This is a gift, yes, for the agent is the Holy Spirit communicating divine grace as supernatural love, but this love is intrinsic to us, it sublates and perfects *us* as we are in our integral, natural, and human structure.[45]

Further, achievement and heritage, development from below and above, do not exist or operate in distinct realities, for they operate in us—they operate *as* us—and "a single structure of human consciousness guides each process, the way of progress moving from experience through understanding and judgment to values, the way of tradition moving in the reverse direction from values through judgment and understanding to mature experience. It is this single structure, and the possibility of traversing it in either direction that provides a real basis for the complementarity of the two ways."[46] Consequently, the "real solution, then, to the problem of integrating . . . has to be found in human nature itself, in the constants of the structure of consciousness . . . it is primarily to the interiority . . . to

---

44. Ibid., 30.
45. Crowe, *Old Things and New*, 14.
46. Ibid., 2.

the subjectivity of the human subject" that provides the solution.[47] In other words, human nature is the constant, and even the supernatural healing of nature operates with reference to human nature, and there is a complete integration of the two ways in human nature.

The supposed un-naturalness of the supernatural, the worry that adding the divine missions to natural law somehow places it beyond natural accessibility, is a problem *only* for conceptualists for whom human nature and the supernatural are reified and static essences or entities articulated as closed concepts, but not a problem for interiority or transcendence. Further, because conceptualists tend to think of natural law as providing a universally accessible set of concepts or propositions, with revelation providing either additional concepts or some sort of spiritual and heavenly awakening, it is a genuine problem to know how to integrate these, just as it is a real problem to know what to do with sin threatening to block access to the concepts. But if nature is not a concept, entity, essence, body, or a physical or biological process, but rather human subjectivity as operational, the issues are radically transposed. The natural law is the principle of movement (transcendental notions) and rest (transcendental precepts) discovered by and discoverable in the thoroughly converted and authentic subject's self-transcendence and conscious operations, and discovered through noetic exegesis. In achievement, the operator *is* the dynamic thrust toward self-transcendence actualized by questions, just as in heritage the operator *is* the same dynamic thrust actualized by questions and remade by love. Natural law is universally accessible through noetic exegesis, and noetic exegesis is possible for any conscious agent who wishes to know, who cares to know.

CONCLUSION

Livio Melina, one of the great contemporary moral theologians, explains that "desire, therefore, shows itself to be anthropologically revelatory of the creaturely indigence constitutive of the human being. We are beings thrown into the world with the original promise that our thirst for the infinite will be quenched," and thus the great drama of human existence begins with our desire, our thrust for self-transcendence.[48] Prior to action, there is love, the

---

47. Ibid.

48. Melina, *Epiphany of Love*, 6.

principle of our every operation—what Lonergan terms the passionateness of being. This love seems to outstrip us, always reaching beyond our grasp towards an infinite horizon with which we seek union, communion, and this is the truth of our meaning. Consequently, "morality can no longer be understood as a simple list of principles directing our choices and helping us to come to correct moral judgments," for this is inadequate to love's reach.[49] Rather than deduction from metaphysics and anthropology, a turn to the perspective of the acting person places us in the drama of human subjects seeking fulfillment and genuine value.[50] Prior to ethical principles is the soul's thirst, an "insurmountable disproportion" of our desire, and natural law begins and ends in love. Not in first propositions, not in anthropology, not in biology, but in love. Created in the image of a Triune God who is the communion of love loving love, we participate in the eternal law (which is love) such that God grants to us a share of His own providence, and natural law is love's capacity to seek for that love which God is, for humans to become fundamentally what they are, lovers.

The natural law is the Great Commandment inscribed in our heart, and such a commandment, while never violating moral principles or acting against the good, is never exhausted by those principles. It is never exhausted, but it is fulfilled by the genuine and full authenticity of persons who are the only creatures made for their own sake. And because God hates nothing he has created, he communicates to persons distorted by inordinate loves and incapable of breaking their evil and inauthentic ways his own Spirit, which is love:

> It is an experience of transformation one did not bring about but rather underwent, as divine providence let evil take its course and vertical finality be heightened, as it let one's circumstances shift, one's dispositions change, new encounters occur, and—so gently and quietly—one's heart be touched. It is the experience of a new community, in which faith and hope and charity dissolve rationalizations, break determinisms, and reconcile the estranged and the alienated, and there is reaped the harvest of the Spirit that is ". . . love, joy, peace, patience, kindness, goodness, fidelity, gentleness, and self-control" (*Gal.* 5:22).[51]

---

49. Ibid., xv.

50. Ibid., xvii.

51. Lonergan, *Third Collection*, 33.

The Fruits of Prejudice, the Workings of Love

One theme prevalent in the current discussion about natural law is its apparent fecklessness in persuading those not already committed. While a good many of those objections rather artlessly assume that self-evidency is tantamount to obviousness, others, such as those of David Bentley Hart, raise serious points about whether natural law is a live option for the person of modern sensibility. Even then, however, it was not obvious that Hart had differentiated the various explanations of the natural law or if he had conflated them into a somewhat incoherent mélange, a response made by myself and Edward Feser. There is only one natural law, yes, but there are many accounts of its workings, and objections or rejections of the natural law are generally rejections of one or more of the accounts, but since the accounts differ in important ways arguments against one version may or may not apply particularly well to another. It is, I would claim, incumbent on the objectors to carefully delineate which account they reject—*Which* natural law? *Whose* explanation?

The purpose of this text was to provide something of a primer on the array of natural law accounts, utilizing the modes of meaning provided by Bernard Lonergan to classify and distinguish natural law articulated in the modes of common sense, theory, interiority, and transcendence. Certainly I have not provided an exhaustive discussion of all the major thinkers in each of the modes, nor the inner workings and viewpoints of each the thinkers over for a whole range of important issues. As a work in metatheory, my method is concrete because based on the operational workings of the individual persons that each of us are, but most of the first-order issues remain to be investigated and adjudicated. I recognize this, but my purpose was to stress and insist that those who object to the natural law ought not do so with blanket generalizations about what natural lawyers posit about the meaning of nature, law, first principles, self-evidency, autonomy, accessibility, and the effects of sin, among other things. More particularly, while the so-called Protestant Prejudice against the natural law, which I summarized under three main categories of objections—(1) natural law's autonomy, (2) natural law's inadequate commitment to Christocentrism, and (3) the noetic effects of sin—are fair and coherent, they also operate as boundary-markers, evidence of group membership and loyalty sometimes repeated without adequate understanding, nuance, and differentiation. And while I am not particularly persuaded by the Prejudice, and never have been, I grant the importance and sensibility of the objections; they aren't pointless or obviously wrong arguments, particularly against certain accounts of natural law. But are they as relevant to every articulation? Or are there versions of natural law which can grant the objections, or even incorporate them directly into the account, such that continuing to posit the objections as serious problems for natural law would be an exercise in missing the point?

I think so, and have attempted to make a case for that claim through this primer in taxonomy, providing a theory of difference and providing brief overviews or introductions to exemplary thinkers of each category of meaning:

1. Natural law operates within stages of meaning, and thus there are natural law accounts articulated from the standpoint of common sense, theory, and interiority. Each mode of meaning brings different emphases and implications for the account.

2. The usual Protestant objections to natural law—the "Protestant Prejudice"—are objections directed toward natural law as it developed within the theoretical mode of meaning, and as such are reasonable and sensible objections, even if not entirely persuasive.

3. Contemporary natural law—John Paul II, Martin Rhonheimer, the so-called new natural law (NNL), and the cosmopolitanism of Bernard Lonergan—have moved beyond the theoretical mode into interiority. While these versions are not reducible to each other, and in fact

disagree on several important issues, particularly in application, all operate from within the mode of interiority rather than theory.

4. Natural law understood from the mode of interiority and transcendence is quite able to include the effects of sin on intellect and will, the role of grace, the importance of community, history (including salvation history) and the centrality of the Gospel. For Protestants to continue the usual objections without differentiation is to commit a straw man, attacking natural law as *theory* as if this defeats natural law as *interiority* and as *transcendence.*[1]

5. An account of natural law incorporating history, sin, grace, and Gospel remains natural law, but it is natural law opening to a further mode of meaning beyond interiority. I am here attempting to articulate the broad outlines of natural law in a new mode, namely, from transcendence, *the perspective of love.*

Somewhat briefly, I'll summarize my response to the three objections: (1) autonomy, (2) insufficient Christocentrism, and (3) sin.

AUTONOMOUS NATURE?

Is the natural law a humanist project illicitly committed to hopes of reconciliation independent of grace and thus in competition with the gospel, and does it's static and universal achievement nullify the need for Christian virtue and the work of the Church?

First, natural law claims and exercises the rightful autonomy of reason and nature. There's nothing incompatible with the doctrine of creation and natural law, for nature is proportionate to our finite perfection and finality, which is in no way God's absolute perfection and finality, and our perfection does not—cannot—compete with God since he is transcendent and since it was He who gifted to us our finite natures and our share of providence or self-governance. Yes, we are created as persons, the only creature God willed for its own sake, and there is a rightful integrity and autonomy proportionate to persons. For interiority, that nature can be grasped through noetic exegesis and is the integral structure of human spirit, the operator of our eros, from which we can—without divine assistance—know ourselves, our directed intentionality, the normative precepts which follow, and can

---

1. This is an argument I posited in "Protestant Prejudice," 21–30. See also my "Thomism and Noetic Sin, Transposed," 7–28.

develop positions and reverse counter-positions as they relate to epistemology, metaphysics, ethics, and theology. There is a way of achievement or development from below upwards as we move from experience to understanding to judgment to choice.

Second, at the same time, there is development from above downwards; the pouring out of God's love through the Holy Spirit to radically remake our horizons, transvalue our values, and subsequently reshape our judgments, understandings and experiences even as conditioning our intellectual and moral conversions to that we might move into full authenticity. This supernatural gift is not proportionate to our nature, but it does sublate and perfect our nature *as* nature. The two vectors of development both operate in and as human nature, which always remains this nature while retaining its own proper functions (horizontal finality) and developmental potency (vertical finality) as well as its passive potentiality to the supernatural gift of God's love. There is autonomy, but autonomy is not independence from God but rather the liberty to overcome alienation and attain authenticity.

Third, two things are necessary for faith, both the beliefs and doctrines proposed "in order than man believe anything explicitly" (*fides ex auditu*), as well as the will to believe and assent which is "God moving man inwardly by grace" (*fides ex infusione*).[2] Of these, the second is the invisible mission of the Spirit moving our values and love through faith, the knowledge born of religious love, while the first, ultimately, depends on the visible mission of the Son in which He is the "sacrament of man's encounter with God ... the way to the new creation ... Emmanuel, God with us," and who sent the disciples on a mission to teach and proclaim that Word in history.[3] The way of heritage, then, includes the will or love given to us by grace, *and* the tradition, beliefs, and community in which we are in-formed and formed in our affections, values, beliefs, understandings, and experiences. Natural law *in no way* assumes or requires us to be disembodied intellects free of history, community, language, and guidance; instead, the turn to the concrete subject acknowledges our embodiment, sociality, historicality, and hermeneutical access to ourselves. Every person begins in the way of heritage in that they are social and dependent animals, and as plain persons they are formed by families, schools, the laws, social norms, and so on, taught what to value, trained how to feel, believe, think, and sense so they can appropri-

2. Aquinas, *ST* II-II 6.1; cf. Lonergan, *Third Collection*, 32.
3. Lonergan, *Third Collection*, 32.

ate that same singular and unified subjectivity which they are and move into the way of achievement as autonomous. Such heritage has as a prime example the Christian family to which the Word is mediated through the tradition, creeds, sacraments, social practices, narratives, and Scriptures which we are moved to love and accept by the gift of God's love through the Spirit. Because there is only one subject who moves by achievement or heritage, whether that heritage is the natural one of the family and polity or the supernatural one of the Church, it is *our nature* which is formed and redeemed such that progress is again possible.

Fourth, while the fruits of authenticity operate in human nature, even when given from above downwards, presupposing and perfecting that one nature, our ability to believe and do certain moral duties, even those duties discovered by reason, may require faith. As Martin Rhonheimer explains, even though the basic requirements of morality are not derived from revelation, if we consider the morally good only from the perspective of how we experience our own capacities absent being-in-love, there will be an inability to fully accept the requirements of morality, and they will be lessened and even denied.[4] Nothing in principle denies natural knowledge, but we *will* not accept what we consider ourselves *incapable* of doing without authenticity. Finnis makes a similar point about refusing to do intrinsically evil acts even when they seem justified by grave danger or threat, for the one resting in the providence of God *will* accept that basic human values ought never be directly and knowingly harmed, even though this is naturally knowable to all. But this *will* to accept is the gift of love, the remaking of horizons, the invisible mission of the Spirit (*fides ex infusione*), even though performed humanly.

Autonomy is never denied, but neither does autonomy preclude grace, for decline results in our alienation and failure of autonomy while redemption brings with it the liberty of vertical finality, the overcoming of alienation, and freedom to be who and what we are. Grace brings with it both faith (as love) and belief (as tradition) as well as the community of Christian fellowship, imagination, and sacramental life, none of which is foreign to the natural law, for nature is open to grace and grace redeems all of life. Old models of extrinsicism, two-storey realities, and rigid conceptual and metaphysical domains are transposed by interiority, and so too should the usual objections be transposed, and perhaps put to rest.

---

4. Rhonheimer, *Perspective of the Acting Person*, 11.

History, Drama, Christocentrism

Interiority does not begin from theoretical anthropology or classical theory of soul. It does not accept faculty psychology with set and separate faculties. It uses but does not cede all meaning to deductive logic. It does not start from universal first propositions of science from which particulars are deduced. Instead, it begins with the concrete subject operating and performing as a result of the dynamic tendencies of consciousness. By adverting to our directed intentionality, the objectives or goods which we seek in knowing and choosing, we are able to note the operations and levels of consciousness which we ourselves are. But while there is an integral and foundational structure which does not change in its transcendental possibilities, the structure is intrinsically dynamic, developmental, historical, and temporal—it is subject, not soul; method, not logic; noetic exegesis, not first propositions; levels of consciousness in their integral unity, not faculties. The *whole* mode of interiority is dramatic and historical.

While certain versions of theory may risk becoming static and enclosed, thus creating a sphere of pure nature poorly integrated with salvation history, interiority is not so static, even articulating the need for transcendence. The dialectics of history and the dialectics of the subject include the differentials of progress/development, decline/sin, and redemption—a dramatic understanding of the existential subject as they are in themselves, in community, and in history. Further, each of the differentials is governed by a form of love and its order and disorder. Insofar as we are governed by the dynamic desire to know, the *Sorge* of meaning, the thrust to self-transcendence, the further question, the transcendental notions, then we are governed by our nature, the principle of motion. In following love, we follow natural law, but this is a drama of self-development and motion toward rest. However, insofar as our loves are bent, limited, skewed, repressed, inhibited, sclerotic, biased, or self-satisfied, then the order of love is refused and we become inauthentic. But insofar as God's love pours into our hearts, we are being-in-love, a radical shaking of our horizons by love and for love, and this radical, total loving, remakes us at every level of our consciousness and every operation, experience, understanding, judgment, and decision. We are new creatures, with hearts of stone become hearts of flesh.

Philosophically, we can turn to the experience of love and unpack it phenomenologically. Theologically we can explore it as religious. As Christians, we understand and name this love as the missions of the Son and

Spirit, as the Word made flesh who sends both his disciples and Spirit into the world to remake loves and allow for progress and authentic humanity once again. Thus, when the Spirit gives us an inclination to faith, a heart of love, we meet the Son, our love is the love of God, and we become authentically ourselves insofar as we meet, follow, and obey the love of God infused into us. Such natural law in no way rejects, and in fact joyously embraces and requires Christ as the redeemer reveals not only God but also "man to himself." [5] Without that revelation, there is only inauthenticity.

THE NOETIC EFFECTS OF SIN

Absent God's love, inauthenticity is our only possibility because we are under the reign of sin. The objection that natural law requires sanguinity about sin, even a semi-Pelagian optimism that while will might be harmed the intellect is still pristine, or even a belief that while grace was lost we are still perfect in our natures, makes decent sense in response to theoretical modes. Concepts and natures do not have histories or change because of sin; they remain what they are.

For interiority and transcendence, sin is a disruption of love, and love is that which brings unity, directionality, normativity, and functionality to the entire structure of our subjectivity. With sin, we do not love, do not will to know, do not want self-transcendence, and thus are captive to the reign of sin. Held by dramatic bias which censors, represses, and inhibits those images and affects leading to insights we do not wish to. Held by individual bias seeking only satisfaction and not the common good. Held by group bias refusing insights, questions, and contributions, shorting itself on the full range of intelligence and reasonableness necessary for progress while avoiding disruptions, shocks, and short patterns of decline. Held by general or practical bias forcing intelligence to serve the master of short term practicality, of gain, of satisfaction, of pleasure, rather than allowing the exigencies of our nature to work themselves out in keeping with our fundamental intentionality. So bent, we lose the civilizational and cultural resources to ask good questions, seek data, form hypotheses, seek adequate reasons, perform responsibly, and in the lacunae of intelligence our actions, judgments, policies become ever less ordered, even opening up the longer pattern of decline and its long decline into incoherence, violence,

---

5. John Paul II, *Redemptor Hominis*, 10.

and barbarism. We can, and do, subvert the scale of value; we can, and do, flee from understanding; we can, and do, reject insight; we can, and do, love darkness rather than light. We are disharmonized by original sin, and basic sin is a rejection of the pure question, of love, and so we capitulate to the reign of sin from which we can only be redeemed but are powerless to escape by our own achievement. We relentlessly dig our own graves, and reason suffers the totality of depravity.

In short, I see almost no reason for the trump card of the noetic effects of sin to be trotted out against natural law. We've changed suits, and the former trump is just another card, and one easily handled, sublimated, and incorporated. For interiority and transcendence, sin is not an objection to natural law but a differential of the human good which natural law seeks and notionally anticipates. There is, now, for us, no natural law without sin, just as there is, now, for us, no natural law without redemption. There is sin, and there is redemption. If anything, the real issue is about limited atonement, for natural law accepts the totality of depravity, just as it accepts that the Word is offered to all who wish it and the Holy Spirit pours out love to any who would have it, to any who would be authentic. As Hopkins knew, "And for all this, nature is never spent; / There lives the dearest freshness deep down things; / And though the last lights off the black West went / Oh, morning, at the brown brink eastward, springs— / Because the Holy Ghost over the bent / World broods with warm breast and with ah! bright wings.//"

The Further Question

As with all endeavors, this is partial and incomplete. I suspect its readers will have queries, objections, issues, disagreements. I've misconstrued or misunderstood, they'll think, and perhaps so. Or I should have consulted this source or that thinker, and perhaps so. Or metaethics is too abstract, whatever my claims about the concrete subject, and at the end of the book we have no there there; we've sharpened a knife but not cut anything, and it's impossible to know the fruits of natural law until we do something with it, tackled some concrete ethical issues—and perhaps so.

These are further questions, and like all such questions, they appeal to data, reach understandings, make judgments, and exercise choice. Like all questions, they manifest the Further Question, the pure disinterested desire to know, the transcendental notions. Like all questions, they manifest the integral structure of the human spirit and are thereby performative demonstrations of the truth of natural law. Whatever the failings of the project, the objections and questions are proof of my central claim which can in no way be refuted without performative contradiction.

That is natural law in a new mode, the perspective of love.

Bibliography

Aeschylus. *Aeschylus I: Oresteia: Agamemnon, The Libation Bearers, The Eumenides.* Edited by David Grene and Richmond Lattimore. Chicago: University of Chicago Press, 1991.

Anderson, Matthew Lee. "Assorted Thoughts on Evangelicals and Natural Law." *Mere Orthodoxy* (March 28, 2011). http://mereorthodoxy.com/assorted-thoughts-on-evangelicals-and-natural-law/#sthash.hKXD3P22.dpuf.

———. "Why Natural Law Arguments Make Evangelicals Uncomfortable." *Christianity Today* (March 2011). http://www.christianitytoday.com/ct/2011/marchweb-only/naturallawarguments.html.

Aquinas, Thomas. *Summa Contra Gentiles.* Notre Dame: University of Notre Dame Press, 1975.

Aristotle. *The Basic Works of Aristotle.* Edited by Richard McKeon. New York: Random House, 1941.

Arkes, Hadley. *First Things: An Inquiry into the First Principles of Morals and Justice.* Princeton: Princeton University Press, 1986.

Baer, H. David. "Some Reflections on the Problem of Natural Law." *Journal of Lutheran Ethics* 10 (March 2010). http://www.elca.org/What-We-Believe/Social-Issues/Journal-of-Lutheran-Ethics/Issues/March-2010/Some-Reflections-on-the-Problem-of-Natural-Law.aspx.

Ballor, Jordan J. "Natural Law and Protestantism—A Review Essay." *Christian Scholar's Review* 41 (2012) 193–209.

Bamforth, Nicholas, and David A. J. Richards. *Patriarchal Religion, Sexuality, and Gender: A Critique of New Natural Law.* New York: Cambridge University Press, 2008.

Barden, Garrett. "Insight and Mirrors." *Method: Journal of Lonergan Studies* 4 (1986) 85–104.

Barmen Declaration. In *The Church's Confession Under Hitler*, edited by Arthur C. Cochrane, 237–42. Philadelphia: Westminster, 1962. http://www.sacred-texts.com/chr/barmen.htm.

Benedict XVI. "The Regensburg Address." http://www.vatican.va/holy_father/benedict_xvi/speeches/2006/september/documents/hf_ben-xvi_spe_20060912_university-regensburg_en.html.

Bennett, Jana Marguerite. "Stanley Hauerwas's Influence on Catholic Moral Theologians." *Journal of Moral Theology* 1 (2012) 148–69.

Blackwood, Jeremy. "Love and Lonergan's Cognitional-Intentional Anthropology: An Inquiry on the Question of the 'Fifth Level of Consciousness.'" PhD diss., Marquette

University, 2012. http://epublications.marquette.edu/cgi/viewcontent.cgi?article=11 96&context=dissertations_mu.

Boyd, Craig A. *Shared Morality: A Narrative Defense of Natural Law Ethics*. Grand Rapids: Brazos, 2007.

Boyle, Joseph. "Natural Law and the Ethics of Traditions." In *Natural Law Theory: Contemporary Essays*, edited by Robert P. George, 3–30. Oxford: Clarendon, 1992.

Braaten, Carl E. "God in Public Life: Rehabilitating the 'Orders of Creation.'" *First Things* (December 1990). http://www.firstthings.com/article/2007/10/004-god-in-public-life-rehabilitating-the-orders-of-creation-36.

———. *Principles of Lutheran Theology*. Philadelphia: Fortress, 1983.

———. "Protestants and Natural Law." *First Things* (January 1992). http://www.firstthings.com/article/2007/12/002-protestants-and-natural-law-28.

———. "A Response." In *A Preserving Grace: Protestants, Catholics, and Natural Law*, edited by Michael Cromartie, 31–40. Washington, DC: Ethics and Public Policy Center, 1997.

Brennan, Michael McKinley. "Asking the Right Questions: Harnessing the Insights of Bernard Lonergan for the Rule of Law." *Journal of Law and Religion* 21 (2006) 1–38.

Budziszewski, J. *The Line Through the Heart: Natural Law as Fact, Theory, and Sign of Contradiction*. Wilmington, DE: ISI, 2009.

———. *What We Can't Not Know: A Guide*. Dallas: Spence, 2003.

———. *Written on the Heart: The Case for Natural Law*. Downers Grove, IL: InterVarsity, 1997.

Buttiglione, Rocco. *Karol Wojtyla: The Thought of the Man Who Became Pope John Paul II*. Translated by Paolo Guietti and Francesca Murphy. Grand Rapids: Eerdmans, 1997.

Byrne, Patrick. "What Is *Our* Scale of Value Preference?" *Lonergan Workshop* 21 (2008) 43–64.

———. "Which Scale of Value Preference? Lonergan, Scheler, Von Hildebrand, and Doran." In *Meaning and History in Systematic Theology: Essays in Honor of Robert M. Doran*, edited by John D. Dadosky, 19–49. Milwaukee: Marquette University Press, 2009.

Carter, Joe. "Why Aren't Natural Law Arguments More Persuasive?" *First Thoughts* (March 28, 2011). http://www.firstthings.com/blogs/firstthoughts/2011/03/28/why-aren%E2%80%99t-natural-law-arguments-more-persuasive/.

Catechism of the Catholic Church. 2nd ed. Washington, DC: Libreria Editrice Vaticana, 1997.

Charles, J. Daryl. "Burying the Wrong Corpse: Protestants and the Natural Law." In *Natural Law and Evangelical Political Thought*, edited by Jessie Covington et al., 3–27. Lanham, MD: Lexington, 2012.

———. "Protestant Bias against the Natural Law: A Critique." *Journal of Lutheran Ethics* 10 (March 2010). http://www.elca.org/What-We-Believe/Social-Issues/Journal-of-Lutheran-Ethics/Issues/March-2010/Protestant-Bias-against-the-Natural-Law.aspx.

———. "Protestants and the Natural Law." *First Things* (December 2006). http://www.firstthings.com/article/2007/01/protestants-and-natural-law-39.

———. *Retrieving the Natural Law: A Return to Moral First Things*. Grand Rapids: Eerdmans, 2008.

Compendium of the Social Doctrine of the Church. Compiled by the Pontifical Council for Justice and Peace. http://www.vatican.va/roman_curia/pontifical_councils/

justpeace/documents/rc_pc_justpeace_doc_20060526_compendio-dott-soc_
en.html.

Couenhoven, Jesse. "Karl Barth's (Rejection of) Natural Law: An Eschatological Natural
Law Theory of Divine Command." In *Natural Law and Evangelical Political Thought*,
edited by Jesse Covington et al., 35–56. Lanham, MD: Lexington, 2012. http://www
.academia.edu/2204978/Karl_Barths_Eschatological_rejection_of_Natural_Law_
An_Eschatological_Natural_Law_Theory_of_Divine_Command.

Covington, Jesse, et al., eds. *Natural Law and Evangelical Political Thought*. Lanham, MD:
Lexington, 2012.

Cromartie, Michael, ed. *A Preserving Grace: Protestants, Catholics, and Natural Law*.
Washington, DC: Ethics and Public Policy Center, 1997.

Crosby, John F. *The Selfhood of the Human Person*. Washington, DC: Catholic University
of America Press, 1996.

Crowe, Frederick E. *Appropriating the Lonergan Idea*. Edited by Michael Vertin. Toronto:
University of Toronto Press, 2006.

———. *Old Things and New: A Strategy for Education*. Atlanta: Scholars, 1985.

Crysdale, Cynthia. "Revisioning Natural Law: From the Classicist Paradigm to Emergent
Probability." *Theological Studies* 56 (1995) 464–84.

DiNoia, J. A., and Romanus Cessario. *Veritatis Splendor and the Renewal of Moral
Theology*. Princeton: Scepter, 1999.

Dooyeweerd, Herman. *In the Twilight of Western Thought*. Nutley, NJ: Craig, 1980.

Dreher, Rod. "Why Natural Law Arguments Fail." *American Conservative* (February
20, 2013). http://www.theamericanconservative.com/dreher/why-natural-law-
arguments-fail/.

Feser, Edward. "A Christian Hart, a Humean Head." *First Things* (March 6, 2013). http://
www.firstthings.com/onthesquare/2013/03/a-christian-hart-a-humean-head.

———. "Sheer Hart Attack: Morality, Rationality, and Theology." *Public Discourse* (April
24, 2013). http://www.thepublicdiscourse.com/2013/04/9978/.

Finnis, John. *Aquinas: Moral, Political, and Legal Theory*. New York: Oxford University
Press, 1998.

———. *Fundamentals of Ethics*. Washington, DC: Georgetown University Press, 1983.

———. *Intention and Identity: Collected Essays, Volume II*. New York: Oxford University
Press, 2011.

———. *Moral Absolutes: Tradition, Revision, and Truth*. Washington, DC: Catholic
University of America Press, 1991.

———. *Natural Law and Natural Rights*. Oxford: Clarendon, 1980.

———. *Reason in Action: Collected Essays, Volume I*. New York: Oxford University Press,
2011.

———. *Religion and Public Reasons: Collected Essays, Volume V*. New York: Oxford
University Press, 2011.

Finnis, John, and Anthony Fisher. "Theology and the Four Principles of Bioethics: A
Roman Catholic View." http://www.ewtn.com/library/PROLIFE/4PRINCES.TXT.

Fitzpatrick, Joseph. *Philosophical Encounters: Lonergan and the Analytical Tradition*.
Toronto: University of Toronto Press, 2005.

Flanagan, Joseph. *Quest for Self-Knowledge: An Essay in Lonergan's Philosophy*. Toronto:
University of Toronto Press, 1997.

Francis. *Encyclical Letter Lumen Fidei. The Light of Faith*. Boston: Pauline, 2013.

George, Robert P. *In Defense of the Natural Law*. New York: Oxford University Press, 1999.

———. *Natural Law Theory: Contemporary Essays.* Oxford: Clarendon, 1992.

Gilson, Etienne. *Methodical Realism.* Front Royal, VA: Christendom, 1990.

———. *The Philosophy of St. Thomas Aquinas.* New York: Dorset, 1929.

Girgis, Sherif, et al. "What Is Marriage?" *Harvard Journal of Law and Public Policy* 34 (2010) 245–87.

Goheen, Michael G., and Craig G. Bartholomew. *Living at the Crossroads: An Introduction to Christian Worldview.* Grand Rapids: Baker Academic, 2008.

Gómez-Lobo, Alfonso. *Morality and the Human Goods: Introduction to Natural Law Ethics.* Washington, DC: Georgetown University Press, 2002.

Grabill, Stephen J. *Rediscovering the Natural Law in Reformed Theological Ethics.* Grand Rapids: Eerdmans, 2006.

Griffiths, Paul. "The Nature of Desire." *First Things* (December 2009). http://www.firstthings.com/article/2009/11/the-nature-of-desire.

Grisez, Germain G. "The First Principle of Practical Reason: A Commentary on the *Summa Theologiae*, 1-2, Question 94, Article 2." *Natural Law Forum* 10 (1965) 168–201.

Grisez, Germain, Joseph Boyle, and John Finnis. "Practical Principles, Moral Truth and Ultimate Ends." *The American Journal of Jurisprudence* 32 (1987) 99–151.

Hadot, Pierre. *What Is Ancient Philosophy?* Translated by Michael Chase. Cambridge, MA: Belknap, 2002.

Hall, Pamela M. *Narrative and the Natural Law: An Interpretation of Thomistic Ethics.* Notre Dame: University of Notre Dame Press, 1994.

Hart, David Bentley. *The Beauty of the Infinite: The Aesthetics of Christian Truth.* Grand Rapids: Eerdmans, 2003.

———. "Is, Ought, and Nature's Laws." *First Things* (March 2013) 71–72.

———. "Nature Loves to Hide." *First Things* (May 2013) 71–72.

Hart, H. L. A. *The Concept of Law.* 2nd ed. New York: Oxford University Press, 1994.

Hauerwas, Stanley. *A Community of Character: Toward a Constructive Christian Social Ethic.* Notre Dame: University of Notre Dame Press, 1981.

———. *The Peaceable Kingdom: A Primer in Christian Ethics.* Notre Dame: University of Notre Dame Press, 1983.

Heidegger, Martin. *Being and Time.* Translated by John Macquarrie and Edward Robinson. New York: Harper & Row, 1962.

Henry, Carl F. H. "Natural Law and a Nihilistic Culture." *First Things* (January 1995). http://www.firstthings.com/article/2008/08/004-natural-law-and-a-nihilistic-culture-28.

Hittinger, Russell. *A Critique of the New Natural Law Theory.* Notre Dame: University of Notre Dame Press, 1987.

———. *The First Grace: Rediscovering the Natural Law in a Post-Christian World.* Wilmington, DE: ISI, 2003.

———. "Natural Law and Catholic Moral Theology." In *A Preserving Grace: Protestants, Catholics, and Natural Law*, edited by Michael Cromartie, 1–40. Grand Rapids: Eerdmans, 1997.

Jacobs, Alan. "More on Natural Law Arguments." *American Conservative* (February 20, 2013). http://www.theamericanconservative.com/jacobs/more-on-natural-law-arguments/.

Jaeger, Werner. *Paideia: the Ideals of Greek Culture.* Vol. 1, *Archaic Greece: The Mind of Athens.* Translated by Gilbert Highet. New York: Oxford University Press, 1945.

Jensen, Steven J. "Thomistic Perspectives? Martin Rhonheimer's Version of Virtue Ethics." *American Catholic Philosophical Quarterly* 86 (2012) 135–59.

John Paul II. *Encyclical Letter Redemptor Hominis. The Redeemer of Man.* Boston: Pauline, 1979.

———. *Encyclical Letter Veritatis Splendor. The Splendor of Truth.* Boston: Pauline, 1993.

Johnson, Thomas K. *Natural Law Ethics: An Evangelical Proposal.* Bonn: Kultur und Wissenschaft, 2005.

Kaczor, Christopher. *Proportionalism and the Natural Law Tradition.* Washington, DC: Catholic University of America Press, 2002.

Kallenberg, Brad J. *Ethics as Grammar: Changing the Postmodern Subject.* Notre Dame: University of Notre Dame Press, 2001.

Knippenberg, Joseph. "Evangelicals and Natural Law Update." *First Thoughts* (March 28, 2011). http://www.firstthings.com/blogs/firstthoughts/2011/03/28/evangelicals-and-natural-law-update/.

Kramer, Matthew H. "What Good Is Truth?" *Canadian Journal of Law and Jurisprudence* 309 (1992) 309–19.

Lawrence, Frederick G. "Finnis on Lonergan: A Reflection." *Villanova Law Review* 57 (2012) 849–72.

———. "Lonergan and Aquinas: The Postmodern Problematic of Theology and Ethics." In *The Ethics of Aquinas,* edited by Stephen J. Pope, 437–55. Washington, DC: Georgetown University Press, 2002.

Lewis, C. S. *The Abolition of Man.* New York: HarperOne, 2001.

Lisska, Anthony J. *Aquinas's Theory of Natural Law: An Analytic Reconstruction.* Oxford: Clarendon, 1996.

Lonergan, Bernard. *Grace and Freedom: Operative Grace in the Thought of St Thomas Aquinas.* Edited by F. Crowe and R. Doran. Collected Works of Bernard Lonergan 1. Toronto: University of Toronto Press, 2000.

———. *Insight: A Study of Human Understanding.* Edited by F. Crowe and R. Doran. Collected Works of Bernard Lonergan 3. Toronto: University of Toronto Press, 1992.

———. *The Lonergan Reader.* Edited by Mark D. Morelli and Elizabeth A. Morelli. Toronto: University of Toronto Press, 1997.

———. *Method in Theology.* New York: Seabury, 1972.

———. *Philosophical and Theological Papers, 1965–1980.* Edited by Robert C. Croken and Robert M. Doran. Collected Works of Bernard Lonergan 17. Toronto: University of Toronto Press, 2004.

———. *A Second Collection: Papers.* Edited by W. F. J. Ryan and B. Tyrrell. Toronto: University of Toronto Press, 1974.

———. *A Third Collection: Papers.* Edited by Frederick E. Crowe. New York: Paulist, 1985.

———. *Topics in Education: The Cincinnati Lectures of 1959 on the Philosophy of Education.* Edited by F. Crowe and R. Doran. Collected Works of Bernard Lonergan 10. Toronto: University of Toronto Press, 1993.

———. *Understanding and Being: The Halifax Lectures on Insight.* Edited by Elizabeth A. Morelli and Mark D. Morelli. 2nd ed. Collected Works of Bernard Lonergan 5. Toronto: University of Toronto Press, 1990.

———. *Verbum: Word and Idea in Aquinas.* Edited by F. Crowe and R. Doran. Collected Works of Bernard Lonergan 2. Toronto: University of Toronto Press, 1997.

Long, Steven A. "A Brief Disquisition Regarding the Nature of the Object of the Moral Act According to St. Thomas Aquinas." *The Thomist* 67 (2003) 45–71.

———. "Natural Law or Autonomous Practical Reason: Problems for the New Natural Law Theory." In *St. Thomas Aquinas and the Natural Law Tradition: Contemporary Perspectives*, edited by John Goyette et al., 165–93. Washington, DC: Catholic University of America Press, 2004.

———. *The Teleological Grammar of the Moral Act*. Naples, FL: Sapientia, 2007.

Lubac, Henri de. *Augustinianism and Modern Theology*. Translated by Lancelot Sheppard. New York: Crossroad, 2000.

———. *A Brief Catechesis on Nature and Grace*. Translated by Richard Arnandez. San Francisco: Ignatius, 1984.

MacIntyre, Alasdair. "Theories of Natural Law in the Culture of Advanced Modernity." In *Common Truths: New Perspectives on Natural Law*, edited by Edward B. McLean, 91–115. Wilmington, DE: ISI, 2000.

———. *Three Rival Versions of Moral Enquiry: Encyclopedia, Genealogy, and Tradition*. Notre Dame: University of Notre Dame Press, 1990.

Maritain, Jacques. *Natural Law: Reflections on Theory and Practice*. Edited by William Sweet. South Bend, IN: St. Augustine's, 2001.

May, William E. *An Introduction to Moral Theology*. 2nd ed. Huntington, IN: Our Sunday Visitor, 2003.

McCormick, John F. *Scholastic Metaphysics*. Part 1: *Being, Its Division and Causes*. Chicago: Loyola University Press, 1940.

McCormick, Richard A. "Some Early Reactions to *Veritatis Splendor*." *Theological Studies* 55 (1994) 481–506.

McGraw, Bruan T. "The Doctrine of Creation and the Possibilities of an Evangelical Natural Law." In *Natural Law and Evangelical Political Thought*, edited by Jesse Covington et al., 57–84. Lanham, MD: Lexington, 2012.

McInerny, Ralph. "The Principles of Natural Law." *American Journal of Jurisprudence* 25 (1980) 1–15.

McNeill, John T. "Natural Law in the Teaching of the Reformers." *Journal of Religion* 26 (1946) 168–82.

Melina, Livio. *The Epiphany of Love: Towards a Theological Understanding of Christian Action*. Grand Rapids: Eerdmans, 2010.

———. *Sharing in Christ's Virtues: For a Renewal of Moral Theology in Light of* Veritatis Splendor. Translated by William E. May. Washington, DC: Catholic University of America Press, 2001.

Milbank, John. *The Suspended Middle: Henri de Lubac and the Debate Concerning the Supernatural*. Grand Rapids: Eerdmans, 2005.

———. *Theology and Social Theory: Beyond Secular Reason*. Malden, MA: Blackwell, 2006.

Millman, Noah. "What's Natural about Natural Law?" *American Conservative* (February 25, 2013). http://www.theamericanconservative.com/millman/whats-natural-about-natural-law/.

Mohler, Albert. "Moral Argument in Modern Times: A Conversation with Robert P. George." *AlbertMohler.com* (January 24, 2011). http://www.albertmohler.com/2011/01/24/moral-argument-in-modern-times-a-conversation-with-robert-p-george-2/.

Moroney, Stephen K. "How Sin Affects Scholarship: A New Model." *Christian Scholar's Review* 28 (1999) 432–51. http://www.asa3.org/ASA/topics/ethics/CSRSpring-1999Moroney.html.

———. *The Noetic Effects of Sin: A Historical and Contemporary Exploration of How Sin Affects Our Thinking*. Lanham, MD: Lexington, 2000.

Murphy, William F., Jr. "Aquinas on the Object and Evaluation of the Moral Act: Rhonheimer's Approach and Some Recent Interlocutors." *Josephinum Journal of Theology* 15 (2008) 205–42.

Novak, Michael. "Bernard Lonergan: A New Approach to Natural Law." *Proceedings of the American Catholic Philosophical Association* 41 (1967) 246–49.

O'Donovan, Oliver. *Resurrection and Moral Order: An Outline for Evangelical Ethics*. 2nd ed. Grand Rapids: Eerdmans, 1994.

Pearcey, Nancy. *Total Truth: Liberating Christianity from Its Cultural Captivity*. Wheaton, IL: Crossway, 2005.

Pinckaers, Servais. *The Sources of Christian Ethics*. Translated by Mary Thomas Noble. Washington, DC: Catholic University of America Press, 1995.

Plato. *The Collected Dialogues of Plato*. Edited by Edith Hamilton and Huntington Cairns. Princeton: Princeton University Press, 1989.

———. *Theatetus*. Edited by Bernard Williams. Translated by M. J. Levett and revised by Myles Burnyeat. Indianapolis: Hackett, 1992.

Potemra, Michael. "A Bracing Challenge to Conservative Natural-Law Theorists." *National Review Online* (February 13, 2013). http://www.nationalreview.com/corner/340579/bracing-challenge-conservative-natural-law-theorists-michael-potemra.

Reimers, Adrian J. *Truth About the Good: Moral Norms in the Thought of John Paul II*. Ave Maria, FL: Sapientia, 2011.

Rhonheimer, Martin. *Natural Law and Practical Reason: A Thomist View of Moral Autonomy*. Translated by Gerald Malsbary. New York: Fordham University Press, 2000.

———. *The Perspective of Morality: Philosophical Foundations of Thomistic Virtue Ethics*. Translated by Gerald Malsbury. Washington, DC: Catholic University of America Press, 2011.

———. *The Perspective of the Acting Person: Essays in the Renewal of Thomistic Moral Philosophy*. Edited by William F. Murphy Jr. Washington, DC: Catholic University of America Press, 2008.

———. "Practical Reason, Human Nature, and the Epistemology of Ethics: John Finnis's Contribution to the Rediscovery of Aristotelian Ethical Methodology in Aquinas's Moral Philosophy: A Personal Account." *Villanova Law Review* 57 (2012) 873–87.

Rommen, Heinrich A. *The Natural Law: A Study in Legal and Social History and Philosophy*. Indianapolis: Liberty Fund, 1998.

Rorty, Richard. *Philosophy and Social Hope*. New York: Penguin, 1999.

Rowland, Tracey. "Augustinian and Thomist Engagements with the World." *American Catholic Philosophical Quarterly* 83 (2009) 441–59.

———. *Culture and the Thomist Tradition: After Vatican II*. New York: Routledge, 2003.

———. "Natural Law: From Neo-Thomism to Nuptial Mysticism." *Communio* 35 (2008) 374–96.

Schaeffer, Francis. *Escape from Reason*. Downers Grove, IL: InterVarsity, 1968.

———. *How Should We Then Live? The Rise and Decline of Western Thought and Culture*. Wheaton, IL: InterVarsity, 1968.

Schindler, David L. *Heart of the World, Center of the Church: Communio Ecclesiology, Liberalism, and Liberation*. Grand Rapids: Eerdmans, 1996.

Schmitz, Kenneth L. *At the Center of the Human Drama: The Philosophical Anthropology of Karol Wojtyla/Pope John Paul II*. Washington, DC: Catholic University of America Press, 1993.

Schockenhoff, Eberhard. *Natural Law and Human Dignity: Universal Ethics in an Historical World*. Translated by Brian McNeil. Washington, DC: Catholic University of America Press, 2003.

Schreiner, Susan E. "Calvin's Use of Natural Law." In *A Preserving Grace: Protestants, Catholics, and Natural Law*, edited by Michael Cromartie, 51–76. Washington, DC: Ethics and Public Policy Center, 1997.

Second Vatican Ecumenical Council. "Declaration on Religious Freedom *Dignitatis Humanae*." Edited by Walter M. Abbott. Piscataway, NJ: New Century, 1966.

———. "Pastoral Constitution *Gaudium et Spes*." http://www.vatican.va/archive/hist_councils/ii_vatican_council/documents/vat-ii_cons_19651207_gaudium-et-spes_en.html.

Smith, Christian. "'More Realism—Critically'—A Reply to James K. A. Smith's 'The (Re) Turn to the Person in Contemporary Theory.'" *Christian Scholars Review* 40 (2011) 205–10.

Snell, R. J. "Desires Natural and Unnatural: A Reply to Paul Griffiths." *Public Discourse* (February 10, 2010). http://www.thepublicdiscourse.com/2010/02/1138/.

———. "Natural Law Is neither Useless nor Dangerous: A Response to Hart and Potemra." *Public Discourse* (February 28, 2013). http://www.thepublicdiscourse.com/2013/02/9233/.

———. "Performing Differently: Lonergan and the New Natural Law." *Lonergan Workshop* 37 (forthcoming).

———. "Protestant Prejudice: On Natural Law." *The City* (Winter 2013) 21–30.

———. "Saving Natural Law from Itself." *Public Discourse* (November 7, 2012). http://www.thepublicdiscourse.com/2012/11/5994/.

———. "Teaching for Cosmopolis: Authentic Subjectivity and the Liberal Arts Today." In *Liberal Arts in America*, edited by Lee Trepanier, 95–112. Cedar City: Southern Utah University Press, 2012.

———. "Thomism and Noetic Sin, Transposed." *Philosophia Christi* 12 (2010) 7–28.

———. *Through a Glass Darkly: Bernard Lonergan and Richard Rorty on Knowing without a God's-Eye View*. Milwaukee: Marquette University Press, 2006.

———. "Understanding Natural Law: A Response to Hart and Potemra." *Public Discourse* (February 27, 2013). http://www.thepublicdiscourse.com/2013/02/9227/.

Snell, R. J., and Steven D. Cone. *Authentic Cosmopolitanism: Love, Sin, and Grace in the Christian University*. Eugene, OR: Pickwick, 2013.

Stebbins, J. Michael. *The Divine Initiative: Grace, World-Order, and Human Freedom in the Early Writings of Bernard Lonergan*. Toronto: University of Toronto Press, 1995.

Steinmetz, David C. *Luther in Context*. 2nd ed. Grand Rapids: Baker Academic, 2002.

———. "What Luther Got Wrong." *The Christian Century* (August 23, 2005) 23–25. http://www.religion-online.org/showarticle.asp?title=3267.

Strauss, Leo. *Natural Right and History*. Chicago: University of Chicago Press, 1953.

Tollefsen, Christopher. "Is a Purely First Person Account of Human Action Defensible?" *Ethical Theory and Moral Practice* 9 (2006) 441–60.

Torrance, T. F. *Calvin's Doctrine of Man*. London: Lutterworth, 1949.

Tracy, David. *The Achievement of Bernard Lonergan*. New York: Herder & Herder, 1970.

Traina, Cristina L. H. "What Has Paris to Do with Augsburg? Natural Law and Lutheran Ethics." *Journal of Lutheran Ethics* 10 (March 2010). http://www.elca.org/What-We-Believe/Social-Issues/Journal-of-Lutheran-Ethics/Issues/March-2010/What-Has-Paris-to-Do-with-Augsburg.aspx.

VanDrunen, David. *Natural Law and the Two Kingdoms: A Study in the Development of Reformed Social Thought*. Grand Rapids: Eerdmans, 2010.

Voegelin, Eric. *Anamnesis*. Translated and edited by Gerhart Niemeyer. Columbia: University of Missouri Press, 1978.

———. *Plato*. Baton Rouge: Louisiana State University Press, 1966.

Walsh, Brian J., and J. Richard Middleton. *The Transforming Vision: Shaping a Christian Worldview*. Downers Grove, IL: InterVarsity, 1984.

Wells, Samuel. *God's Companions: Reimaging Christian Ethics*. Malden, MA: Blackwell, 2006.

Westberg, Daniel. "The Reformed Tradition and Natural Law." In *A Preserving Grace: Protestants, Catholics, and Natural Law*, edited by Michael Cromartie, 103–17. Washington, DC: Ethics and Public Policy Center, 1997.

Westphal, Merold. *God, Guilt, and Death: An Existential Phenomenology of Religion*. Bloomington: Indiana University Press, 1984.

———. *Overcoming Onto-Theology: Toward a Postmodern Christian Faith*. New York: Fordham University Press, 2001.

Wiley, Tatha. *Original Sin*. New York: Paulist, 2002.

Wojtyla, Karol. *The Acting Person*. Translated by Andrzej Potocki. Boston: Reidel, 1979.

———. *Man in the Field of Responsibility*. Translated by Kenneth W. Kemp and Zuzanna Maslanka Kieron. South Bend, IN: St. Augustine's, 2011.

———. *Person and Community: Selected Essays*. Translated by Theresa Sandok. New York: Peter Lang, 1993.

Yoder, John Howard. *Body Politics: Five Practices of the Christian Community Before the Watching World*. Scottdale, PA: Herald, 2001.

Made in the USA
Middletown, DE
13 August 2015